A DIRECTORY OF RELIGIOUS BODIES IN THE UNITED STATES

GARLAND REFERENCE LIBRARY
OF THE HUMANITIES
(VOL. 91)

A DIRECTORY OF
RELIGIOUS BODIES
IN THE UNITED STATES

compiled from the files of
The Institute for
the Study of American Religion

J. Gordon Melton
with James V. Geisendorfer

GARLAND PUBLISHING, INC. • NEW YORK & LONDON
1977

Library of Congress Cataloging in Publication Data

Melton, J   Gordon.
  A directory of religious bodies in the United States.

  (Garland reference library of the humanities ; v. 91)
  Bibliography: p.
  1. United States--Religion--Directories. I. Geisen-
dorfer, James V., joint author. II. Institute for the
Study of American Religion. III. Title.
BL2530.U6M44   200'.25'73   76-52700
ISBN 0-8240-9882-X

To the memory of
Elmer Talmage Clark
and
Arthur Carl Piepkorn

without whose pioneering research and direct contri-
butions this work could never have been brought to
fruition

CONTENTS

TABLES AND GRAPHS

ix

ACKNOWLEDGMENTS

The development of a Directory of religious bodies in the United States has been a major task of the Institute for the Study of American Religion since its founding in 1969. Beginning with lists developed by Elmer T. Clark, Frank S. Mead, and the Yearbook of American Churches, we have built the expanded list reproduced below, which is four times the size of the original. In the early 1970s, two researchers who had been working independently of the Institute, James V. Geisendorfer and the late Dr. Arthur C. Piepkorn, added their efforts to the Institute's work. Dr. Piepkorn had been working on a major revision of F. E. Mayer's *The Religious Bodies of America*, while Mr. Geisendorfer had compiled a large collection of materials on Unusual Religious Groups, now housed at the Bethany Lutheran Seminary at Mankato, Minnesota.

In addition to establishing a research library on the religious bodies of the United States and compiling a Directory, the Institute has become the focus of some new formulations and methods of research on several persistent problems in American religious studies—the nature of religious groups, the basic structures of American religious life, and the role of cults and sects, to mention only a few. These new formulations, some of which are included in the text below, appeared first in my Ph.D. dissertation at Northwestern University, "The Shape and Structure of the American Religious Experience" (1975).

It is hoped that in the very near future, the Institute will be able to produce a major reference work with descriptions and analysis of each of the different groups mentioned in the Directory, many of which have generated no descriptive literature to date.

xi

Acknowledgments • xii

Over the years many people have helped to collect the materials from which this Directory has been compiled and have offered valuable critiques of the new formulations, thus adding to whatever strength they may have. Among those who have been most helpful in the dialogue that has produced the new formulations are Donald Tinder, associate editor of *Christianity Today*, and David Barrett, Secretary of Research, Church of the Providence of East Africa, Nairobi, Kenya. I am always amazed at the patience of Dr. Frederick A. Norwood, my advisor while in graduate school and chairman of my dissertation committee. I am thankful for his efforts in working with me and for his encouragement in my research. The members of my graduate committee, Drs. Walter Muelder, Egon Gerdes, and Edmund Perry, each contributed new insights or posed a fruitful area for exploration that led to an important addition to the theoretical framework.

Among the important contributors of resource material are several whose ongoing concern and helpfulness have been essential to this Directory's successful completion, and to whom special thanks are due. That list must be headed by John Batsel, head librarian, and Ted Martin Young, assistant librarian of Garrett Evangelical Seminary Library. They, by their concern and help over the years, have created a debt I can never repay. Thanks are also due to Dr. Marcus Bach, Carl Hagensick, John Paerson, Bishop Karl **Pruter**, Barbara Mraz, David Techter, and Tim Zell.

I regret that space limitations do not permit me to name the many individuals who have donated materials to the Institute. They number in the hundreds and coming to know them, most of whom are members of groups whose life is so different from my own United Methodist heritage, has added immeasurably to the richness of my life.

J. Gordon Melton
Evanston, Illinois
January 1977

INTRODUCTION:
How to Use This Directory

This Directory attempts to meet the long-standing need for an exhaustive listing of the addresses of America's religious bodies. Such a listing, in alphabetical order, of over 1,200 groups makes up the bulk of the volume. Each entry includes the address of the headquarters (or contact point) of each group and the name(s) and address(es) of the group's major periodical(s). In addition to the basic Directory (Chapter III), supporting material has been incorporated in Chapters I, II, IV, and V.

Because this Directory goes beyond a mere listing of Christian Churches and includes many non-Christian groups, a rationale for inclusion and exclusion from this list had to be determined. This rationale is presented in Chapter I, where the definition of the "primary religious group" is developed. The term "primary religious group" is inclusive of and replaces the former categories of "church," "sect," "denomination," and "cult," some of which have pejorative connotations. This Directory is, in effect, a directory of the 1,275 primary religious bodies currently functioning in the United States.

With so many groups, some means of grouping or classifying them seemed necessary. Previous methods, which had been used with only a fraction of the number of groups included in this Directory, proved unworkable here, so a new system was devised. The rationale for this new system is given in Chapter II, where religious "Family groups" are defined and described.

The actual delineation of the family groups, both those within and those outside of the American religious consensus, is given in Chapters IV and V. Each family group is defined in terms of its shared heritage, thought world, and life style. Each member of the family is listed in its appropriate subfamily grouping.

Although particular information on the unique origin and belief of each group has been omitted because of space limitations, by locating a group within its family, you will learn something of its essential life and focus.

Before each group's name in both the Directory and family-groups listing, there is a five-digit number. These numbers have been assigned to facilitate identification. Many groups have similar names, and often several groups go under one popular designation. These numbers will prevent confusion from arising. The first two digits refer to the family group to which the individual group has been assigned. For example, the first two digits for the Aaronic Order are "19." This is the family-group number for the Latter-Day Saints or Mormons. The third digit refers to the subfamily of Latter-Day Saints of those groups associated with the Utah Mormons. The final two digits are assigned to new groups as they are located.

The name and five-digit number function as a cross-reference system: the Directory lists groups in alphabetical order, while Chapters IV and V list them in numerical order. Thus, if you know the name of a group, by using the number you can locate its family group and other similar bodies. If you know, in general, the characteristics of a group, its exact name can be located in Chapters IV and V, and by cross-reference, its address can be found in the Directory.

A DIRECTORY OF
RELIGIOUS BODIES
IN THE UNITED STATES

CHAPTER I

THE PRIMARY RELIGIOUS GROUPS

The basic structure in American religious life is the
"primary religious group," more popularly called by various
names--sect, denomination, church, and cult.[1] Among the
myriad forms of religious life which have emerged in American
society in its two centuries of religious freedom, the primary religious groups, the associations which seek the primary
religious allegiance of its members, began as transplanta-
tions, emerged as splintering developed, and appeared as new
belief structures blossomed in a new land. The primary
religious groups are thus distinct in structure from the
even more numerous "secondary religious groups," formed to
serve or supplement some aspect of primary group life
(education, evangelism, literature, missions, etc.), and
the "tertiary religious groups," which are essentially
groups of groups (i.e., ecumenical associations).

The history of American religion focuses on the development of its over 1,200 primary religious groups. These
derive from three basic sources. The largest number of
groups have migrated to these shores from another country.
Such immigrant bodies range from old line groups such as
the Roman Catholic and Episcopal Churches to the recent
Hindu and Buddhist groups. The second large set of primary

1

religious bodies have formed by schism of the immigrant bodies. These groups include many "sects." The third set have been formed around individual charismatic leaders who have put together new religious gestalts. While drawing on several previous options, Joseph Smith, Phineas P. Quimby, Andrew Jackson Davis, and others created genuinely new group structures.

The Rise of Denominations

The great crisis that set the stage for the development of America's new religious world was the Revolutionary War. The Revolution relieved the initial issue confronting American religion--the right to exist in schism from a state church. After the recovery from the war, the problem of reclaiming the nation of new non-church members became the vital issue and was the major cause of the formation of new religious bodies. Schism occurred because of the adoption of new evangelistic tools, such as camp meetings, and new attitudes that no longer assumed that one was working from a "Christian" societal base. The audience needed salvation, not just revival of a weak experience.

The basic issue of "salvation" and the claiming of new members versus "spiritual awakening" of a nominal membership is the difference between the First and Second Great Awakening. The era of the Second Great Awakening was a time of growth and expansion by those bodies existing prior to 1800 and the formation of several new ones. That the older bodies grew faster than new ones were formed is shown by the declining ratio of groups per million of population during the first decades of the century.

In the early part of the nineteenth century two leaders created new family groups. Joseph Smith--psychic, charismatic leader, and prophet--called people together around the Book of Mormon, which is supposedly translated from ancient American records, and his frequent revelations. There are now twenty-three groups which can trace their origin to him. William Miller, the first great prophet of apocalypticism in the New World, brought together people expecting the end of the world in 1843-44. The failure of the prophecy led to the splintering, not disbanding, of the original following. Today fifty-three groups have derived from Miller's initial inspiration. Smith, Miller, and Barton Stone, founder of the Disciples of Christ, were three basically Baptist leaders whose teaching created followings during the nineteenth century and two new family groups and a sub-family in the twentieth.

Not to be forgotten is the wave of communal utopianism that gripped the country in the 1840s. Beginning with the experiment at Brook Farm and the work of the French socialists, there was a decade which flowered with attempts at social reorganization. A second such era is just drawing to a close in the 1970s.

The middle of the nineteenth century was the great time of European immigration and the settling of the mid-continent by groups who brought their Protestant faiths with

3

them. Numerous Lutheran and Reformed churches, which
quickly began a process of consolidation, came out of these
settlements. By the last third of the century Americanization initially led to their splintering. Complete Americanization in the twentieth century supplied a basis for re-
union.

Urbanization began to be a major factor in reshaping
and spurring new forms of religious life by the late nineteenth century. The pressures of the city were felt in many
ways. Educational levels, science, urban problems, mechani-
zation, mobility, and the freedom of the city all placed
pressures on established religion, resulting in schism.
Three reactions were made to these pressures. A reactionary
approach emphasizing tradition eventually caused the Holiness
groups and the Fundamentalists to leave their former homes
and form new family groups. Liberals accepted the challenge
of urban life and championed education and ethics. The older
bodies found an uneasy peace in the midst of these pressures,
but were continually losing conservative elements as urban
values came to dominate.

The coming to dominance of urban centers in the twentieth century provided more than just new values to strain
denominational structures. It brought masses of people
together in a small space and created a new potential for
freedom. While religious freedom had been declared after
the Revolution, in actual fact the scope of deviation that
was allowed was small. Social pressure in an agricultural,

4

small-town setting worked to keep new ideas to a minimum. Further, a person with a new notion had to be highly motivated and mobile in order to collect any following at all.

In the city the religious situation changed. The more anonymous social structure allowed a greater diversity of religious ideas without the community's feeling threatened. Also, potential converts were abundant. As cities grew, a following for almost any non-conventional idea or practice could be formed.

Immigration has always been the major source of new religious bodies. In early twentieth-century America the influx of Western and Northern European religions was replaced by Eastern European and Mideastern ones. During this era, the Orthodox churches were all established as were several Moslem groups. The Jewish community went through reorganization that set its major structures in the present day.

Religious experience is continually reasserting itself as an entity of some force. In the early years of the twentieth century it manifested itself in two movements-- Pentecostalism and Spiritualism. Both movements grew and expanded after embryonic forms had surfaced throughout the nineteenth century.

The varieties of religions set in the early twentieth century by immigration, urbanization, and religious freedom continued a steady growth throughout the years between the world wars. Each family group showed a slowly growing

5

fragmentation until 1940. Then for some reason, possibly related to the war, schisms slowed down markedly for five years (Graph I-1). Several reasons for this can be suggested. First, immigration almost totally stopped, so no new groups were being imported. Second, many Oriental and German groups were slowed by both official and unofficial inhibitions. Third, the war became a "religious" crusade in itself and thus claimed a significant portion of the energy that might have led to new movements. Finally, many potential converts were out of the country fighting a war. That the soldiers were prime potential converts is aptly illustrated by the post-war religious history.

The trends created in the early twentieth century and slowed by World War II were revived and phenomenally accelerated after the war. The reorganization of society around urban complexes, tied to each other by swift communication and transportation systems, was completed. Almost intuitively grasping the fact of this reorganization, the new religions of the post-war period adapted to the structure and grew with it. Such action is illustrated by the growth of non-Christian missions in the land.

After World War II, Hinduism, Buddhism, and various Oriental religions, primarily brought home by servicemen stationed in Asia, began to view America as a prime mission field. Missionaries, who made their homes in either coastal cities or with known friends, were dispatched. Upon gathering a small following as a base, "city-hopping" began. The

Buddhists operated from Los Angeles to San Francisco, Portland, and Seattle. From there, Denver, Chicago, and New York became targets. Hindus started in New York City and worked west. The rural areas between the cities were almost totally neglected, except for the building of an occasional retreat center for urban followers. The newer psychical religious groups have followed a similar pattern of growth.

Primary Religious Groups-- Statistically Considered

A study of the 1,200-plus primary religious groups has yielded the three tables included below. Table 1 contains a summary of the basic working data on these bodies and the totals on the number of groups formed during each five-year period from 1800 to 1975. Horizontal line "n.d." shows figures for groups whose date of origin cannot be determined. Columns 1 to 13 show the breakdown for the various family groups (see Chapter IV and V) and Column 14 shows those groups which cannot be classified at this time. Column 15 gives the totals for the other 14 columns. Column 16 shows the totals for now-defunct bodies, most of which are ante-cedent bodies of presently existing groups. Plus figures in Column 16 show the formation of these groups while minus figures show their demise. Column 17 contains totals of Columns 15 and 16, and shows the number of primary religious bodies in existence during any given five-year period.

Line A shows the total number of bodies in each family group in existence on November 1, 1976, for which a date of

TABLE I-1

AMERICAN RELIGIOUS GROUPS STATISTICALLY CONSIDERED

	1 Liturgical and Lutheran	2 Protestant	3 Holiness and Pentecostal	4 Liberal	5 Adventist	6 Mormon	7 Communal	8 Ind. Fundamentalist	9 European Free Church	10 New Thought	11 Psychic	12 Magical	13 Non-Christian	14 Miscellaneous	15 Sub-Total	16 Defunct	17 TOTAL
1600																	
1700	2	10					1		3		1				17	19	36
1800																	
1805		1													1	4	5
1810		1							2						3	-	3
1815		1													1	2	3
1820		2													2	2	4
1825		3	1						1						5	3	8
1830		1				1									2	-	2
1835																-1	-1
1840		1			1	1	1		2						6	2	8
1845	2								1					1	4	8	12
1850	1	3	1				2							2	9	7	16
1855		2					1		2						5	4	9
1860		1	2		2	1		1	2						9	-	9
1865		3			1	1			2		1				8	1	9
1870	1	3			2	2	1		5						14	-1	13
1875		2	1			1					1	1			6	1	7
1880		3	2						2			3		1	11	-1	10
1885		3	4	1	1	2					1	1	1	1	15	2	17
1890	1	4	6					1			1	1	3	1	18	2	20
1895	2	1	6									1	3	1	14	1	15
1900	2	1	8	1				2	1		1			7	23		23
1905	2	8	9	1				2						3	25	2	27

	1 Liturgical and Lutheran	2 Protestant	3 Holiness and Pentecostal	4 Liberal	5 Adventist	6 Mormon	7 Communal	8 Ind. Fundamentalist	9 European Free Church	10 New Thought	11 Psychic	12 Magical	13 Non-Christian	14 Miscellaneous	15 Sub-Total	16 Defunct	17 TOTAL
1910	2	1	9		1				1		1		6	2	23	1	24
1915	6	2	11	3					2	3	1		3		31	7	38
1920	6	6	11		2			1	1	3	5		5		40	-6	34
1925	6	3	8	1	2	1		5	1	1	8		7		43		43
1930	4	4	11		3	1		3	1	2	9		7	3	48	-4	44
1935	3	6	14		2	1		4	2	2	10		3	1	48	-4	44
1940	2	2	10	2	2	2	2		1	2	5		4	3	37	-6	31
1945	4	6	12		4	1	2	3	1	2	4		5	2	46	-5	41
1950	6	5	12		2	1	3	1	2	2	16		9	3	62	-6	56
1955	6	7	13	1	5	3		3	3	2	21		1	14	79	-9	70
1960	21	3	17	2	2		3	3	5	2	28	9	22	10	128	-4	124
1965	11	5	17	3	2	1	9	3	1	5	39	12	27	15	150	-11	139
1970	9	6	1	2	7		3			1	23	30	27	14	123	-11	112
A TOTAL	99	109	188	12	45	18	30	33	45	29	184	53	151	59	1055		1055
N.D.	12	16	20	3	18	6	1	9	2	7	44	27	40	15	220		
B TOTAL	111	125	208	15	63	24	31	42	47	36	228	80	191	74	1275		1275

origin is known. The last figure in the line gives the total (1,055). Line B gives the total for all religious bodies in each family group known to be in existence on November 1, 1976, and the final figure is the grand total (1,275).

Several related family groups are shown together in Columns 1, 2, and 3. The Liturgical and Lutheran families are placed together in Column 1. The Reformed-Presbyterian, Pietist, and Baptist families are in Column 2; the Holiness and Pentecostal in Column 3.

Population is a significant factor in the development of American religious groups. While more detailed information about defunct groups in the period 1880-1940 would enhance the value of tentative conclusions, at least one working hypothesis can be projected: in a religiously free society, the number of primary religious organizations is a factor of population and population density. (See Table I-2).

Graph 1 shows visually the figures in Column 17 of Table 1 and covers the years 1855 to 1970. This graph reveals the thirty- to thirty-five-year cycle that American religion has gone through in the last century.[2] Religious activity has peaked in the 1840s, the 1870s, the first decade of this century, the late 1930s and the 1970s (a period just ending). During these periods, many groups were born, but only a percentage survived. (It should also be noted that the period of greatest ferment and new formation does not necessarily coincide with media interest and focus.

10

TABLE I-2

RELIGIOUS GROUPS AND POPULATION

Year	Number of Bodies on January 1	Population (by millions)	Percent in Urban Area	Number of Groups Per Million Population
1800	36	5.3	6	4.6
1810	41	7.2	7	5.6
1820	47	9.6	7	4.7
1830	59	12.9	9	4.3
1840	60	17.1	11	3.3
1850	80	23.2	17	3.3
1860	105	31.5	19	3.2
1870	123	39.9	26	3.0
1880	143	50.3	28	2.8
1890	170	63.1	33	2.7
1900	205	76.1	39	2.7
1910	255	92.4	46	2.7
1920	317	106.5	50+	2.9
1930	394	123.1	56	3.3
1940	482	132.0	57	3.7
1950	554	151.2	63	3.7
1960	680	179.3	71	3.8
1970	943	203.2	73	4.5
1976	1055			

GRAPH I-1

NUMBER OF NEW GROUPS FORMED PER FIVE YEAR PERIOD 1855-1970

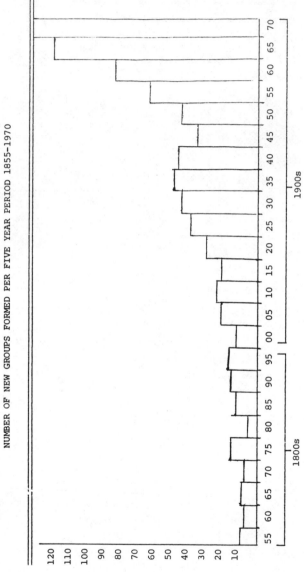

Media focus on religious ferment usually begins as the movement peaks and begins to decline.)

A word about the unique role that Hawaii and California have played in American religious development is in order. While each of the fifty states has made a unique and significant contribution to the story of American faiths, Hawaii is a convenient laboratory of religious life and California has attained an almost mythic position as an apparent source of new religious bodies.

Hawaii's uniqueness appears in a cultural situation where Christianity faces its greatest challenge to religious hegemony. The old faith of the Islands, a magical polytheistic religion, was all but destroyed by the Hawaiian royalty who became Christians, but it is currently undergoing a revival. Hawaii is also home to a large Oriental population (over one-third of the population) who have brought with them their Shinto, Buddhist, and various Chinese religions. Because of the large Oriental population, Hawaii has become the missionary gateway to the West for many Japanese groups. After a foothold on the Islands is established, missionaries find the trip to the Mainland fairly easy. Today the only American gatherings of some bodies are to be found in newly formed groups in Hawaii.

David St. Clair quoted a San Francisco astrologer as saying, "Didn't you hear that God picked up the United States right under the East Coast and lifted it into the air? When he did, the loose nuts rolled into California."[3] How

13

California developed such a reputation is yet to be determined. It has, of course, been the home of some famous non-conventional religious bodies--Aimee Semple McPherson and the Four-Square Gospel Church; Frank Ballard and the I AM; Krishna Venta; and the AMORC Rosicrucians. The degree to which the myth reflects reality needs some examination, however.

California shows far more continuity than discontinuity with American religious life. A quick look at the Yellow Pages of Los Angeles and San Francisco shows, as in any Eastern city, an abundance of mainline Christian Churches and Jewish Synagogues. Traveling through any California suburb offers the observer no hint that the community is "different." This fact is balanced by the obvious presence in any large urban area of a wide range of non-conventional religions. In Chicago, for instance, there are "congregations" of the Bahaists, Zen Buddhists (both Soto and Rinzai), Moslems (at least four varieties), the True Temple Solomon Church, the School of Human Divinity, the Uranus Temple, and the Vivekananda Vedanta Society, to name only a few. As a matter of fact, a recent study has concluded that there is a larger psychic/metaphysical/mystical community functioning in Chicago than in either Los Angeles or San Francisco.[4]

There is reason to believe that the myth of California as the home of most of America's "weird" religions is just that--a myth, created by the media and fed by the Hollywood movie focus. The media image has over the years become to a

limited extent a self-fulfilling prophecy. Religious transients have sought their own Haight-Asbury or Sunset Strip
only to disperse around the country in a few years. But
enough remain to add to the image.

The Primary Religious Group--Defined

Any cursory examination of American religious life
reveals not only the wide variety of beliefs but the wide
variety of structures which have emerged to embody those
beliefs. The major discussions of the problem have focused
on a definition of "sect," and of what is seen as a sectarian
frame of mind. The use of the term, especially as it has
derived from the "church-sect" categories of Troeltsch, has
been dominated by a rather narrow range of problems to which
it was an answer. These problems centered on how a "sect"
deviated from the norms of mainstream Christianity. In
recent years, however, the concern for some understanding
of the social forms of religious life in an increasingly
heterogeneous religious situation has come to the fore. This
emerging concern has pointed to some weakness in the use of
the term sect and the need to develop a terminology to replace it and its associated terms--church, cult, and
denomination.

A major reason to discard the terms "sect," "cult,"
"church," and "denomination" is the value judgments which
they of necessity carry. Sect and cult carry definite
pejorative connotations, while church and denomination con-
note the opposite. Secondly, all of the terms assume a

15

definite Christian bias. Sect and cult are seen basically as deviations, schisms, and alteregos of churches or denominations. Sects grow into churches as they mature. As non-Christian groups become a major concern, the sect-cult categories lose their functionality. Finally, as the issues of sectarian religion have been debated, a complete lack of consensus on the use of terms such as "sect" and "cult" have resulted, so that it is difficult to find even two writers who agree.

The focus on pinpointing the differences between churches, sects, and cults has also obscured another very real structural cleavage in American religious life, the difference between those groups which are the primary object of religious allegiance and those other forms of the religious life that serve auxiliary functions. The role of these secondary structures is an almost unexplored area in American religion, but perhaps highlighting their positions in relation to the primary groups will promote study of them. Those groups which seek primary allegiance are also to be distinguished from the ecumenical bodies which have formed a diverse and yet significant role in the religious scene. Again, from a structural perspective, our knowledge is slight as to how councils of churches and ministerial associations function.

The term to replace what has in the past been called sect, denomination, church, or cult shall be <u>primary religious group</u>. Since distinguishing it from secondary and

16

tertiary bodies is a basic concern, a single standard emerges immediately as an adequate starting point. The primary religious group claims the exclusive or primary religious affiliation of its members. It attempts to serve the overall needs of its members, as opposed to secondary and tertiary bodies that serve specialized needs. It also attempts to minister to its members on a regular, weekly, or even daily basis, while other bodies come into the picture at less frequent intervals and often make contact only through the primary bodies.

A second standard in determining the basic religious organizational unit is that it is a social entity, rather than an individual philosophy or a purely temporary local organizational schism by a small group from a local congregation. In possibly the most subjective part of the definition, the basic unit must pass one of three tests as to size and/or scope of its work. If it is congregationally oriented, it must have at least two congregations or groups in which members meet for worship or instruction or fellowship; if it has only one congregation or group, it must have at least 2,000 members and be making a measurable outreach through mass media beyond its geographic region; or if it is non-congregationally organized, groups must have a membership that crosses a state line or, as in the case of groups headquartered in metropolitan areas such as Kansas City, that extends beyond the metropolitan area.

It is thought, based on wide observation, that no

independent congregations of fewer than 2,000 members really
exist. This hypothesis is especially relevant in relation to
so-called independent Baptist churches and unaffiliated
gospel temples. Quite apart from those churches that are
members of congregational associations, such as the
Independent Fundamentalist Churches of America, no independent congregation has yet been investigated that does not
have an affiliation with other like-minded congregations by
its attachment to certain service bodies upon which it de-
pends for essential parts of its life. These include attach-
ments to select Bible colleges, Sunday School literatures,
and ministerial licensing agencies. At a minimum, the leadership will know the other congregations that are within its
"group."

Independent congregations that arrive at the status of
being truly independent are usually those built upon either
a distinct task or goal, such as interracial fellowship, or
charismatic leadership. The Moody Bible Church, the
Cathedral of Tomorrow, and the Church of All Faiths are
prominent examples.

Non-congregationally organized groups that qualify as
primary religious groups do exist; their structure is organized around mass media. Such groups include the mail
order "cult" which consists of a central office, a mailing
list, and members, scattered around the country, who receive
religious lessons regularly from the office. Such groups
as Life-Study Fellowship and the Mayans are examples. The

18

AMORC Rosicrucians, who are often encountered in media ads, is a mail order group whose enlarged membership has allowed local conclaves to emerge.

While few independent congregations exist, communal groups and groups whose religious perspective significantly differs from the overall religious milieu do exist. Communal groups by their very nature are small and live off the intimacy which the group nurtures. In actual fact, many communal groups, especially those which survive, have more than one center. The Hutterites have almost two hundred centers. Also in existence are small bodies whose religious perspective is so distinct that they have been limited in growth to one center, usually urban. Such groups, including various non-Christian, magical, and psychical groups, are included in this survey although they are recognized as exceptions to the size requirements.

Finally, the group is a proponent of a unique point of view on one or more issues vital to its life. (This unique point of view eliminates from consideration independent efforts by individual members of larger groups.) Included with the definition of "a unique point of view" is a strong difference of opinion on the manner in which the policy of a religious group is implemented. Schism is rarely over doctrine but often over the implementation of disciplinary machinery, personality conflicts, or parochial modes of behavior.

These three standards--exclusiveness, size and scope,

19

and unique perspective--will determine the type of ninety-
nine percent of America's religious bodies. In order to
dissipate any doubt which may remain after the first three
criteria are applied, several supplementary questions can
be posed.

1.   Do you have religious functionaries who perform
     marriages and burials?

2.   Do you see your group growing by the addition of
     new centers of religious life in the near future?

3.   Do you see your teachings or perspectives as
     radically distinctive from other groups around
     you?

4.   Are you affiliated with a foreign-based religious
     body which could be described as a "sect"?

5.   Are you actively proselytizing for members in
     your group?

Two or more affirmative answers place the group in the category as one of the basic organizations to be counted among
the groups to be treated in the remainder of this work.

     In order to complete a picture of religious structures
in the United States,[5] other than the primary religious
groups with which this study is primarily concerned, one
must also give consideration to the second and tertiary
religious organizations. These structures, which have never
been enumerated in any way approaching completeness, consume
a significant amount of the time and money given to religious
groups in the country. Both secondary and tertiary

organizations differ from primary religious groups in that they seek out members of primary religious groups for support and membership.

Secondary religious groups are service agencies which perform tasks for one or more primary groups which they cannot do for themselves. Typical of the secondary religious group is the faith mission agency which allows small primary religious bodies to participate in a foreign mission program without building a missionary agency of its own. A primary religious group of fewer than 50,000 members would be hard-pressed to develop the variety of structures that a million-member group can. Secondary religious organizations can draw strength from several closely related groups. Secondary groups typically receive support from only one or two family groups, although they may be advertised as totally non-denominational.

At least six kinds of secondary organizations can be distinguished, although individual agencies may combine several functions into one structure. The best documented of the secondary structures are the mission societies. These organizations raise funds and recruit missionaries for work in foreign lands. While not forming primary religious structures in the United States, they do so in their mission field. In Africa and southern Asia, primary religious groups supported in large part by United States funds form a large part of the religious milieu.

In the United States, domestic missions abound. They

21

are focused on various minority groups--Jews, Indians, children, urban transients, and the poor. These groups seek to convert unbelievers and then channel them into related primary religious structures. While most domestic missions remain small, some, such as Child Evangelism, Inc., and the American Board of Missions to the Jews, are quite large.

Making a largely hidden impact apart from the few prominent examples are numerous evangelistic and teaching associations. Some, such as those formed around evangelists Billy Graham and Oral Roberts, are far larger and more influential than most primary religious bodies. But like most of the smaller evangelistic structures, they are built around one or more leaders who are members of primary bodies (Graham is a Southern Baptist and Roberts, a United Methodist) and support is drawn from a narrow range of those bodies.

Institutions--orphanages, homes for senior citizens, and, most importantly, schools (Bible schools, seminaries, and colleges)--have received the support of primary religious groups. Among the smaller bodies, seminaries and Bible schools are significant in helping to define family membership, as schools tend to draw from a narrow range of groups for students and groups draw on a narrow range of schools for their ministers and leaders.

Similar to the institutions which service primary religious groups are the multitude of publishers of religious literature. These range in scope from small

22

publishers of limited circulation periodicals to major publishers of books (Zondervan, Baker, and Revell) and church
school literature (Scripture Press, David C. Cook, and Union
Gospel).

Smaller groups specializing in various services have
also arisen in the twentieth century. Not included strictly
in the above would be Bible publication societies, communications specialists, and numerous supply houses (both whole-
sale and retail) offering a wide variety of religious
articles.

Tertiary religious organizations differ from secondary
groups in the following ways. Instead of helping to implement
the program of primary religious groups in reaching prospec-
tive members and constituencies, they try to change primary
religious groups by promoting a particular concern. The
typical tertiary group is the ecumenical body which attempts
to bring a variety of primary religious bodies together over
one or more issues. Based on an assumed consensus, ecumenical groups (the National Council of Churches and the National
Association of Evangelicals) have drawn from the several
families which make up the established Christian consensus
in the United States, although a significant number of the
larger bodies have remained aloof from any conciliar structures.

The most vigorous of the ecumenical structures are the
intrafamily group structures and the task-oriented groups.
The intrafamily ecumenical organizations are found in every

family of American religious life. Included are not only
the better-known organizations, such as the Christian
Holiness Association, the Pentecostal Fellowship of North
America, and the World Baptist Alliance, but also the
International New Thought Alliance, the American Council of
Witches, the Council of Themis, and the Buddhist Council of
Hawaii.

Task-oriented groups can be found gathered around any
issues broad enough to affect a wide range of religious
people. Currently operating are long-standing groups concerned with peace (Fellowship of Reconciliation); creation
versus evolution (Bible Science Association, Inc.); the
psychic (Spiritual Frontiers Fellowship); spiritual healing
(International Order of St. Luke, the Physician); pentecostalism (Full Gospel Businessmen's Fellowship, International);
and sabbatarianism (Bible Sabbath Association).

With the distinction between the primary, secondary,
and tertiary religious organizations in mind, a more comprehensive look at the shape and structure of American religion
from the perspective of primary religious groups can be made.

CHAPTER II

TOWARD A CLASSIFICATION OF AMERICAN RELIGIOUS BODIES

Having defined the basic religious group (i.e. the

primary religious body) and having presented our list of

over 1,200 groups presently functioning in the United

States, the next task is finding some means of classifying

them. Scholars have made building typologies and classi-

fications a favorite activity. Die Soziallehren der
1
Christlichen Kirchen and Grappen of Ernst Troeltsch

published in 1911 launched modern attempts and most modern

efforts have derived from his theoretical framework. Be-

low we shall briefly review classifications schemas from

Troeltsch to the present as a prelude for offering an

alternative approach.

Troeltsch on Church and Sect

In setting out to write The Social Teachings of the

Christian Churches, Troeltsch had three separate concerns.

All,

. . . readily became unified when the sociological
formulation of the problem was applied to the whole
sweep of history of the Christian Church . . . At
the same time this led me to a peculiar conception
of the nature of Christianity, its history and its
relation to the general history of civilization.
This again led to progress in my whole formulation
of the theological problem in general . . . .[2]

Troeltsch wished to bring his understanding of the

scope of history, in particular the social perspectives of

the Church through the ages, to bear on the solution of

the problem. The book dealt in broad strokes with the

major tendencies in the Church's understanding of

the social milieu.

In the course of his discussion Troeltsch developed his classic distinctions between the Church, the sect, and mysticism. Each is a type of social form or organization which emerged as an embodiment of Christian thought. All were rooted in tendencies within the Primitive Church and representatives of the various tendencies have appeared throughout the Church's history.[3] Each form also has a distinctive view of the doctrine of Christ, which relates directly to the sociological manifestation.

Troeltsch saw three basic tendencies in the church's life. One was the radical tendency which was based in the purely religious impulse of primitive Christianity. Ethically early Christianity was characterized by an un-qualified individualism. It was a movement based on religious ideals and the relation with God, and evolved without concern for the on-going social situation. "There is no thought of the state at all."[4] The form that the radical ethic took was a new social order--the visible community of love which practiced a communism of consumption. The new order, however, was confined to the Church itself. The radical tendency continually reappeared as sectarian movements within the history of the Church. It was manifest, for example, in the apocalypticism of the Montanists and in Donatism and monasticism.

The second tendency, conservatism, began to develop as soon as the Church moved out into the larger

world of the Mediterranean Basin. In this world the state
could not be ignored, and the communism of love proved
impossible in the larger corporate group. One must come
to terms with the general life of the world. The view
was developed that the state and the structures of society
must be accepted, albeit with a certain hostility. They
were expressions of God-given Natural Law (a concept
borrowed from the Stoics). The structures have been
corrupted by sin (violence, avarice, etc.) and thus laws
emphasizing compulsion, the reaction against corruption,
and the legal structuring of inequalities (slavery, male
patriarchalism) have resulted. The state is seen in its
positive aspects as an institution which cares for order,
justice and external morality. The church submits to God
and His Will, in a world whose basic structures (war,
social control, inequalities of wealth, etc.) are permitted
by God and hence are to be endured. Thus the Church, as
it grows into a large organization, develops an ambiguous
attitude of patient waiting for the kingdom and positive
action in using the ordinances of society as a means of
attaining its own ends. From this tendency develops the
medieval all-pervasive Church whose concerns and activities
reach into every area of life, all classes of humankind,
and all centers of power.

It was the development of the medieval synthesis
that set the context for the new outburst of the radical
tendency which Troeltsch termed "the new type of the

sect."[5] The medieval sect's point of departure is dated
to the Gregorian reform and typical examples include the
Cathari, the Waldensians, the Francisians, the Lollards,
and the Hussites. Of course, the Anabaptist movement
represented a new burst of radicalism. In the context
of the medieval manifestations of the conservative and
radical tendencies, Troeltsch included his classic discussion of church and sect.

In developing his understanding of the church and
sect, Troeltsch turned to his colleague Max Weber for some
insight and then greatly enlarged upon what he had learned.
Weber, in his classic Die Protestantische Ethik und der
Geist des Kapitalismus,[6] had developed the idea of the
sect type in order to deal with the Baptists which he saw
as a "second independent source of Protestant asceticism"
(which produced capitalism). Sects were to be contrasted
with the church out of which they grew and to which they
reacted. A sect was a group in which "only those adults
who had personally gained their own faith should be
baptized." They would emphasize separation from the world
and individual salvation. Weber developed the idea of sect
for his own purposes. It is to both Weber's and
Troeltsch's credit that they moved beyond the earlier
definitions of sect as a separated group, outside of
corporate Christianity and hence to be regarded as "in-
ferior side-issues, one-sided phenomena, exaggerations or
abbreviations or ecclesiastical Christianity."[7] Their

28

ability to move from this interpretation was in part due
to the studies on sect life by such scholars as J.J. Ignaz
von Dollinger.

According to Troeltsch, the sect was a form which
appeared as a reaction to the medieval form of the church.
The post-Gregorian Church was seen as a conservative
social body, universal in its scope and accepting of the
secular order which it used as a means to its own ends.
Its acceptance of the social order meant also an acceptance of the evils of society as the result of sin's influx into the structures of Natural Law. From the view-
point of the sects, such acceptance is seen as a modification of the moral law of Jesus which compromised with the
world order. The church included within it the radical
(and mystic) tendencies. For example, Troeltsch noted
that Luther first gained his personal certainty of salvation through mysticism and his views of ethics which
focused on the Sermon on the Mount and the priesthood
of all believers were similar to sectarianism.

The church has its own particular emphasis in
Christology. Christ is the redeemer, who in his work of
salvation has achieved Redemption, once and for all;
working marvelously through the ministry, the Word, and
the sacraments in the church, He imparts to individuals
the benefits of His Saving Work. The church is the
Kingdom of God in the world and, as a result of the
redemption completed, possessed the power to transmit

29

remission of sins to those within its system.

The sect was contrasted to the church in every
way.[8] It was small with an emphasis on fellowship within the group instead of the attempt to reach out in im-
personal control of the masses. For a number of reasons
the sect was hostile to the state. It had experienced
persecution because of a conformist ideal of religion
and had doctrines which were hostile or passive toward the
social order, such as pacificism or refusal to acknowl-
edge the courts. The sect found its major thrust in the
lower class. It pointed people toward a supernatural goal
and taught an ascetic approach to life. It was critical
of the sacramental means of grace.

The two most important characteristics of the sect
were its voluntary nature and its approach to the law of
Christ. The sect, not wishing to involve itself in the
secular order, was composed only of those who made a
specific choice to join it. The church, which has mass
membership, included all as a matter of course. Rejecting
any common secular order, the sect taught a type of
perfectionism. It was not willing to compromise the law
(of Christ), which the relativizing process of the state
church accomplished, and thus further decreased the number
of potential members.

Like the church, the sect tended toward a distinctive Christology. Christ was seen primarily as Lord,
the example, the lawgiver, the One with authority and

dignity. Christ allows his people to pass through the

pilgrimage of earthly existence but will complete His

work at His coming and the establishment of the Kingdom

of God. The fulfillment of Christ's work is thus in the

future.

Often overlooked by Troeltsch's interpreters is

the third tendency--mysticism. There is some justifi-

cation for this lapse, in that in his discussion of the

primitive and medieval church he talks only of a radi-

cal and conservative tendency,[9] but leaves his discussion

of mysticism until the Reformation section. Prior to

the Reformation, Troeltsch notes, mysticism,

> had no influence upon the life of the religious
> community, nor had it yet any critical significance
> in connection with the idea of the Church, or with
> doctrine. Mysticism was still under the protection
> of the Church, or it was connected with the Religious
> Orders. It never stood alone.[10]

With the Reformation's ideal of the priesthood of all

believers, it was able to exist independently.

The mystic group, like the sect, was small, but

the individual nature of the mystic experience greatly

modified the nature of in-group fellowship. Mystics were

associated in loose organizations of the like-minded

sharing a spiritual fellowship. They emphasized the

invisible church (the sect and the church were both quite

visible). The mystic was indifferent to the world. The

sectarian, while hostile or passive, was rarely in-

different. The mystic was most tolerant in beliefs and was

the source of the ideal of freedom of religion. Finally,

31

in relation to the law the mystic had a tendency toward antinomianism.

To the mystic, Christ is viewed as an inner spiritual principle who stirs religious feelings and is experienced in the influence of the Divine spark within. While incarnated in the Christ of History, He is only truly known in inner experience. The Kingdom of God is the inner kingdom of the dominion of the Divine Spirit. Redemption is the process of the soul's union with God of which Christ is the quickening agent.

It should be noted that while Troeltsch moved beyond the off-the-cuff rejection of the sects, he did have a definite preference for the church as opposed to the forms of both sect and mysticism. The church is the only form of Christianity capable of fostering a popular religion and to include within itself the varied degrees of Christian attainment and maturity. The church's universal outlook, its institutionalization within the centers of power, and its possibilities of continually drawing on the energy of the grace of the Body of Christ allow it alone to grasp the social problem (as elucidated by Troeltsch) and to influence society in any continued manner and to extend the scope of its social and ethical ideas and energies.

Troeltsch's description of the church-sect-mystic tricotomy (even though the mystics were usually forgotten) had some inherent weaknesses as applied to the American scene.

32

TABLE II-1

THE TROELTSCH TRICHOTOMY

Church	Sect	Mysticism
Universal - for the masses	small-fellowship in group	individual - spiritual fellowship
Christ as Redeemer	Christ as Lord	Christ as inner spiritual principle
Accepts secular order	hostile or passive to the state	indifferent to the world
Kingdom equals Church	Kingdom is yet to come	Kingdom is within
Relativized moral and natural law	absolute law of Christ	antinomian
State church	visible church	fellowship with God - invisible church
All classes	lower class	
Secular as means conservative	perfectionist supernatural aim to life anti-sacramental voluntary	loose organization toleration freedom

Troeltsch was writing a description of historical
realities on the continent where the state church was
pervasive. The sect whose existence was based on its
relation to the church lacked many pure examples beyond the Reformation groups. In the United States, which
had a real church establishment for only two brief instances,[11] the sect never really existed. The classic sect
bodies were a major component in Pennsylvania society and
were remolded by the lack of persecution and pressure from
above. It is often forgotten that Troeltsch was decidedly
not trying to describe religious forms as a sociologist
or history of religions scholar might do. Had he been
trying to do so, he certainly would not have neglected
the synagogue, a very present reality in western Europe
in the early part of the century.

Troeltsch in America

After the publication of The Social Teachings of
the Christian Churches, and especially after the English
translation in 1931, most classifications adapted his
categories. There were alternatives by those who wished
to use either a psychological or doctrinal perspective.
Noteworthy among the former was H.C. McComas[12] who built
a classification based on (1) observable data such as
group history, doctrine and liturgy, and (2) the type
of personality attracted to the group.

A number of doctrinal approaches to religious groups
have appeared, though most are polemic works from a

34

conservative Christian perspective. A major exception
is F.E. Mayer's The Religious Bodies in America.[13]

Mayer classified bodies into eleven theological families.
The system ultimately fails in bringing into close prox-
imity groups which share a similar formal doctrine, but
differ radically otherwise.

Increasingly, however, the problem of understanding
religious dynamics and the shape and structure of religious
experience came to the fore, and in this quest, the categories of Troeltsch were much more suggestive.

As Joachim Wach suggested, "It would be interesting
to review the saga of religion as a more or less successful struggle for the adequate manifestation and expression
of religious experience."[14] Religious classifications
thus became a means of understanding the life of any
religious body through the interaction of their thought
forms (termed by Wach, their "theoretical expression")
and their life style (their "practical and sociological
expressions"). Also integral to most considerations was
a discussion of various religious functionaries--the
priest, the shaman, the saint, the true believer. Missing
in most discussions was the role of particular religious
traditions as modifiers and limiters of religious
behavior.[15]

Two systems, those of Howard Becker and J. Milton
Yinger, have dominated discussions of classification of
religious groups. Howard Becker[16] expanded Troeltsch's

categories into a fourfold classification system. The four types of religious groups were the ecclesia, denomination, sect, and cult. The ecclesia is essentially the state church of Europe and represents the twentieth-century form of Troeltsch's church. The sect, which stands in contrast to the ecclesia, is small, exclusive, personal and ethical in emphasis. The demonination is Troeltsch's sect after growth, time and adjustment to society have taken the edge away from its protest. The cult is a group emphasizing private, personal religion within a loose social organization. Becker's classification with additions by Yinger is pictured in Table II-2.

Yinger,[17] as a prelude to his sixfold modification of Troeltsch, criticizes the church-sect dichotomy on two points. First, two concepts, or three, if mysticism is added, are too few to describe adequately the range of data concerning religious groups. Secondly, Yinger criticizes Troeltsch for not being a sociologist. By the time Yinger was writing, Troeltsch was being treated as a sociologist. But as was pointed out above, Troeltsch was an historian doing an historian's work. Yinger wrote of Troeltsch,

> He notes they all (the churches and the sects)
> stem from fundamental Christian ideas and
> describes their relationship to social crises
> and historical movements; but he is more
> concerned with their variations as religious
> systems than in specifying sharply the social
> and personality factors involved in the various
> religious-group types.[18]

In this quote Yinger highlighted a primary reason for the
dead end to which much sociological work in sect classification had led. Troeltsch was not writing as a sociologist
about contemporary church forms of organization. He was
describing a group of forms which were prominent in the
sixteenth century but which have become less so to this
very day even in their European settings. In the United
States they never existed at all in pure form.

Yinger's schemata outlined below include six cate-
gories--four from Becker and two added by Yinger. The
Universal Church and the ecclesia are two forms of the
state church, neither of which exist in America, and only
the second in Europe. There is some doubt as to whether
the former ever existed; but if it did, the Roman Catholic
Church of the 1200s was it. The denomination is the
ecclesia limited in universality by social factors like
race, social class, or regional boundaries. The Established Sect is a denomination that could not adjust to
society at one point and remains alien because of it. It
originates in a sect with a "social protest" orientation.
The sect is the same as in Becker, except that three kinds
of sects are distinguished. Cult is significantly re-
defined but applies to the same groups that Becker described.

37

TABLE II-2

A CLASSIFICATION OF RELIGIOUS BODIES
BY J. MILTON YINGER

The Universal Church	Relatively successful in supporting the integration of society--combining both church (social) and sect (individual) tendencies.
	ex: 13th century Roman Catholic Church
Ecclesia	Seeks universality and obtains formal allegiance on all levels of society. Cannot incorporate sect tendencies as well as the universal church.
	ex: European national churches
Denomination	Ecclesia further limited in ability to hold sect tendencies and also socially limited by class and race.
	ex: Lutheran Church in America
Established Sect	A sect which has accommodated itself to the culture over time, but less than a denomination. Originates as a social protest sect.
	ex: Quakers
Sect	Small voluntary group protesting church's inability to meet their needs. Usually a lower class phenomena.
Cult	Similar to sects; but make a sharp break religiously from the dominant religious tradition of society.
	ex: Black Muslims

Since Yinger's classification system appeared in
1957, there has been a continuing dialogue on the
viability of the church-sect dichotomy and upon Becker's
and Yinger's modifications. One thrust was the attempt
to isolate a scale by which churchness or sectness could
be measured.[19] The total effect of the effort has been to
confuse the theoretical work by offering a multiplicity of
definitions, most of which are subjectively based. The
major problem of all the definitions is their inappli-
cability to the full range of "sectarian" religious
activity. For example, Benton Johnson's scale (based upon
acceptance or rejection of the social order) will have
United Methodists, the Oxford Group (Buchmanites) and
Zen Buddhists arrayed against Black Muslims, the Amish
and the Assemblies of God--hardly an ideal system.

In an exciting exchange on church-sect typologies
which appeared in the Journal for the Scientific Study of
Religion, Erich Goode, N.J. Demerath III, and Allan W.
Eister have offered a number of valid critiques that have
furthered the debate. Goode began the dialogue with:

> As it (the church-sect concept) stands today,
> it is a hodge-podge of definitions and empirical
> correlates and empirical non-coorelates. It has
> no power to explain or elucidate. Unless it
> undergoes a radical revision which is universally
> accepted by researchers and theorists in the
> field, church-sect must be seen as a dead concept,
> obsolete, sterile, and archaic.[20]

Without being as quick to shelve the church-sect
classification altogether, Demerath does offer some further

critique, primarily of the way that allegiance to it has
tended to hold back research. Sociologists have concen-
trated on sects and little work has been done on the
"churches." Also the insight that could be obtained from
comparative analysis of non-religious institutions has not
yet appeared. He finally suggests, "We might very well be
at our best in abandoning the specifically religious formulation in favor of similarly wide-ranging constructs."[21]
By "similarly," he means a reference to Weber's constructs
on social institutions.

Eister, in calling for complete abandonment of the
church-sect category, is the most radical of all. It has,
asserted Eister, been unreliable but more importantly,
"excessive and insufficiently critical, reliance upon it may
well have blocked more vigorous and impressive development
of a sociology of religious phenomena."[22]

From all sides the seeming result of the massive critique of the church-sect dichotomy is to manifest its inade-
quacy even when modified to deal with the problem of
describing the shape and structure of religious life. It
has certainly proved a hindrance to researchers actually
approaching members of religious bodies for purposes of
gathering information. Such terms as "sect" and "cult"
carry an implicit value judgment against the very group
whose cooperation is sought. Therefore, Eister's proposal
to abandon these concepts altogether (for the time being, at
least) seems the only viable alternative. They are beyond

40

recovery as useful and meaningful categories.

Sect Classifications

Besides Yinger and the church-sect dichotomy there have been a lesser number of attempts to deal with just the "sect" groups--though each author had a somewhat different idea of what constituted a sect. Of this number, three stand out in the effect that they have had and are having on sectarian scholarship.

In 1940 Robert Friedmann[23] published a classification of primarily Christian sect groups. He grounded his work on Johannes Kühn[24] who had developed a schema for European groups based on their attitude toward the toleration issue (see Figure II-3). Friedmann pointed out the specialized nature of Kuhn's study and wished to expand it to include more possibilities of reaction. A new starting point was needed, but one which would keep Kuhn's basic insights.

> This new starting point can be formulated as
> a question: What attitude does one take toward
> the Holy Bible and especially the New Testament?
> What does one think of it or which part of it
> has been chosen as the definite truth and pattern of
> one's life?[25]

Table IV-3 shows how the schema works in practice. There are some obvious errors. Spiritualism does not relate primarily to John but to the miracle stories in the Synoptics and Acts (as does Pentecostalism which is missing from the schema). There are also obvious flaws in that the overwhelming majority of religious bodies are in one category--St. Paul's Epistles. Of course, Friedmann was

41

TABLE II-3

A CLASSIFICATION OF SECT BODIES BY
ROBERT FRIEDMANN

The Christian refers to the New Testament as his proper basis, but mostly chooses only one part of it as decisive for his life.				The New Testament is not needed in the main for religious guidance.

He chooses:

Synoptics	Johannine Prologue	St. Paul's Epistles	Revelation of St. John

"Old evangelical brotherhoods"	Mystics Christian Theosophy (Bohme, Parcelsus)	Teaching of grace and redemption	Millenarians (Eschatology, Apolyptic) Taborites	"Schwarmer" Enthusiasts, New Prophets, Dreamers, (Muntzer,
Franciscans (Fraticelli) Waldenses Evangelical Anabaptists	Neo-Platonism	Theology of salvation All churches	Munsterites Harrison (Fifth Monarch) Mostly antinomian	David, Joris, etc.) Mostly antinomian.
(love and cross)	Spiritualism (Single)	Majority of sects (even Donatists)		

Quakers combine 1, 2 & 5		Pietism has some evangel. tones but remains Paulinistic, Methodism too.
Humanistic ethics (rationalism, Tolstoy)		

42

trying to deal primarily with Anabaptists and saw his task
as separating them from other Reformation groups of which
he disapproved (Millenarians, Taborites, and Schwarmer).
As a study of Anabaptist and related groups, it is a
thorough job, only recently improved upon by George H.
Williams. But as an attempt to understand religious forms
in a broad way, it is of limited value.

Leland Jameson refined Friedmann's concept and proposed making "what a group does with the Bible" the
"measure of sectness."[26] He propounded Friedmann's
classification as the principle of selective emphasis
and noted that many groups had a monolithic concentration
on some aspect of Biblical teaching. Beyond the Catholic
and Reformation tradition groups, however, there were
others which Jameson added: 1) those with an esoteric
principle or method of Biblical interpretation; 2) those
with a supplementary revelation (Mormons, Christian
Science); and 3) those outside the orb of Biblical faith.[27]
Elmer T. Clark, for many years the one central
source for American sectarian studies and actual information
about United States' sects, published his work in 1938
(revised in 1949). Clark's interest grew out of his study
of revivalism and the psychology of religion.[28] From this
primal concern he continued to collect data on a number of
varied United States' sect bodies, and his analysis of the
material resulted in one of the few attempts to understand
sects from a survey of their life and faith. The variety

of sect life experienced directly, not just through their services and talking to their leaders, led Clark to see the problems which other researchers missed. When he arrived at the process of classification, Clark wished to classify along the lines of his psychological heritage. But he recognized factors that modified psychological processes—most significantly the teaching process of churches which modified the expressed needs of converts.

He finally arrived at a classification which was aesthetically unappealing but which fitted his data better than any classification before or since. The seven categories corresponded to significant issues around which groups have organized and orientations which groups have used to determine a major structure of their lives. As seen in Table II-4, Clark almost instinctively selected doctrinal, behavioral and social categories by which to understand the sect groups. The distinct advantage of this system is that Clark's basic categories say something significant in the term that classifies a group. Those classifications based solely on one set of criteria work very well for those groups under primary concern (Friedmann and the Anabaptists) but always end by categorizing many groups in a way completely irrelevant to their life.

Clark's schema is not perfect by any means, even though it fits the data of American sects better than others with which it competes. The system needs more categories to deal with the multiplicity of groups listed

44

TABLE II-4

TYPES OF SECT BODIES ACCORDING TO
ELMER T. CLARK

Pessimistic or Adventist	Disinherited who see no future in this world and hence look for a catastrophic end and replacement with a heavenly kingdom.
Perfectionist or Subjectivist	Oriented on moral perfection, spiritual holiness and the total eradication of sinful desire.
Charismatic or Pentecostal	Oriented upon special experiences and blessing of the Holy Spirit as manifested in speaking in tongues, healings, etc.
Communistic	Withdrawn groups, secure in communal social existence.
Legalistic or Objectivist	Stress certain definite performable rules, rituals and observances as essential to true religion.
Egocentric or New Thought	Seek physical comfort and peace of mind as main goals.
Esoteric or Mystical	Claim to understand a "revealed" truth not possessed by the ordinary.

under legalistic or objectivist sects. There is something questionable about lumping Greek Orthodox and Primitive Baptists in the same basic category. Finally, Clark slighted two of his categories, the metaphysical and the occult, which are treated almost as suspect groups. They are given but four pages of listing at the end of the book with no analysis or history.

The most recent attempt to classify the sects has been by Bryan Wilson,[29] who has emerged as the sociologist of sectarian life. Wilson's ideas are, however, dominated by the continued existence of the state church in Britain which determines partially his definition of sect and to that extent the usefulness of his categories on the American scene. For example, he emphasizes that sects are voluntary. Voluntarism is not a meaningful category with which to begin study in the United States, because all groups are voluntary. Wilson's Britishisms, however, should not detract from the genuine contribution he has made (and continues to make) to sectarian studies.

Wilson's basic category is the religious response to the world. Different sects--because of their history, economic conditions, leadership, and other factors--react in various ways to their environment. Wilson, assuming that certain "institutionalized procedures and rituals" are normative, uses the word "deviant" to describe these reactions. The deviating responses, however, can be observed and classified and seem to fall into seven

46

groupings.

Conversionist sects emphasize the need of a new life for the individual centered on a "conversion" experience. Only a large number of conversions will lead to a better world. Revolutionist or transformative sects look to the imminent overthrow of the evil world by God or divine activity. Introversionist sects abandon and withdraw from the evil world. Manipulationist sects seek salvation in the world but by an unusual or generally unknown means. Thaumaturgical sects seek a personal release from present ills without reference to the world. This release is through supernatural elements. Two other responses are also possible as religious options, though neither is inherently religious. Reformist sects seek possible elimination of present social ills by reform. Utopian sects wish to reconstruct society radically.

Wilson admits that these categories are types which in practice mix in complex ways but which do give meaningful help in dealing with sect groups. Some typical examples of each can be given:

1. Conversionist   Methodists and Baptists

2. Revolutionist   Jehovah's Witnesses

3. Introversionist   Hutterites, Amish

4. Manipulationist   Christian Science, Scientology

5. Thaumaturgical   Spiritualism, Snake Handlers

6. Reformist   Quakers

7. Utopian   Bruderhof (Society of Brothers).

47

One must question Wilson's categories on two points, especially in relation to their usefulness in the United States. First, one can question the comprehensiveness of the list in dealing with the variety of religious responses to the world. For example, the life of the contemplative and the ethnic traditionalist both seem to be missing. Secondly, one can also question the adequacy of the categories in describing distinct modes of response. Thus, Introversionist sects and Utopian sects seem to be largely the same phenomena. There is also room for greater clarity between Manipulationist and Thaumaturgical bodies. Possibly some of the confusion is because of the examples Wilson uses. Scientology's response to the world seems much closer to Spiritualism than Christian Science. Is the major religious response of Quakers their social activism or the idea of the "inner light?"

In the critique, however, one must not miss the genuine contribution of Wilson's method of approaching religious bodies. In selecting the category that he does, religious response to the world, he, more adequately than any sociologist before him, has chosen categories which seem actually to say something important about the groups under consideration. Such an important insight is not to be missed.

Anthropology Suggests an Alternative Direction

In the 1950s anthropologists began a process of seeking a means to classify nativistic groups which closely

48

parallels the attempts of sociologists with religious
forms.[30]   The particulars of the various systems and

revisions are of no importance to this study as they refer

to different data.   But, in attempting to systematize

understanding of a much broader variety of groups within

the whole scope of world culture, they have highlighted

the factors which seem to be necessary to classify properly

such widely variant groups as Sikhs, Indian Shakers,

Chandi's movement, and cargo cults.   The method of approach-

ing data is extremely suggestive of new categories by which

to arrange American groups.

More important, within the discussions of particular

classifications was a discussion of the limits of classifi-

cation systems, which evolved into a discussion of what

could be termed a philosophy of classification.   A summary

and major contribution to this discussion was made by Igor
Kopytoff.[31]

Kopytoff noted that in the years since Ralph Linton

began to classify nativistic groups, anthropologists had

experienced similar problems in classification to those

that sociologists had--oversimplified systems with too few

categories.   Several alternative classification systems of

a more complex sort had been attempted with limited success.

The general model, of which there were several varieties,

used a biological evolutionary scheme, which classified

groups according to origin.   Ideally, an all-embracing

schema was possible.   In practice, it did not work.   Dogs

49

and children do not merge to form new species. Reformed and Congregationalists do merge to form new churches. The generic system broke down in syncretism and mixed traditions. The classification could operate in local situations or among single tradition groups but not in the complexity of world religion.

The matrix approach to classification treats each group as a more or less random cluster of several kinds of traits. The problem was that the addition of traits expanded the system geometrically and soon there were more categories than groups. This approach also continued the problem of placing together groups that possessed vastly different dynamics.

Kopytoff wished to replace former classifications with what he called the analytical profile approach. This approach would, said Kopytoff, "recognize formally what has been happening in fact--that all along we have been classifying not movements but some of their aspects and that the multiplicity of existing terms stem to a large extent from concentration on different variables."[32] What was needed was the collection of data both objective (evaluation by an outside observer) and subjective (views of the movement's members). This data would cover a wide range of interests, including organizations, environment, ideology, goals, and tools. These characteristics could then be related to geography, history, cultural settings, and politics for emerging patterns.

Kopytoff was "dubious" that any satisfactory classification system was possible and wished to see characteristic types and to view movements as more or less partici-
pating in their type. Such characteristics as reactions
to domination, synthetic beliefs, millennial dogma, and
prophetic leaders, did exist. Each group in its total
gestalt might participate more or less in one or more of
these characteristics.

The critique aimed by Kopytoff at anthropologists
had, of course, equal significance for sociologists and
psychologists. One of the prime reasons for the number of
definitions of church and sect was the choice of different
characteristics by which sects could be classified. Thus,
given a particular concern (vindication of Anabaptists,
ethnic structures, illumination of societal norms,
description of religious genius, or any number of polemic
ends), any set of characteristics might be applicable and
valid as a source for a typology. The characteristics
chosen to highlight, however, would determine the limits
of information one could receive and use.

Utilizing the insights of McComas, Clark, Wilson and
Kopytoff, a new approach to a definition of the shape and
structure of religious experience, with particular
reference to its American setting, may be undertaken. The
question for the researcher becomes, "What set of
characteristics and categories will most adequately
illuminate the structure and dynamics of the groups

51

themselves?"

Some Necessary Elements in an Adequate
Classification Schema or Typology

The possibility of an adequate typology of religious
groups must meet squarely the weaknesses of past classifications, including the issues raised by Kopytoff. If
these weaknesses are to be overcome, there are several
criteria which must be met. First, the typology must be
empirically based. There is a tension in working with
typologies between logical neatness and symmetry and the
demands of empirical data. The tension must give way to
the data. Typologies must be based on the widest range
of knowledge both from a local and world-wide perspective.
Anything less is intellectual edifice-building.

At this point Kopytoff's insight about classifying
characteristics instead of groups is pertinent. Previous
attempts at classifications have picked meaningless "characteristics" by which to seek understanding of a group.
For example, there is no question that the Jehovah's
Witnesses and the Divine Light Mission of Guru Maharaj Ji
are radically different movements. Yet, if one chooses
such basic characteristics as belief or non-belief in the
divinity of Jesus, relation to the political structure,
relations with non-members, apocalypticism, or orientation
on a charismatic leader, they will be seen as almost
identical. The categories supply true but incomplete data
in understanding the two groups.

52

Secondly, an adequate typology must, like the definition of the basic religious group, be open to the variety in forms of religious life it will encounter and be free from any preconceived theological perspective of judgment. Classification systems with a theological bias can emerge even in the most sophisticated research. Value judgments about a class or type of culture can reappear as a subtle condemnation. On a personal level the researcher cannot help but accept or reject certain forms of religious behavior (such as animal sacrifice). However, such prejudices must remain outside the classification system.

The group in itself must figure prominently in any adequate typology. If classification of groups is to occur, based upon a classification of their characteristics, then a knowledge of the working dynamics of the particular groups must be assumed from the beginning. Obviously, adequate knowledge of all groups is a heuristic goal, but work must begin with information already available.

Merely overcoming these acknowledged weaknesses of past studies may seem sufficient, but such is not the case. Building typologies is significant only if it serves a purpose. Hence, the adequate typology must meet other criteria. First, it must supply meaningful data, that is data that highlights central and important aspects of the group. There are many questions one can ask and answers one can receive about a group which are true but contribute little or nothing toward understanding the essential

53

features of its religious life. Most theologically oriented sect studies fail at this point. Ananda Marga's understanding of the Bible, a psychic's understanding of sin, and a Mormon's understanding of predestination are all data to be received and eventually considered in a detailed study of a group. To classify on this basis is meaningless, however, because these items are of such peripheral concern to these groups. A meaningful classification will say something essential about the life of each member of a class with the very first statement.

Secondly, the classification must in itself supply useful knowledge, that is data helpful to the broader concerns of the religious researcher, and be a tool in supplying further knowledge. It has been the strength of sociological typologies to give useful knowledge. If one visits a sect which has been classified conversionist or communal or cultist, at least one will have some information about what to expect. The weakness of the sociological classifications has been its limited use as a basis for further study. It has placed strangely dissimilar groups together and separated some that by most standards seem very close.

Any particular group will manifest dominant behavior patterns--particular expressions of religious experience (speaking in tongues, morality or mysticism), secular activities (social activism, communal living, withdrawal, work or conspicuous consumption) and worship (liturgy,

54

magick, or personal interaction). Together they consti-
tute the collective forms of the religious life.[33]

Each group has two histories, one which is evident
to the observer and another accepted by the group as its
personal story. Often these two closely conform, but
sometimes they are strikingly different. Some groups
attempt to build a history far surpassing their span of
existence. Others wish to hide their origins in a parent
group in order to assert the "originality" of their own
group. Most importantly, inherited forms become the
easiest to adopt and where unchallenged will become highly
determinative for any new group. That which is inherited
from the past puts boundaries on growth, and new religious
births tend to be the children of their parents.[34]

Not to be missed in the survey of any group's thought
world, life style and heritage is the gap which often
exists between its articulate spokespersons (theologians,
official leadership) and its membership. The larger the
group, the larger that gap may be. Also the leadership may
be completely out of touch with the needs that the group
is filling for its members. Thus an analysis of religious
structures must include the "popular" expression of ideas
by second eschelon leaders (such as pastors, Sunday School
teachers, and evangelists). For those groups with a longer
history, there will also appear a gap between official
statements and current ideology. The literature meant to
be distributed to the larger membership (periodicals and
church school booklets) is the best evidence of such gaps.

An adequate classification would be able to pin-point areas in which new religious groups would be most likely to arise and which would be most likely to survive once they were formed. It should also be able to delineate the course of particular religious bodies based upon their significant characteristics, the debates with their closest rivals, and the subcultural milieu in which they chose to exist.

The Family Group

In answering the question of which characteristics most adequately delineate the shape and structure of a given group's religious experience, at least three continually emerge as important--life style, thought world, and heritage.[35] Other characteristics, such as types of religious authority and leadership, relations with other religious bodies, ethics, and class, ethnic, and racial origins, seem secondary. Beginning with the unique and particular religious body, one can see it in its special relations to other religious bodies and its culture and subculture. That relationship is best understood as one of ideas, behavior and history.

The ideological expression of religion is present from the beginning of a religious movement's life. Religious groups respond to symbols, archetypes, and myths.[36] They also respond to the particular content of language in which the movement develops. Take the writings of a religious leader into a new time and place, and its

56

meaning changes. Wesley's writings on sanctification gave

an ideological thrust which, when shifted to nineteenth-

century America, took on new meaning and became a basis for
37
the Holiness Movement and even the Pentecostal Movement.

Also allegiance to particular ideas will allow or inhibit

a group's growth. Given the present context of religion

in America, no group can prosper (including a Hindu or

Buddhist group) without a positive view of Jesus, and any

group for whom Jesus is unimportant will remain on the

fringe.

A number of primary religious groups which share a

common thought world, life style, and heritage will be

called a family group. At present in the United States,

with 1,275 primary religious groups, there are

17 family groups with 74 primary religious groups listed

as unclassifiable due to lack of data. The prime question

remains, however, does the above type of grouping overcome

the weakness of past classifications? Or does it carry as

yet undiscovered weaknesses?

Obviously, it overcomes the problem of insufficient

categories as in many previous systems. It begins with

seventeen categories and is open to others as they emerge.

It also chooses three items, not just one, as a basis of

classification, thus refusing to classify by a supposed

common response to a common religious issue, such as
doctrine.

The typology based on family groups overcomes the
problem of too many categories, as in the matrix system.
There are only as many categories as the material justifies.
There are no null categories which come from symmetrical
system-building. Only those categories that can with some
degree of logic and accuracy describe a number of religious
groups are used.

The system is open in a number of respects. It is
open to functional groups which can come in under their own
ideas of what is important. The many small Marxist
political sects in America can easily be seen as a family
group. It is open to the change of a group from one family
to another through time. Unlike the generic classification
which classifies primarily on origin, this system sees not
only history or origin as a significant item but also the
acceptance of an identifying history which can and does
change in time. Of course, this system is open to the
emergence of new family groups and the disappearance of
others.

The family group idea supplies pertinent information
about the life style of each group listed as a member. It
also provides a basis for understanding the seemingly
insignificant issues of belief and behavior which have
become rallying points for schismatic groups. One can
never grasp the reason for condemning the wearing of

58

neckties without understanding the course of the whole

debate on dress, which has been accepted as a major

concern by the Holiness churches. One cannot understand

the search for contemporary types of the Biblical Elijah

and Elisha without some comprehension of the question as

raised in the 1890s in the Bible Student Movement of

Pastor Russell.

Only time will tell if the family group idea will

be a tool for gaining further knowledge. At present it

does provide a means of keeping up with the myriad movements and groups with some degree of understanding.[38]

It does offer one excellent piece of insight for the

researcher; it points him to the community, the thought

world, and the life style of the sect as a beginning point.

Adequate understanding of any particular group, because of

the very nature of group religion, cannot be received from

merely objective observation. There must be emphathetic

contact, an attempt to grasp the inner logic of what may

at first seem to be a completely illogical set of beliefs

and ways.

The family group idea will hopefully provide a common

meeting ground upon which sociologists, psychologists,

historians, and other religious theoreticians can meet to

share their equally valid, if sometimes limited, insights.

Historians, all too prone to look at the organizational

history of a group, are called to examine the history

accepted by the group as a functioning reality.

59

Sociologists should cease to ignore the historical factors determining structures and present relations. Religious theoreticians are called to account for cultural determinants in group life. Psychologists must deal with the search for religious truth as a factor of equal importance with personality traits in determining the nature of religious life. If the family group idea can bring a point of focus to the various disciplinary approaches to the interdisciplinary task of understanding religious bodies, it will be a tool of immense importance in furthering knowledge.

The Family Group and Social Issues

The family group can be seen as the essential structure in American religion by providing the more or less stable orientation for reaction to more ephemeral issues that rise and wane. Its importance can be shown in relation to the ecumenical movement whose impetus toward merger of various Christian bodies has produced only one such merger across family group lines (the Congregational-Christian Church merger in 1931). Family groups remain while issues like war, the role of women, political corruption, Sunday Schools, alcohol, and unconventional religious forms come and go. While such issues occasionally split a particular group, they rarely lead to the creation of new religious gestalts (i.e., produce new family groups).

Among the large body of miscellaneous groups to be listed below seem to be several which could produce new family traditions in the next quarter century. Although

60

homosexual churches have become a national phenomena,

only time will tell if they will be integrated into

mainline Christianity or not. A similar question remains

for the Jesus People. Churches built on the experience

of psychedelic drugs remain in a tenuous state. Many

other religious bodies are built on such shallow perspec-

tives or ephemeral issues that they cannot survive without

drastic change. Some have been born and died during the

course of this particular study.

Social ethics, the active involvement of religious

bodies in efforts to directly change the structures of

society, is the only contemporary issue that has been able

to divide family groups significantly. The importance of

social ethics can be traced to the religious restructuring

caused by the American Revolution, the most determinative

force in the overall structure of American religions.[39]

For the first time in many centuries, religious

bodies in the last decade of the eighteenth century found

themselves cut off from government support and to a large

extent (for the classical sects) government interference.

Such freedom forced all groups into a competition

for members and a reorientation on evangelism; only those

groups that either succeeded in such reorientation

(Methodists, Baptists) or gained enough adherents through

immigration from Europe grew (Roman Catholics, Lutherans).

One of the implications of the new form of religious

life, for Christianity at least, was the necessity of

61

finding new ways to influence the social order. Prior to
the Revolution, the ministerial leadership had direct
entree to the power centers of society. Such access gave
to the priesthood the responsibility for a Christian social
ethic. Thus, Luther could write his Duties of a Christian
Prince. It took over a generation for the adjustment to
responsibility in a democratic free-church society to
become a major issue. The first to articulate the new
stance was Charles Finney, professor of theology at
Oberlin. Out of his work grew the social imperatives of,
first, the Holiness Movement, and then the Social Gospel
Movement of the late 1880s.[40] This social imperative
differs from the evangelistic imperative, in that it was
not forced upon the church by the same kind of survival
response.

The perspective on social responsibility is crucial
to the form of religious bodies. While missions, Sunday
schools, and charitable institutions shifted religious
structures, they were primarily additions to the evangelistic thrust. Social ethics requires a major reformation
of church structure and the time-consuming involvement
of membership in "secular" affairs. Such involvement
requires priority attention to education on political,
economic and social issues and concerns. Such attention
must necessarily distract from a central concern with
cultus and evangelism.

Much of the last two centuries of American religious

62

history could be seen as the growth and maturation of a
social philosophy in an increasingly democratic religious
context. A wide variety of bodies were involved in the
crusades leading up to the Civil War. They continued as
a predominate form for social involvement until the rise
of the social gospel at the turn of the century. The
social gospel called for a social involvement beyond the
crusade to actualize a single value (peace, freedom) in
a societal context. Such involvement meant a real shift
of priorities away from evangelism and worship toward
education on social, political and economic concerns. This
one issue has consistently divided religious bodies in
America since 1900.[41]

The involvement in social issues has led to further
demonstration of the role of family groups as the continuing structure of American religious life. First, the
social gospel itself has produced only a few groups for
whom the social gospel has become the prime issue. These
groups,[42] located on the extremes of the political spectrum,
are in agreement on the overriding priority of the social
question. In most cases, the issue of the validity of
social questions has actually been a cover for deep, if
passing, disagreement on particular social issues. The
demand of the Methodist Episcopal Church, South, in the
1850s and 1860s for the church to remain free of political
issues was a means of justifying its stand of slavery.
It did not keep them from promoting political activity on

63

other issues. Also where dissent on social issues has
occurred, a reassertion of family group values has arisen
as each side attempts to justify its position from the
family group's consensus.

The existence of such groups as the Ecumenical
Institute and the Church of the Christian Crusade may be
the sign of the emergence of a new family group. It may
even be the clue pointing toward the existence of a social
activist family group which would include the ideological
political groups, such as the Trotskyites and the Ku Klux
Klan. Only time and further research will tell. The real
difficulty of building structures based on the priority
of social activism is, of course, the ephemeral nature of
any given social issue. The issues which call together
groups of concerned religionists pass quickly as success
or new priorities or exhaustion overtakes individuals.

The involvement of the religious bodies on the
American scene with social issues offers a challenge to
Troeltsch's understanding of a sect as being indifferent
"toward the authority of the State and the ruling classes,"
and "separating . . . the religious life from the economic
struggle."[43] The American scene has continually produced
religious groups on either end of the political spectrum.
Such groups as the Wesleyan Methodists were abolitionist
in orientation while the Methodist Episcopal Church, South,
was pro-slavery. A coalition of many of the "sect" bodies
was able in the early twentieth century to become a major

64

force in producing prohibition. A social vision, accompanied by various degress of political skill, is characteristic of many of America's religious bodies.

A Picture of a Family Group

Any given religious body will manifest a particular heritage, life style and thought world. In actual practice, one of these will predominate. When one examines the 1,275 religious bodies in the United States, the overwhelming majority of them share one of seventeen sets of characteristics, and from these seventeen sets, seventeen family groups have been distinguished. They are named for their dominant characteristics.

Some family groups are particularly distinguished by their allegiance to an historical tradition. Most pointedly, the Lutherans and the Liturgical Churches are so characterized. To a lesser extent the other Christian family groups are oriented upon their tradition. They are partially defined by their founder who is well known among members. Some groups--such as the Pentecostals, the Communalists, and the Psychics--have a very nebulous history.

A second group of religious bodies can be defined primarily by the adoption of a characteristic life style. Immediately the Communal groups are brought to mind. Group ownership of property and certain self-imposed disciplines are the ideals that override other considerations. The Holiness Churches--characterized by a particular moral

65

imperative, the life of perfect love--would also be similarly distinguished.

Religious experience is a prime factor determining the life style of the Pentecostals and Psychics. Both are oriented upon particular kinds of parapsychological phenomena which each member at some time in varying degrees is expected to manifest. For the Liberals, religious experience is all but a dead issue; and for the Pietists, a notable shift away from an emphasis on it has occurred throughout their history.

The final priority around which the family group converges is thought world, or more narrowly, theology. The Protestant churches, especially those which can be traced to John Calvin's reformed theology, are so characterized. Fundamentalism has a doctrinal imperative from which some Reformed, Baptist, and Fundamentalist Churches can judge all other groups.

The sharing of a thought world should not be taken to mean theological uniformity so much as: 1) a common acceptance of the issues about which argument is important and 2) a mutual agreement of distinctives to be defended. Adventists all agree that Christ is expected to return soon, but violently argue about the nature of the return, the possibility of pinpointing the date, and the significance of certain world events as signs of that coming. Jargon will develop within a family. Words, descriptive of important concepts, will take on distinctive connotations

66

so that only the "initiated" can follow the full impact of
conversation.

Not to be overlooked in considering each religious
body's central concern is its other, but lesser, priorities.
A group whose priority is a particular life style will also
have a heritage and a world-view. A group which is centered on perpetuation of a tradition will also give that
tradition form and theology. A group centered on a thought
world will look back to a tradition (though often vaguely)
and will be structured around some definite ideas. Each
individual group, then, must be considered from all three
aspects, and only then classified.

Upon the basis of the above criteria some seventeen
family groups have been identified. Each group shares a
common religious tradition (or in one case the rejection of
a common tradition), a similar life style and a common
thought world. With some eclectic groups and others that
have changed family groups,[44] a careful analysis of all
three factors is necessary before determining to which
family group any particular group is to be assigned.
Polemics are an important indicator of a group's family.
Repeated arguments on one subject will occur only on items
of importance and characteristic of family group matters.
Secondly, with groups which have existed in America for any
length of time, contemporary publications, particularly
those aimed at training youth, are necessary in delineating
shifts of doctrine and emphases from historical statements

and standards. Thirdly, actual visits to group gatherings and interviews with members and leaders are often the only way to determine the true nature of a group. Some groups function as religious groups while denying their religious base. Other dislike denominational labels, and still others do not produce written materials for non-members.[45]

Ritual, in the narrow sense of worship forms, has emerged as a helpful tool in delineating subfamily membership. Ritual, one of the few literary products of some smaller groups, tends to be highly derivative. It requires great artistic skill to write successful ritual, and the few successful creations become widely used in slightly altered forms. Thus the tradition of a group can be traced through the unchanged forms of its worship.[46]

In assessing the characteristics of each religious body, the group's own self-understanding and image of itself has assumed an important role. Most religious bodies know who their closest imitators are and which other groups share their heritage, though world and life style. But while a group's own self-image is significant, it by no means fully determines into which family group any particular group is assigned. There is often a gap between self-image and seemingly plainly observable facts.

Some groups so stress their uniqueness that they would deny any relationship to any other group. Often members, and to a lesser extent, leaders, are quite unaware of an historical continuity of ideas. In groups that are

receiving revelations from a psychic or "supernatural"
source, content will come from a common pool of ideas
(Spiritualism, Theosophy, angelology, etc.) which have
been previously absorbed from books, lectures and
conversations.

Some groups have attempted to rewrite or deny some
aspects of their life style or history. Many Pentecostal
bodies speak of having been founded in 33 A.D. and only
intense probing will reveal their more limited history.
Some groups try to cover up the career of their founder
prior to the emergence of the group. Such leaders as
David Berg (Children of God), Ron Hubbard (Scientology),
(Miracle Revival Fellowship) and Sun Myung Moon
(Unification Church) have all led or still lead lives
different from their present role.

Members of some groups might possibly deny the
correctness of the family group into which they have been
placed. For example, some Holiness groups might argue
that they are in the Pietist Family and vice-versa. The
United Methodist Church is among several large inclusive
bodies which includes major membership segments which deny
or do not possess family group characteristics. Many
Methodists would see themselves more at one with the social
action churches (miscellaneous) or might wish to construct
a Liberal Protestant Family. However, an examination of
the United Methodist Church reveals an emphasis on
Wesleyan symbols, literature and church school material with

69

a focus on religious experience, and an openness to small spiritual-growth groups, such as those promoted by the Disciplined Order of Christ, the Prayer Life Movement, and the World Literacy Prayer Group.

There is recognizable in the United States a dominant religious perspective, which functions as a milieu within which religious groups and families function. That faith is defined by a consensus of ideas and a range of behavior patterns found within the larger religious bodies.[47] The faith, while not possessing legal and political powers to enforce its views, does, by having the allegiance of most Americans, possess tremendous social pressure. Groups will more or less identify with this dominant faith.

The faith is decidedly Christian and affirms belief in God, Jesus Christ, the Bible, and the Ten Commandments. Its adherents tend to worship on Sunday (Saturday is allowable) in a service led by a priest or minister. They baptize their members and partake of the Lord's Supper. Worship occurs in a building called a church. Variation is allowed within individual groups, but too many variations defines a group outside of the dominant faith.

Of the sixteen family groups, ten are within the dominant faith, although individual members may be out-side. In some families, such as the liberals and communal groups, one finds a great variation in relation to the dominant faith. Among "out" groups, splintering occurs over accommodation to the dominant faith. New Thought

70

churches are among the most acceptable of the "out" groups
while the Satanists would possibly be the least acceptable.

The Family Group Internally

As an actual entity, family groups seem to share
some common structures. Each has one or more dominant
or influential members. In the Pietist Family the United
Methodist Church is such a group, and among the Baptists
the Southern Baptist Convention and the American Baptist
Church so function. Of factors that measure dominance
and influence size certainly is the most important. Any
group which can claim over half the members of a family,
as do the United Methodist Church or the Roman Catholic
Church (or for that matter any group that can claim as many
as one million members), moves on that account into the
role of a dominant and influential family member.

For smaller family groups other characteristics are
helpful in spotting influential members. Influence is
directly related to access to media, including both self-
generated media (measured by quality and number of circulated periodicals and radio and television time) and
coverage over a period of years by the national news
services. One must measure access to media of communication over a period of years, possibly two years at the
minimum, as some very small and unimportant bodies can
generate a significant amount of short-term coverage (with
48
publicity campaigns and stunts).

Access to media becomes particularly important as

71

it becomes the source of information around which a "reactive" program can be geared. The emergence of the International Society of Krishna Consciousness and the Divine Light Mission as major items of media attention in the late 1960s and early 1970s has forced the other Hindu groups to differentiate themselves strongly from these two and has forced each of the two to develop stances vis-a-vis the other.

Dominant family members are usually the parent groups for most other members, which will direct polemic toward them. In many cases, of course, other family members who originated as protest movements in the dominant body, must seek justifications in the weaknesses of their parent for their own existence. As a corollary to this characteristic, a rise to dominance usually is accompanied by a decreasing need for self-justifying polemics.

Finally, influential members serve as the group from which other family members build their self-image. Schismatic groups share most points of history, life style, and thought world with the parent body. They identify themselves as Lutherans, Baptists or Calvinists, but differ at a few points. (This fact often accounts for the lengthy names of some groups.)[49]

Each family is generally host to some subfamily groupings. Typical are the Adventists with subgroupings among: 1) those bodies who look primarily to William Miller and 2) those who look primarily to Charles T. Russell, a

latterday improvisor on Miller's apocalyptic theme. In
many cases there can be legitimate argument that the sub-
group might be a new family group. Over a period of time
they often become so. If, however, the criteria of
defining a family group is followed, most decisions can
be reached by analysis of a group's heritage, thought world
and life style.

Subgroups are collections of members within a single
family group who differ with other family members on some
issue. They often modify the general family history by
a secondary identification with the founder of their particular subfamily group. They may group around a significant doctrinal issue, as the trinitarian and non-trinitarian
Pentecostals do. There may be variation in rigidity of
behavior (holiness), the interpretation of history (dispensationalism), church organization (non-Episcopal
Methodism), or response to various social forces (pro- and
anti-slavery churches).

Subgroups can emerge on any issue which becomes
dominant in the family group's discussions. The issues may
be inherent in the family (like discussion of the nature of
charismatic phenomena in the psychic family) or be posed
by the culture (the race question) or by particular historical events (the UFO phenomena in the late 1940s). The
subfamily groups represent a minority family response to a
particular but significant issue.

The family groups must constantly be seen in their

73

growth, process, and developmental aspect. Just as children are seen as members of one family but usually take on other designations in later life, so the whole process of forming family (and subfamily) groups, keeping them, or losing them, is continuing. To present a picture of them in 1970 is not necessarily to see them fixed for 1980. Some family groups have shown marked tendencies self-consciously to eliminate some subfamilies (such as those formed on race). Others show marked tendencies to create new subfamilies or even to split into two families (the psychics).

The marked degree of constancy actually present in families is due in large part to the overwhelming conservatism of most religious institutions, which had rather lose dissident members than change. Jumping family groupings is rare because patterns once set in the past (be they theological, organizational, or historical) tend to perpetuate themselves. Institutions certainly adjust to the ever changing environment, but such changes tend to be made begrudgingly and only to stave off a threat to vital processes.

74

CHAPTER III

THE DIRECTORY

Listed below are 1,275 primary religious bodies currently (Summer, 1976) existing in the United States. This list has been compiled over the last seven years by the Institute for the Study of American Religion. Included are almost all of the primary religious groups known to be functioning in the United States, including some rather large groups which have been omitted from standard reference works such as Frank Mead's Handbook of Denominations and the Yearbook of American Churches. Such omissions have included the million and a half member Baptist Bible Fellowship, the World Baptist Fellowship and the Holy Spirit Association for the Unification of World Christianity. Excluded from this survey are several occult groups which operate in secret and have requested that no names and addresses be published, and the American Indian groups, for reasons considered elsewhere.

For easy cross-reference to Section IV, the five-digit computer identification number has been included with the directory listing.

An attempt has been made to standardize the listing of each group under its official name. Where popular names of various groups have become widely known, they are listed with cross references to the proper name. In some cases, particularly among some loosely organized groups, there is no official name, only more-or-less in-group definitions. For example, among the Primitive Baptists, there are very definite fellowship lines drawn on doctrinal issues so that letters of communion are passed only between associations of like-mind. Yet there is no official name for the different "sets" of associations. Like situations exist for the Plymouth Brethren, Christadelphians, the Christan Churches and Churches of Christ, many bodies that use the term "Church of God" or "Church of Christ" and several Bible Churches such as the groups that refer to themselves as just "some Members of the Body of Christ." In the case of these confusing and often overlapping designations, the best-known designation of the group has been adopted, and a modifier has been added in parenthesis. The parenthetical additions should not be understood as part of the group's name. They will be based on headquarters location, founder, characteristic, or popular designation.

75

Jewish groups are listed under the various rabbinical
associations such as the Union of Orthodox Rabbis of the
United States and Canada, instead of the congregational
associations such as the Union of American Hebrew Congregations.

For each group included below both a headquarters
address and major periodical is listed. If the periodical
address is different from the headquarters address, it is
given separately. In many cases there is no official "headquarters." In those cases, a contact address is given. Such
a contact address is given also where the headquarters
changes annually, such as is the case with several of the
black Baptist groups.

Though this Directory is the most complete published to
date, religious structures in the United States are as mobile
and dynamic as the society in general. New religious bodies
are constantly being formed and dying. Many groups, especially those on the fringe of culture, are continually in flux,
changing form, dividing and merging with like groups, and
changing addresses from one member's apartment to another.
Many groups have operated in the anonymous city for many
years without being discovered by either media or scholars.
Therefore, it is to be expected that there are some groups
missing from this list and that between the date of last
checking the address and publication, some addresses will
become obsolete.

It will also be noted that in a few instances no address has been located for a religious group. In these cases,
at least two independent sources have confirmed the existence
of those groups, but direct contact has not been made. They
are included both to complete the picture of American religious life and in the hopes that addresses can be secured in
the near future.

The Institute for the Study of American Religion is
endeavoring to keep an up-to-date file of such changes, and
would welcome any corrections and additions to this list.
Also, where addresses prove inadequate, we would be happy to
supply alternate contacts to the different groups. It is
also to be expected that the publication of this Directory
will stimulate letters of information to the various groups,
letters that the groups have no facilities to handle. ISAR
will, for cost, be happy to supply information on these
groups from its files. Direct all correspondence to:

Institute for the Study of American Religion
P.O. Box 1311
Evanston, Illinois 60201

18222   A Candle
         Box 2325
         Lehigh Valley, Pennsylvania   18801

19115   Aaronic Order
         c/o Robert J. Conrad
         P.O. Box 7095
         Salt Lake City, Utah   84107

                        Aaron's Star (bi-m)
                        6268 South 1300 West
                        Salt Lake City, Utah   84107

18110   Advent Christian Church
         P.O. Box 23152
         Charlotte, North Carolina   28212

                        Advent Christian News (w)

                        Advent Christian Witness (m)

21610   The Aeth Priesthood,
            Franternitas Rosae Crusis/
            Church of Illumination
         Beverly Hall Corporation
         Quakertown, Pennsylvania   18951

21730   Aetherius Society
         6202 Afton Place
         Hollywood, California   90028

                        Cosmic Voice (bi-m)

12350   African Methodist Episcopal Church
         414 Eighth Avenue, South
         Nashville, Tennessee 37203

                        Christian Recorder

                        AME Review (q)
                        3004 North Cincinnati Avenue
                        Tulsa, Oklahoma   74106

12353   African Methodist Episcopal Zion Church
         P.O. Box 1047
         Charlotte, North Carolina   28201

                        Star of Zion (w)

                        Quarterly Review (q)

10169   African Orthodox Church
         International Chancery
         122 West 129th Street
         New York, New York   10027

12355   African Union First Colored
      Methodist Protestant Church
      602 Spruce Street
      Wilmington, Delawrae 19801

14529   African Universal Church
      c/o Abp. C.C. Addison
      14 Webster Place
      East Orange, New Jersey 07018

22210   Afro-American Vodoun
      (no address available)

21153   Agasha Temple of Wisdom, Inc.
      460 North Western Avenue
      Los Angeles, California 90004

21574   Agni Yoga Society, Inc.
      319 West 107th Street
      New York, New York 10029

23715   Ahmadiyya Movement of Islam
      2141 Leroy Place, N.W.
      Washington, D.C. 20008

                    Moslem Sunrise

10125   Albanian Orthodox Archdiocese
        in America
      c/o Archdiocean Chanccry
      523 East Broadway
      South Boston, Massachusetts 02127

                    The Vineyard (q)
                    Metropolitan Fan S. Noli
                      Library
                    529 East Broadway
                    South Boston, Massachusetts 02127

10126   Albanian Orthodox Diocese in America
      54 Burroughs Street
      Jamaica Plains, Massachusetts 02130

                    True Light (m)
                    P.O. Box 18162
                    Station A
                    Boston, Massachusetts 02118

21974   Aletheia Foundation
      c/o Jack Schwarz
      515 N.E. Eighth
      Grants Pass, Oregon 97526

22351   Alexandrian Witchcraft
        c/o Roy Dymond
        Box 978
        Station F
        Toronto, Ontario
        Canada

22353   Algard Wicca
        c/o Mary Nesnick
        520 East 20th Street
        New York, New York   10009

                        Algard Newsletter

24059   All Faith Fellowship
        c/o Swami Nityanada
        502 South Bois d'Arc
        Tyler, Texas   75701

30965   All Freedom Church
        225 Turk Street
        San Francisco, California   94102

30901   All One Faith in One God State
        c/o Dr. H.E. Corey
        213 South Tremont Street
        Oceanside, California   92054

14527   Alpha and Omega Christian Church
        3023 Clifton
        Baltimore, Maryland   21216

14906   Alpha and Omega Christian Church
            and Bible School
        96-171 Kamehameha Highway
        Pearl City, Honolulu
        Hawaii 96782

20110   Amana Community of Inspirationists
        c/o President Charles L. Selzer
        Homestead, Iowa   52236

                *   Amana Society Bulletin

19150   American Association for the
            Advancement of Atheism, Inc.
        1223 12th Avenue
        San Diego, California   92101

                        Truthseeker (m)

11953   American Atheists, Inc.
        c/o Mrs. Madalyn Murray O'Hair
        P.O. Box 2117
        Austin, Texas   78767

16120   American Baptist Association
        4605 North State Line Avenue
        Texarkana, Texas   75501

                        Missionary Baptist Searchlight
                        Box 663
                        Little Rock, Arkansas   72203

15101   American Baptist Churches in the USA
        Valley Forge, Pennsylvania   19481

                        American Baptist (m)

25560   American Buddhist Mission
        P.O. Box 536
        Atlantic Beach, Florida   32233

25517   American Buddhist Order
        c/o Rev. Eugene Wagner
        153 Bradford Street
        San Francisco, California   94110

25445   American Buddhist Society and
            Fellowship, Inc.
        c/o Dr. Robert E. Dickhoff
        Apartment 56
        Maitreyamantaka
        600 West 157th Street
        New York, New York   10032

10108   The American Carpatho-Russian Orthodox
            Greek Catholic Church
        249 Butler Avenue
        Johnstown, Pennsylvania   15906

                        Cerkovny Vistnik-Church
                            Messenger (bi-w)
                        145 Broad Street
                        Perth Amboy, New Jersey   15963

10310   American Catholic Church
        c/o Archbishop Hugh Michael Strange, Primate
        218 Mira Mar
        Long Beach, California   90803

10170   The American Catholic Church,
         Archdiocese of New York
         c/o Most Rev. James Francis
         Augustine Lashley, Primate
         457 West 144th Street
         New York, New York 10031

10311   The American Catholic Church
         (Syro-Antiochean)
         St. Peter's Cathedral
         1811 Northwest Fourth Court
         Miami, Florida 33136

         OR

         c/o Most Rev. Archbishop
           Herbert F. Wilkie
         St. Mary Magdalene Catholic Church
         189 Lenox Avenue
         New York, New York 10027

10409   American Eastern Orthodox Church
         c/o Most Rev. Thomas Martin,
           Metropolitan Archbishop
         Archdiocese of Divine Love
         1580 Bledsoe Lane
         Las Vegas, Nevada 89110

10407   American Episcopal Church
         Camperdown Building
         One Cleveland Street
         Greenville, South Carolina 29602

                         Ecclesia
                         840 Derry Street
                         Knoxville, Tennessee 37917

11905   American Ethical Union
         Two West 64th Street
         New York, New York 10023

                         Ethical Culture Today

                         Ethical Culture Forum

14911   American Evangelical Association
         2200 Mt. Royal Terrace
         Baltimore, Maryland 21217

                         World Evangelical Magazine

                         81

17223   American Evangelical Christian Churches
        Waterfront Drive
        Pineland, Florida 33945

21213   American Grail Foundation
        12315 Saginaw Street
        Mt. Morris, Michigan   48458

        OR

        2181 Hasler Lake Road
        Lapper, Michigan   48466

11907   American Humanist Association
        125 El Camino del Mar
        San Francisco, California   94121

                        The Humanist (bi-m)
                        923 Kensington Avenue
                        Buffalo, New York   14215

14758   American Indian Evangelical Church
        1823 Emerson Avenue, North
        Minneapolis, Minnesota   55411

11010   American Lutheran Church
        422 South Fifth Street
        Minneapolis, Minnesota   55415

                        The Lutheran Standard (bi-m)

30903   American Mission for Opening
            Closed Churches
        Olcott, New York   14126

22325   American Order of the Brotherhood
            of Wicca
        c/o Lady Sheba
        P.O. Box 3383-G
        St. Paul, Minnesota   55165

10322   American Orthodox Catholic Church
        c/o Bishop Robert S. Zeiger
        12033 West Maryland Drive
        Lakewood, Colorado   80228

10175   American Orthodox Catholic Church,
            Archdiocese of New York
        c/o Most Rev. John A. Christian, Archbishop
        National Cathedral Church of the
            Holy Resurrection
        675 East 183rd Street
        New York, New York   10458
                        American Church Life

10187   American Orthodox Catholic Church,
         Diocese of Wisconsin
         c/o Most Rev. Michael Bent, D.D.
         300 South Maple Avenue
         Green Bay, Wisconsin 54303

10179   American Orthodox Church
         c/o David Baxter
         Rogers, Arkansas 72202

13131   American Rescue Workers
         2827 Frankford Avenue
         Philadelphia, Pennsylbania 19134

                        Rescue Herald (q)

20545   American School of Mental Vivology
         Cedar Heart of the Ozarks
         Thornfield, Missouri 65762

21955   American Universalist Temple
         of Divine Wisdom
         Route 4
         Box 301
         Escondido, California 92025

                              Bulletin

24268   American Vegan Society
         Malaga, New Jersey 08328

                               Ahisma

10176   American World Patriarchs
         c/o Archbishop Uladyslau Ryzy-Ryski
         P.O. Box 482
         Wren Place
         Scrub Oak, New York 10588

                              Quincena

11954   Americans First, Inc.
         Box 60511
         Oklahoma City, Oklahoma 73106

21554   Amica Temple of Radiance
         c/o Mr. Roland T. Hunt
         Box 304
         Ojai, California 93023

24246   Ananda Marga Yoga Society
         854 Pearl Street
         Denver, Colorado   80203

                    Sadvipra (m)

                    Vistara (q)

24057   Ananda Meditation Retreat
         c/o Swami Kriyananda
         Alleghany Star Route
         Nevada City, California   95959

                    Spirit of Nature (bi-m)

14240   Anchor Bay Evangelistic Association
         P.O. Box 188
         New Baltimore, Michigan   48047

21618   Ancient and Mystic Order of
            Rosae Crucis (AMORC)
         Rosicrucian Park
         San Jose, California   95114

                    Rosicrucian Digest (m)

10409   Anglican Church of America
         c/o Most Rev. J.H. George
         P.O. Box 727
         Spartanburg, South Carolina   29301

10412   Anglican Episcopal Church
         P.O. Box 11782
         Santa Ana, California   92711

                    Anglican Episcopal Digest (q)

10406   Anglican Orthodox Church
         c/o Most Rev. James Parker Dees,
            Presiding Bishop
         P.O. Bos 128
         Statesville, North Carolina   28677

                    Anglican Orthodox Church News (m)

17701   Anglo-Saxon Federation of America
         Haverhill, Massachusetts   01830

                    Destiny

84

21241   Anthropological Research Foundation
         c/o Ray and Jack Fletcher, Presidents
         P.O. Box 7203
         San Diego, California   92107

         Anthropological Society
         (See Christian Community)

20555   Antioch Association of Metaphysical Science
         13580 Orleans Street
         Detroit, Michigan   48203

10145   Antiochean Orthodox Christian
            Archdiocese of All North America
         c/o Metropolitan Philip
         358 Mountain Road
         Englewood, New Jersey   07631

                          The Word (m)

30905   Apostolic Christian Church (Nazarean)
         c/o Apostolic Christian Church Foundation
         P.O. Box 622
         Akron, Ohio 44309

30313   Apostolic Christian Church of the
            United States and Canada
         (no address available)

30907   Apostolic Christian Churches of America
         c/o Elder Roy L. Sauder
         3528 North Linden Lane
         Peoria, Illinois   61604

14255   Apostolic Church
         142 North 17th Street
         Philadelphia, Pennsylvania   19103

14403   Apostolic Church of Jesus
         1825 East River Street
         Pueblo, Colorado   81001

                          Jesus--Only News of the
                            Apostolic Faith (q)

14415   Apostolic Church of Jesus Christ
         (no address available)

10403   Apostolic Episcopal Church
         c/o Most Rev. Harold F.A. Jarvis
         Wesley Avenue
         Shelter Island Heights
         Long Island, New York   11965

14440   Apostolic Evangelistic Association
         (no address available)

14407   Apostolic Faith
         1043 Middle Street
         Kalihi
         Honolulu, Hawaii 96819

14201   Apostolic Faith
         1009 Lincoln Avenue
         Baxter Springs, Kansas 66713

                        The Apostolic Faith Report (m)
                        Box 133
                        Hardesty, Oklahoma 73944

14125   The Apostolic Faith
         Northwest Sixth & Burnside
         Portland, Oregon 97209

                        Light of Hope (bi-m)

14439   Apostolic Gospel Church of
           Jesus Christ
         1767 Thomas Terrace
         Decatur, Georgia 30032

11040   Apostolic Lutheran Church
         c/o Rev. Andrew MacKelson
         Canal Road
         Houghton, Michigan 49931

                        Christian Monthly (m)
                        Apostolic Lutheran Book Concern
                        Box 126
                        Marks Road
                        Esko, Minnesota 55733

11041   Apostolic Lutherans
           (Church of the First Born)
         (no address available)

11043   Apostolic Lutherans
           (Evangelical #1)
         (no address available)

11044   Apostolic Lutherans
           (Evangelicals #2)
         (no address available)

11045   Apostolic Lutherans
           (Heidemans)
         (no address available)

11042   Apostolic Lutherans
         (The New Awakening)
         (no address available)

12324   Apostolic Methodist Church
         (no address available)

14419   Apostolic Overcoming Holy Church
            of God
         c/o Bishop W.T. Phillips
         2212 Tonlours Drive
         Mobile, Alabama 36617

                          The People's Mouthpiece
                          c/o Phillips Publishing Company
                          Mobile, Alabama

21355   Aquarian Educational Group
         P.O. Box 605
         Reseda, California 91335

22340   Aquarian Family of Covens
         c/o Starrcraft--Moon Star
         P.O. Box 531
         Watertown, New York 13601

21135   Aquarian Fellowship Church
         965 Park Avenue
         San Jose, California 95126

         OR

         P.O. Box 5141
         San Jose, California 95150

20220   Aquarian Research Foundation
         5620 Morton Street
         Philadelphia, Pennsylvania 19144

                          Newsletter (m)

22383   Aquarius Spiritus Templum
         126-1/2 South Main
         Elkhart, Indiana 45614

21354   Arcana Workshops
         407 North Maple Drive
         Suite 214
         P.O. Box 5105
         Beverly Hills, California 90210

21350   Arcane School
        11 West 42nd Street
        32nd Floor
        New York, New York 10036

                    World Goodwill Newsletter (q)

                    The Beacon (bi-m)

10180   Archdiocese of the American Orthodox
          Catholic Church in the U.S. and
          Canada
        c/o Most Rev. R. Zaborowski,
          Archbishop-Primate
        Monastery of St. Gregory
        2803 Tenth Street
        Wyandotte, Michigan 48192

10326   Archdiocese of the Old Catholic
          Church in America
        c/o Most Rev. Walter Xavier Brown
        2915 West Highland Boulevard
        Milwaukee, Wisconsin 53208

                    The Franciscan (q)
                    1636 West Rascher Avenue
                    Chicago, Illinois 60640

21973   Arica Institute
        580 Market Street
        San Francisco, California 94104

10215   Armenian Apostolic Church of America
        138 East 39th Street
        New York, New York 10016

                    Cilicia

10216   Armenian Church of North America,
          Diocese of the
        c/o Most Rev. Archbishop Torkom Manoogian
        630 Second Avenue
        New York, New York 10016

                    The Armenian Church (m)

                    Hayastanyaitz Yeyeghetzy (m)

24242   Arunachala Ashrama
        342 East Sixth Street
        New York, New York 10003

21420   Aryo-Christian Church of St. George
        of Cappadocia
        c/o Rev. George Stasek, Pres. Bp.
        Box 74884
        Los Angeles, California   90004

12330   Asbury Bible Churches
        c/o Rev. Jack Tondee
        P.O. Box 1021
        Dublin, Georgia   31021

21527   Ascended Masters Fellowship
        Box 603
        162 Look-a-Way
        Yarnell, Arizona   85362

14210   Assemblies of God
        1445 Boonville Avenue
        Springfield, Missouri   65802

                         Pentecostal Evangel (w)

18315   Assemblies of "The Called Out Ones"
        of "Yah"
        231 Cedar Street
        Jackson, Tennessee 38301

                    "Called Out Ones" Bible Thought
                       Provocative Massager

14411   Assemblies of the Lord Jesus Christ, Inc.
        3403 Summer Avenue
        Memphis, Tennessee   38122

                         Apostolic Witness (m)

18307   Assemblies of Yah
        P.O. Box 811
        Albany, Oregon   97321

                              The Word

18309   Assemblies of Yahweh
        c/o Jacob O. Meyer
        R.D. 1
        Box 200
        Bethel, Pennsylvania   19507

                    The Sacred Name Broadcaster (m)

14740   Assembly of Christian Churches, Inc.
        c/o Bethel Christian Temple
        7 West 110th Street
        New York, New York

30450   Assembly of Christian Soldiers
          (no address available)

18305   Assembly of Yahvah
          Sixth & Elm Streets
          P.O. Box 35
          Junction City, Oregon   97448

                        The Eliyah Messenger and Field
                        Reporter (m)

                        World Today Analyzed (m)
                        c/o Elder L.D. Snow
                        120 North Zunis Avenue
                        Tulsa, Oklahoma   74110

18301   Assembly of Yahweh
          1010 North Gunnel Road
          Eaton Rapids, Michigan 48827

                        The Faith (m)
                        P.O. Box 102
                        Holt, Michigan   48842

11706   Associate Reformed Presbyterian
             Church (General Synod)
          c/o Associate Reformed Presbyterian
             Center
          Suite 206
          300 University Ridge
          Greenville, South Carolina   29601

                        Associate Reformed Presbyterian
                        Due West, South Carolina   29639

14409   Associated Brotherhood of Christians
          221 East Lowery Street
          Hot Springs, Arkansas   71901

13303   Associated Churches of Christ (Holiness)
          1302 East Adams Boulevard
          Los Angeles, California   90011

18226   Associated Churches of God
          The Clark Building
          Columbia, Maryland   21044

                        Impact (bi-m)

17215   Associated Gospel Churches
          10380 American Avenue
          Detroit, Michigan   48204

                        A.G.C. Reporter (q)

90

21911   Association for Research and
           Enlightenment
         Box 595
         Virginia Beach, Virginia   23451

                    The ARE Journal (bi-m)

                    ARE News (m)

21253   Association for the Understanding
           of Man
         c/o Mr. Ray Stanford
         P.O. Box 5310
         Austin, Texas   78763

                    Journal (q)

11035   Association of Evangelical
           Lutheran Churches
         P.O. Box 9637
         St. Louis, Missouri   63122

16105   Association of Evangelicals
           for Missions
         c/o Rev. Charles A. Hodgman
         24 Granby Road
         Worcester, Massachusetts   01604

                    The New Aurora (bi-m)
                    314 Richfield Road
                    Upper Darby, Pennsylvania   19082

11024   Association of Free Lutheran
           Congregations
         3170 East Medicine Lake Boulevard
         Minneapolis, Minnesota   55427

                    The Lutheran Ambassador (bi-w)

15505   Association of Fundamental Gospel
           Churches
         9189 Grubb Court
         Canton, Ohio   44721

13103   Association of Fundamental
           Ministers and Churches
         c/o Hugh Sawyer
         1927 East Monroe Terrace
         Springfield, Missouri   65802

                    Fundamental News
                    1803 East 55th Street
                    Kansas City, Missouri   64103

12331   Association of Independent
         Methodist Churches
         c/o Mr. John R. Wright, President
         Box 4274
         Jackson, Mississippi 39216

                         The AIM Bulletin
                         530 Woodland Hills Boulevard
                         Jackson, Mississippi 39216

14130   Association of International
         Gospel Assemblies
         2621 Louisiana Avenue
         St. Louis, Missouri 63118

21522   Association of Sananda &
         Sanat Kumara
         P.O. Box 35
         Mt. Shasta, California 96067

14903   Association of Seventh-Day
         Pentecostal Assemblies
         4700 N.E. 119th Street
         Vancouver, Washington 98665

10220   Assyrian Orthodox Church/aka/
         Archdiocese of the Syrian Church
         of Antioch
         c/o Rev. Elias Sugar
         701 87th Street
         North Bergen, New Jersey 07047

21630   Astara Foundation
         216 South Mariposa Avenue
         Los Angeles, California 90004

                         Voice of Astara (m)

21987   Astrological, Metaphysical, Occult,
         Revelatory, Enlightenment (AMORE)
         Church
         Meridian, Connecticut 06450

22239   Atlantion Wicca
         c/o Don F. Sawyer
         4280 Aurora Path
         Liverpool, New York 13088

21988   Aum Temple of Universal Truth
         c/o Nina Fern Dennison, President
         45837 Deva Lane
         Newberry Springs, California 92365

10155   Autocephalous Slavonic Orthodox
         Catholic Church (In Exile)
         c/o Metropolitan-Archbishop Andrew
         2213 Hunter Avenue
         Bronx, New York 10469

30130   Avalon (and Related Jesus People
         Communities)
         174 Portage Drive
         Akron, Ohio 44303

                         Jesus Loves You

21995   Awareness Research Foundation, Inc.
         Box 143
         North Miami, Florida 33161

                         Meet The Lords (m)

18425   Back to The Bible Way
         517 N.E. Second Street
         Ft. Lauderdale, Florida 33301

                    Back To The Bible Way

23901   Baha'i Faith
         National Spiritual Assembly Headquarters
         536 Sheridan Road
         Wilmette, Illinois 60091

                    World Order (q)

16121   Baptist Bible Fellowship International
         Box 106
         Springfield, Missouri 65801

                    Baptist Bible Tribune (w)

10420   Baptist General Conference
         (Swedish Baptist)
         1233 Central Street
         Evanston, Illinois 60201

                    The Standard (s-m)

16123   Baptist Missionary Association
         of America
         716 Main Street
         Little Rock, Arkansas 72201

                    The Advancer (m)

                    The Gleaner (m)

                         93

22117   Bavarian Illuminati
c/o R.A. Wilson
535 Taylor, #104
San Francisco, California 94102

15305   Beachy Amish Mennonite Churches
c/o Amish Mennonite Aid
Lester J. Hershberger
East Rochester, Ohio 44625

22116   Bennu Phoenix Temple of the
Hermetic Order of the
Golden Dawn
c/o Mr. John Phillips Palmer
Box 36
River Road
Lumberville, Pennsylvania 18933

17320   Berean Bible Fellowship
52nd & East Virginia Streets
Phoenix, Arizona 85008

17330   Berean Bible Society
7609 West Belmont
Chicago, Illinois 60635

Berean Searchlight (m)

17245   Berean Fundamental Church
Box 549
North Platte, Nebraska 69101

Berean Digest (m)

30106   Berkeley Christian Coalition
Box 4309
Berkeley, California 94704

Right On (m)

30421   Berkeley Free Church
P.O. Box 9177
Berkeley, California 94709

Win With Love

17217   Bethany Bible Church and Related
Independent Bible Churches of
the Phoenix (Arizona) Area
6060 North Seventh Avenue
Phoenix, Arizona 85013

14443   Bethel Ministerial Association, Inc.
         4350 Lincoln Avenue
         Evansville, Indiana   47715

                        ". . . . Words With Power" (q)

14256   Bethel Temple
         2033 Second Avenue
         Seattle, Washington   98121

15150   Bethesda Mennonite Colony Conference
         Box 537
         Gladstone
         Manitoba ROJ OTO, Canada

                            Believer's Bulletin

18218   Bible Church of God
         826 East Ninth Street
         Des Moines, Iowa   50316

17215   Bible Churches (Classics Expositor)
         c/o Dr. C.E. McLain
         1429 N.W. 100th
         Oklahoma City, Oklahoma   73114

                            Classics Expositor

13164   Bible Fellowship Church
         c/o Pastor W.B. Hottel
         404 West Main Street
         Terre Hill, Pennsylvania   17581

13415   Bible Holiness Church
         (no address available)

18204   Bible Holiness Mission
         (no address available)

                            Truth on Fire (bi-m)

13417   Bible Methodist Church
         c/o Rev. George Vernon
         P.O. Box 187
         Brent, Alabama   35304

                            Bible Methodist

13411   Bible Methodist Connection of
            Tennessee
         P.O. Box 10408
         Knoxville, Tennessee 37919

                            Tennessee Tidings (m)

95

13401   Bible Missionary Church
         2601 North Federal Boulevard
         Denver, Colorado   80211

                          The Missionary Revivalist (m)
                          3501 46th Avenue
                          Rock Island, Illinois   61201

11703   Bible Presbyterian Church
         756 Haddon Avenue
         Collingswood, New Jersey   08101

                          Christian Beacon

12321   Bible Protestant Church
         110 Virginia Avenue
         Audubon, New Jersey   08106

                          Bible Protestant Messenger (m)

14433   Bible Way Church of Our Lord
           Jesus Christ World Wide, Inc.
         1130 New Jersey Avenue, N.W.
         Washington, D.C.   20001

                          Bible Way News Voice (bi-m)

23430   Black Christian Nationalist Church
         c/o Shrine of the Black Madonna
         13535 Livernois
         Detroit, Michigan   48238

24212   Blue Mountain Center of Meditation
         Box 381
         Berkeley, California   94701

                          The Little Lamp (q)

25150   Bodaji Mission
         1251 Elm
         Honolulu, Hawaii 96814

21568   Bodha Society of America, Inc.
         c/o Violet Reed
         Box 144
         Long Beach, California   90801

                          Sun Rays

14908   Body of Christ Movement
         c/o Fellowship of Christian Believers
         210 Third Avenue, N.E.
         Grand Rapids, Minnesota 55744

                          Fellowship Together
                          96

18203   Branch SDAs
         Route 7
         Box 471-B
         Waco, Texas   76705

15502   Brethren Church (Ashland, Ohio)
         524 College Avenue
         Ashland, Ohio   44805

                         The Brethren Evangelist

15511   Brethren in Christ   .
         c/o Evangel Press
         Nappanee, Indiana   46550

                         Evangelical Visitor (bi-w)

21502   Bridge to Freedom, Inc.
         Kings Park
         Long Island, New York   11754

30325   Brotherhood of Peace and Tranquility
         (Church of the Brotherhood)
         P.O. Box 2142
         Costa Mesa, California   92626

                         Pastoraletter (q)

21415   Brotherhood of the Pleroma
         P.O. Box 5220
         Sherman Oaks, California   91403

21705   Brotherhood of the Seven Rays
         (no address available)

20230   Brotherhood of the Spirit
         Shepardson Road
         Warwick, Massachusetts   01378

20235   Brotherhood of the Sun
         808 East Cota Street
         Santa Barbara, California   93103

21634   Brotherhood of the White Temple
         Sedalia, Colorado   80135

                         Light on the Path

                         Brotherhood Truth Sheet

25310   Buddha's Universal Church
         702 Washington Street
         San Francisco, California   94108

97

25355   Buddha's Universal Church and Ch'an
           Buddhist Sangha
           c/o Dr. Calvin Chan Vassallo, Archbishop
           3507-1/2 Louisiana
           Houston, Texas   77002

25330   Buddhist Association of America
           109 Waverly Place
           San Francisco, California   49108

25340   The Buddhist Association of the
             United States
           3070 Albany Crescent
           The Bronx
           New York, New York   10463

25122   Buddhist Churches of America
           1710 Octavia Street
           San Francisco, California   94109

                    Newsletter (m)

25530   Buddhist Fellowship of New York
           c/o Buddhist Church
           331 Riverside Drive
           New York, New York   10025

           OR

           c/o Rev. Boris Erwitt
           309 West 57th Street
           New York, New York   10019

                    Kantaka (m)

25510   Buddhist Vihara Society, Inc.
           5017 16th Street, N.W.
           Washington, D.C.   20011

               Washington Buddhist (bi-m)

25515   Buddhist World Philosophical Group
           c/o Miss Marie Harlowe
           Three Rivers, Wisconsin   49093

16213   Buffalo River Primitive Baptist Association
           (no address available)

22101   Builders of the Adytum
           5105 North Figueroa Street
           Los Angeles, California   90042

               Adytum News Notes

10130   Bulgarian Eastern Orthodox Church
         c/o Bishop Joseph, Metropolitan
         312 West 101st Street
         New York, New York 10025

10131   Bulgarian Eastern Orthodox Church
           Diocese of the U.S.A. and Canada
         c/o Very Rev. Fr. George Nedelkoff
         St. Nicholas Eastern Orthodox Church
         Warsaw & Oxford Streets
         Ft. Wayne, Indiana 46806

10160   Byelorussian Autocephalic Orthodox
           Church in the USA
         c/o Most Rev. Archbishop Andrew
         3517 West 25th Street
         Cleveland, Ohio 44109

10161   Byelorussian Patriarchate of
           St. Andrew the Apostle the
           First Called
         c/o The Most Rev. Prof. Uladyslau
           Ryzy-Ryski, Th. M., Lit. D.
         Pro-Cathedral-Bielorussicum
         Wren Place
         Shrub Oak, New York 10588

25220   California Bosatsukai
         c/o Nakagawa Soen Roshi
         5632 Green Oak Drive
         Los Angeles, California 90068

23720   Calistran Muslims
         (no address available)

17707   Calvary Fellowships, Inc.
         c/o Woodbrook Soul Winning
           Bible School
         14815 Spring Street, S.W.
         Tacoma, Washington 98539

                          Christ Is The Answer (m)

30321   Calvary Grace Christian Churches
           of Faith
         c/o Rev. Herman Keck, Jr.
         271 N.E. 57th Street
         Ft. Lauderdale, Florida 33308

30319   Calvary Grace Churches of Faith, Inc.
         Box 333
         Rillton, Pennsylvania 15678

13216   Calvary Holiness Church
        3415-19 North Second Street
        Philadelphia, Pennsylvania   19140

20548   Calvary Missionary Church
        1515 Steves Avenue
        San Antonio, Texas   78210

                        Light For All   (q)

14218   Calvary Pentecostal Church, Inc.
        c/o Rev. Bruce M. Hughes
        1856 Bigelow Avenue
        Olympia, Washington 98506

                        Calvary Tidings

25234   Cambridge Buddhist Association
        Three Craigie Street
        Cambridge, Massachusetts 02138

14126   Carolina Evangelistic Association
        200 Tuckaseege   Road
        Charlotte, North Carolina 28208

17225   Cathedral of Tomorrow
        P.O. Box 3500
        Akron, Ohio   44310

                        The Answer

30975   Catholic Apostolic Church
        417 West 57th Street
        New York, New York   10019

10340   Catholic Life Church
        c/o Bishop Mark Harding
        2257 West 32nd Avenue
        Denver, Colorado   80200

23012   Central Conference of American
           Rabbis
        790 Madison Avenue
        New York, New York   10021

                        CCAR Journal   (q)

16210   Central District Primitive
           Baptist Association
        (no address available)

15735   Central Yearly Meeting of Friends
        Box 296
        Noblesville, Indiana   46060

                        100

30160   Chicago Metropolitan Jesus
         Peoples Groups
         (no central address)

30190   Children of God
         (no address available)

21580   Children of Light Society
         c/o Trevor and Martha Modecai
         10025 East Girard Avenue
         Denver, Colorado 80231

21835   Children of the Moon
         4611 Upshur
         Bladenburg, Maryland 20710

25345   China Buddhist Association
         102 Mott Street
         New York, New York 10013

25306   Chinese Buddhist Association
         42 Kawananakoa Place
         Honolulu, Hawaii 96817

21901   Chirothesian Church of Faith
         1747 North Normandie Avenue
         Los Angeles, California 90027

18320   Chosen Vessels
         c/o Elder Anna S. Krieter
         1030 "E" Street
         San Diego, California 92101

                              New Age Truth

25555   Chowado Henjokyo
         c/o Rev. Reisai Fugita
         1757 Algaroba Street
         Honolulu, Hawaii 96814

21782   Christ Brotherhood, Inc.
         c/o Tarna L. Halsey
         Box 244
         Logan, Utah 84321

                              Newsletter

10321   Christ Catholic Church
         c/o Fr. Karl Pruter
         1744 West Devon Avenue
         Chicago, Illinois 60660

                         Catholic Life (q)

                         Pastoral Counseling (q)
                         101

30150   Christ Is The Answer
         (no address available)

21957   Christ Light Community
         c/o Dr. Gilbert N. Holloway
         Star Route 2
         Box CLC
         Deming, New Mexico   88030

                        Newsletter (m)

21909   Christ Ministry Foundation
         P.O. Box 9543
         San Jose, California   95157

                     The Seeker's Quest

10320   Christ Orthodox Catholic Exarchate
           of Americas and Eastern Hemisphere
         c/o Most Rev. Peter A. Zurawetzky,
           Archbishop
         946 Leesville Avenue
         Rahway, New Jersey   07065

                     Our Missionary

20525   Christ Truth League
         2400 Canton Drive
         Fort Worth, Texas   76112

16755   Christadelphians-Amended

                     The Christadelphian Tidings (bi-m)
                     P.O. Box 1066
                     Pasadena, California   91102

16750   Christadelphians-Unamended

                     Christadelphian Advocate (m)
                     1530 Yewley Drive
                     Richmond, Virginia   23231

13160   Christian and Missionary Alliance
         350 North Highland Avenue
         Nyack, New York   10960

                     Alliance Witness

30977   Christian Apostolic Church
         c/o Elder Ben Edelman
         Sabetha, Kansas   66534

30978   Christian Apostolic Church
         c/o Elder Peter Schaefer, Sr.
         Forest, Illinois   61741

102

20534   Christian Assembly
         72 North Fifth Street
         San Jose, California   95112

18405   Christian Believers Conference
         1828 South 47th Court
         Cicero, Illinois   60650

                     Kingdom Scribe

18417   Christian Bible Students
            Association
         P.O. Box 724
         Warren, Michigan   48089

                     The Harvest Message   (bi-m)

30909   Christian Catholic Church
         Dowie Memorial Drive
         Zion, Illinois   60099

                     Leaves of Healing   (q)

16701   Christian Church (Disciples of Christ)
         222 South Downey Avenue
         Indianapolis, Indiana   46219

                     The Disciple   (bi-w)
                     Box 179
                     St. Louis, Missouri   63166

16710   Christian Churches-Independent
         c/o North American Christian Convention
         3533 Epley Road
         Cincinnati, Ohio   45239

                     Lookout   (w)

                     Christian Standard   (w)
                     Standard Publishing
                     8121 Hamilton Avenue
                     Cincinnati, Ohio   45231

21550   Christian Community
            (Anthroposophical Society)
         309 West 74th Street
         New York, New York   10023

                     The Christian Community

14241   Christian Church of North America
        General Council
        1818 State Street
        Sharon, Pennsylvania 16146

                         Il Faro (m)
                         P.O. Box 66
                         Herkimer, New York   13350

16735   The Christian Congregation
        c/o Rev. Ora Wilbert Eads
        804 West Hemlock Street
        LaFollette, Tennessee 37766

30115   Christian Foundation
        (no address available)

18810   Christian Israelite Church
        1204 North Rural Street
        Indianapolis, Indiana 46201

                         Notes From Our Church Organ (bi-m)

                         Daily Bible Reading Notes (m)

13217   Christian Kingdom Centers
        c/o Christian Assembly
        P.O. Box 9
        Holly Hill, Florida 32017

                         Ecclesian Truth (m)

12357   Christian Methodist Episcopal Church
        P.O. Box 6447
        531 South Parkway East
        Memphis, Tennessee 38106

                         Christian Index (w)

13161   Christian Nation Church U.S.A.
        c/o Rev. Walter F. Clark, Secretary
        345 Cedar Drive
        Loveland, Ohio 45140

13211   Christian Pilgrim Church
        Coldwater, Michigan

11602   Christian Reformed Church
        2850 Kalamazoo Avenue, S.E.
        Grand Rapids, Michigan 49508

                         The Banner (w)

                         De Wachter (w)

104

17705   Christian Research, Inc.
         2624 First Avenue, S.
         Minneapolis, Minnesota   55408

                        Facts For Action   (bi-m)

         Christian Science
         (See Church of Christ, Scientist)

21187   Christian Spirit Center
         P.O. Box 114
         Elon College, North Carolina   27244

30911   Christian Union
         P.O. Box 38
         Excelsior Springs, Missouri   64024

                        Christian Union Witness   (m)

11902   Christian Universalist Church
            of America
         P.O. Box 323
         Deerfield Beach, Florida   33441

16124   Christian Unity Baptist Association
         c/o Elder Thomas T. Reynolds
         Thomasville, North Carolina   27360

14922   Christ's Faith Mission
         Box 68
         Highland Park Station
         Los Angeles, California   90042

                        Herald of Hope   (bi-m)

30170   Christ's Household of Faith
         c/o Rev. Donald Asbury
         313 Clark Street
         Mora, Minnesota   55051

13140   Christ's Sanctified Holy Church
            (West Columbia, South Carolina)
         CSHC Campground
         Perry, Georgia   31068

13141   Christ's Sanctified Holy Church
         South Cutting Avenue & East Spencer Street
         Jennings, Louisiana   70546

21525   Christ's Truth Church and
            School of Wisdom
         Columbus, New Mexico   88029

                        The Golden Dawn

                    105

21558   Christward Ministry
         c/o Mrs. Flower A. Newhouse
         P.O. Box 1628
         Escondido, California 92025

22375   Church and School of Wicca
         Box 1502
         New Bern, North Carolina 28560

                         Survival

30420   Church for the Fellowship
            of All People
         2041 Larkin Street
         San Francisco, California 94109

                    The Growing Edge

21173   Church of Ageless Wisdom
         c/o Rev. Beth R. Hand
         124 South 13th Street
         Philadelphia, Pennsylvania 19107

22520   Church of All Worlds
         P.O. Box 2953
         St. Louis, Missouri 63130

                    Green Egg (eight per year)

                    The Pagan (a)

21410   Church of Antioch, Malabar Rite
         c/o Most Rev. H. Adrian Spruit
         P.O. Box 1713
         Santa Ana, California 92702

                         Contact

20236   Church of Armageddon
         c/o Love Israel
         617 West McGraw Street
         Seattle, Washington 98119

21917   Church of Basic Truth
         P.O. Box 6084
         Phoenix, Arizona 85005

30195   Church of Bible Understanding
         (no address available)

19415   Church of Christ (Bible and Book of
            Mormon Teaching)
         723 South Chrysler Street
         Indianapolis, Indiana 46224

                         106

19411   Church of Christ (Bronson)
         P.O. Box 146
         Independence, Missouri   64051

                   Voice of Warning (m)

13301   Church of Christ (Holiness) U.S.A.
         329 East Monument Street
         Jackson, Mississippi   39202

                        Truth (m)
                        552 East 44th Street
                        Chicago, Illinois   60658

19411   Church of Christ (Temple Lot)
         Temple Lot
         Independence, Missouri   64050

                        Zion's Advocate (m)
                        Box 472
                        Independence, Missouri   64051

20610   Church of Christ, Scientist
         Christian Science Church Center
         107 Falmouth Street
         Boston, Massachusetts   02115

                   Christian Science Sentinel (w)

                   Christian Science Journal (m)

                   Christian Science Quarterly (q)

19412   Church of Christ with the
            Elijah Message
         c/o Rev. James W. Savage
         608 Lacy Road
         Independence, Missouri   64050

                        Voice of Peace (m)
                        Box 199
                        Independence, Missouri   64051

17230   Church of Christian Liberty
         203 East McDonald Road
         Prospect Heights, Illinois   60070

                        Christian Militant

21556   Church of Cosmic Origin &
            School of Thought
         P.O. Box 257
         June Lake, California   93529

                        Cosmic Frontiers (q)

                        107

21165   Church of Cosmic Science, Inc.
         P.O. Box 61
         Jamul, California   92035

                          Cosmic Light (m)

12328   Church of Daniel's Band
         c/o Rev. Wesley Hoggard
         R.F.D. 2
         Midland, Michigan   48640

21963   Church (and Institute) of
            General Psionics
         2501 Artesia Boulevard
         Redondo Beach, California   90278

18120   Church of God (Abrahamic Faith)
         Oregon, Illinois   61061

                          Restitution Herald (m)

                          Church of God Progress Journal (m)

13102   Church of God (Anderson, Ind.)
         Box 2499
         Anderson, Indiana   46011

                          Vital Christianity (bi-w)

                          Church of God Missions (m)
                          Box 337
                          Anderson, Indiana   46011

14401   Church of God (Apostolic)
         c/o Elder David E. Smith
         125 Meadows Street
         Beckley, West Virginia   25801

14101   Church of God (Cleveland, Tenn.)
         Keith Street at 25th, N.W.
         Cleveland, Tennessee 37311

                          Church of God Evangel (bi-w)

                          Lighted Pathway (m)

13104   Church of God (Guthrie, Okla.)
         c/o Faith Publishing House
         920 West Monsur Avenue
         Guthrie, Oklahoma   73044

                          Faith and Victory (m)

13143   Church of God (Holiness)
          7415 Metcalf
          Overland Park, Kansas   66204

                    The Church Herald and Holiness
                         Banner (w)

18313   Church of God (Jerusalem)
          Box 568
          Jerusalem, Israel

                    Mount Zion Reporter

                    Jerusalem Messenger

14104   Church of God (Jerusalem Acres)
          Box 1207
          Jerusalem Acres
          Cleveland, Tennessee   37311

                    The Vision Speaks (m)

13305   Church of God (Sanctified Church)
          1037 Jefferson Street
          Nashville, Tennessee 37208

          OR

          c/o H.C. Nesbitt
          1501 21st Avenue, N.
          Nashville, Tennessee   37208

18214   The Church of God (Seventh Day)
          79 Water Street
          Box 328
          Salem, West Virginia   26426

                    Advocate of Truth (s-m)

14101   The Church of God (World Headquarters)
          2504 Arrow Wood Drive
          Huntsville, Alabama   35803

                    The Church of God (m)

23401   Church of God and Saints of Christ
          c/o Bishop Howard Z. Plummer
          P.O. Box 187
          Portsmouth, Virginia   23704

                    Weekly Prophet (w)

109

18235   Church of God at Cleveland
        P.O. Box 02026
        Cleveland, Ohio   44102

18219   Church of God-Bible Beacon
        430 Live Oak Street
        Edgewater, Florida   32032

                            Bible Beacon

18230   Church of God, Body of Christ
        c/o Elder Ivan W. Igames
        Route 1
        Box 86
        Mocksville, North Carolina   27028

14912   Church of God by Faith
        3220 Haines Street
        Jacksonville, Florida   32206

                    The Spiritual Guide (m)
                    3125 Franklin Street
                    Jacksonville, Florida   32206

14501   The Church of God in Christ
        958 Mason Street
        Memphis, Tennessee 38126

                        Whole Truth (m)

14502   Church of God in Christ,
          Congregational
        (no address available)

14506   Church of God in Christ,
          International
        1331 Quindare Boulevard
        Kansas City, Kansas   66104

                        The Message

                    The Holiness Call

15113   Church of God in Christ
          (Mennonite)
        420 North Wedel Street
        Moundridge, Kansas   67107

                    Messenger of Truth (bi-w)
                    Lahoma, Oklahoma   73754

14923   Church of God in the Lord
          Jesus Christ
        (no address available)

                            110

14103   The Church of God of Prophecy
         c/o M.A. Tomlinson, General Overseer
         Bible Place
         Cleveland, Tennessee 37311

                    White Wing Messenger (w)

                    Happy Harvester (m)

14129   Church of God of the
         Apostolic Faith
         2530 West Cameron
         Tulsa, Oklahoma 74127

14143   Church of God of the
         Mountain Assembly
         Florence Avenue
         Jellico, Tennessee 37762

                    The Gospel Herald (m)

14145   Church of God of the Original
         Mountain Assembly
         Williamsburg, Kentucky 40769

14144   Church of God of the Union
         Assembly, Inc.
         Box 1323
         Dalton, Georgia 30720

                    Quarterly News (q)
                    Box 345
                    Salome, Arizona 85348

18217   Church of God, Sabbatarian
         P.O. Box 1134
         Hawthorne, California 90250

                    Salt (m)

18228   Church of God Seventh Era
         c/o Larry Gilbert Johnson
         P.O. Box A-1
         Cabot, Arkansas 72023

18226   Church of God, The Eternal
         P.O. Box 775
         Eugene, Oregon 97401

                    Newsletter (m)

14106   Church of God, The House of Prayer
         Cleveland, Tennessee 37311

                         111

14610   Church of God with Signs Fellowship
        (no address available)

20527   Church of Inner Power, Inc.
        P.O. Drawer AA
        Evergreen, Colorado 80439

20560   Church of Inner Wisdom
        c/o Joan Gibson
        Box 4765
        San Jose, California 95126

                        The Voice (q)

19225   Church of Jesus Christ (Allred)
        (no address available)

19920   The Church of Jesus Christ
          (Bickertonites)
        P.O. Box 72
        Sixth & Lincoln Streets
        Monongahela, Pennsylvania 15063

                        Gospel News (m)

19905   Church of Jesus Christ (Cutlerites)
        c/o Mr. Rupert J. Fletcher
        819 South Cottage
        Independence, Missouri 64050

19240   Church of Jesus Christ (Goldman)
        (no address available)

19229   Church of Jesus Christ (Musser)
        (no address available)

19910   Church of Jesus Christ (Strangites)
        c/o Elder Vernon D. Swift
        P.O. Box 522
        Artesia, New Mexico 98210

                        Gospel Herald (q)
                        c/o Voree Press
                        Bruce Flanders
                        Box 194
                        Burlington, Wisconsin 53105

19101   Church of Jesus Christ of
          Latter-Day Saints
        47 East South Temple Street
        Salt Lake City, Utah 84111

                        Deseret News (q)

                        The Ensign (m)
                        112

19235   Church of Jesus Christ of
         Latter-Day Saints (Kingston)
         Bountiful, Utah 84010

19220   Church of Jesus Christ of
         Latter-Day Saints
         (Leroy Johnson)
         Colorado City, Arizona 86021

         OR

         c/o Fred Jessup
         Alldale, Utah

21640   Church of Light
         Box 1525
         Los Angeles, California 90053

                          Church of Light Quarterly (q)

21165   Church of Metaphysical
         Christianity
         2717 Browning Street
         Sarasota, Florida 33577

                          The Metaphysical Messenger

25535   Church of One Sermon
         8135 Lincoln Street
         Lemon Grove, California 92045

14421   Church of Our Lord Jesus Christ
         of the Apostolic Faith, Inc.
         2081 Seventh Avenue
         New York, New York 10027

                          The Contender for The Faith (m)
                          112 East 125th Street
                          New York, New York 10035

21113   The Church of Revelation
         517 East Park Passeo
         Las Vegas, Nevada 89104

22426   Church of Satanic Brotherhood
         P.O. Box 1711
         Dayton, Ohio 45401

                          The True Grimore (m)

113

21927   Church of Spiritual Freedoms
       Association of International
         Dionologists
       c/o Mr. Jack Horner
       1700 Westwood Boulevard
       Los Angeles, California 90024

                 Alternatives (m)

21815   Church of the Awakening
       c/o John Aiken
       P.O. Box 1097
       Socorro, New Mexico 87801

13403   Church of the Bible Covenant
       c/o Dr. Remuss Rehfeldt
       Route 2
       Box 66
       Greenfield, Indiana 46140

                 The Covenanter (m)
                 2127 South Delaware Court
                 Tulsa, Oklahoma 74114

15501   Church of the Brethren
       c/oChurch of the Brethren Central Offices
       1451 Dundee Avenue
       Elgin, Illinois 60120

                 Messenger (m)

                 Brethren Life and Thought (q)

20105   Church of the Brotherhood
       Box 606
       Orange City, Florida 32763

30455   Church of the Christian Crusade
       c/o Rev. Billy James Hargis
       P.O. Box 977
       Tulsa, Oklahoma 74102

                 Christian Crusade Weekly (w)

21939   Church of the Christian
         Spiritual Alliance (CSA)
       Lakemont, Georgia 30552

                 Truth Journal (bi-m)

                 Orion (bi-m)

30459   Church of the Creator
        P.O. Box 5908
        Lighthouse Point, Florida   33064

10210   Church of the East in America
        c/o Patriarchate of the East
        554 Arbullo Drive
        San Francisco, California   94132

                        Light From the East
                        3939 Lawton Street
                        San Francisco, California   94122

22550   Church of the Eternal Source
        P.O. Box 7091
        Burbank, California   91505

                        Khepera

19211   Church of the First Born
        c/o Ross Wesley LeBaron
        500 North State Street
        Sandy, Utah   84070

19210   Church of the First Born of
           the Fullness of Times
        c/o Ervil LeBaron
        Colonia LeBaron
        Galena
        Chihuahua, Mexico

21141   Church of the Four Leaf Clover
        144th Street & 85th Drive
        Jamaica
        Long Island, New York   11432

20541   Church of the Fuller Concept
        1420 16th Street, N.W.
        Washington, D.C.   20036

21983   Church of the Gentle Brothers
           and Sisters
        905 Alma Place
        Oakland, California   94610

21984   Church of the Gift of God
        Magnolia Manor
        Hesperus Circle
        Magnolia, Massachusetts 01930

115

11609   Church of the Golden Rule
         P.O. Box 68
         Mt. Eden, California 94577

         OR

         3351 Arizona Street
         Oakland, California 94602

13204   Church of the Gospel
         c/o Ms. Marion E. Green
         20-1/2 Walnut Street
         Hudson Falls, New York 12839

22113   Church of the Hermetic Sciences
            (Ordo Templi Astarte)
         P.O. Box 3341
         Pasadena, California 91103

                              Seventh Ray (q)

11904   Church of the Humanitarian God
         c/o Mr. Ron Libert
         Box 13236
         St. Petersburg, Florida

21560   Church of the Jesus Ethic
         336 West Colorado Street
         Glendale, California 91209

14902   Church of the Little Children
         c/o Mrs. E.C. Wenglaff, Superintendent
         Route 1
         Black Rock, Arkansas 72415

30957   Church of the Living God
         (no address available)

14512   Church of the Living God
         c/o Chief Bishop F.C. Scott
         801 N.E. 17th Street
         Oklahoma City, Oklahoma 73105

                              National Bulletin (q)

                              Fellowship Echoes (m)
                              4355 Washington Boulevard
                              St. Louis, Missouri 63108

21985   Church of the Lord Jesus Christ, Inc.
            (Ishi Temple)
         P.O. Box 489
         Brisbane, California 94005

                              The Christoid Evangel
                              116

14422   Church of The Lord Jesus Christ
        of the Apostolic Faith
        22nd & Bainbridge Streets
        Philadelphia, Pennsylvania   19146

                        The Whole Truth (m)

11025   Church of the Lutheran Brethren
        of America
        Fergus Falls, Minnesota   56537

                        Faith and Fellowship (m)
                        107 North Middletown Road
                        Nanuet, New York   10954

11026   Church of the Lutheran Confession
        Markesan, Wisconsin   53946

                        Lutheran Spokesman
                        22 North State Street
                        New Ulm, Minnesota   56073

13146   Church of the Nazarene
        6401 The Paseo
        Kansas City, Missouri   64131

                        Herald of Holiness (w)

30913   Church of the New Song
        Purilieu of Tellus
        c/o Dr. Stephen S. Fox, S.R.M.
        Box 2001
        Iowa City, Iowa   52240

        OR

        Church of the New Song
        c/o Mr. Harry W. Theriault, Bp.
        P.O. Box 1000
        Anthony, New Mexico   88021

20145   Church of the Savior
        2025 Massachusetts Avenue, N.W.
        Washington, D.C.   20036

20550   Church of the Science of Religion
        c/o Mrs. Carolyn Barbour LaGalyon
        Hotel Wellington
        Seventh Avenue & 55th Street
        New York, New York   10014

21820   Church of the Tree of Life
        451 Columbus Avenue
        San Francisco, California   94133

                        117

20533   Church of the Trinity
       (Invisible Ministry)
       P.O. Box 571
       San Marcos, California 92069

Tidings

20528   Church of the Truth
       c/o Dr. Ervin Seale
       New York Church of the Truth
       154 West 57th Street
       New York, New York 10019

22307   Church of the Wiccan Rede
       c/o Lady Cybele's Cauldron
       405 West Gilmon Street
       Madison, Wisconsin 53703

21159   Church of Tzaddi
       P.O. Box 3082
       Orange, California 92667

30315   Church of Universal Brotherhood
       6311 Yucca Street
       Department F
       Hollywood, California 90028

13315   Church of Universal Triumph/
       The Dominion of God
       c/o Rev. Lord James Shaffer
       8317 LaSalle Boulevard
       Detroit, Michigan 48206

30425   Church of What's Happening Now
       c/o Sister Imagene Williams
       162 Tennessee Avenue, N.E.
       Washington, D.C. 20002

22355   Church of Wicca of Bakersfield
       c/o Rev. George E. Patterson
       1908 Verde Street
       Bakersfield, California 93304

30927   Church of World Messianity
       3068 San Marino Street
       Los Angeles, California 90006

The Glory

16720   Churches of Christ (Non-instrumental)
         (no central address)

                        Firm Foundation (w)
                        P.O. Box 610
                        Austin, Texas   78767

                        Gospel Advocate
                        P.O. Box 150
                        Nashville, Tennessee 37202

14925   Churches of Christ (Non-instrumental-
         Charismatic)
         (no central address)

         Contact: Elder Dan Peters
                    Hillcrest Church of Christ
                    2420 Hillcrest Drive
                    Thousand Oaks, California   91360

16722   Churches of Christ (Non-instrumental-
         Conservative)
         (no central address)

         Contact: Elder William E. Wallace
                    Affton Church of Christ
                    6939 Weber Road
                    St. Louis, Missouri   63123

16724   Churches of Christ (Non-instrumental-
         Non-Sunday School)
         (no central address)

                        Christian Appeal
                        c/o Gene Shelburne
                        Amarillo, Texas

16726   Churches of Christ (Non-instrumental-
         One Cup)
         (no central address)

         Contact: Elder James W. Russell
                    931 North Blackstone
                    Fresno, California   93701

16728   Churches of Christ (Non-instrumental-
         Open)
         (no central address)

                        Mission (m)
                        Box 15024
                        Austin, Texas   78761

119

16730   Churches of Christ (Non-instrumental-
        Premillenimalist)
        (no central address)

        Contact: Elder H.E. Schreiner
                 Highview Church of Christ
                 6105 East Manslick Road
                 Louisville, Kentucky 40219

                 Word and Work (m)

13203   Churches of Christ in Christian Union
        Box 30
        459 East Ohio Street
        Circleville, Ohio 43113

                 Advocate (bi-w)

                 Missionary Tidings (m)

13145   Churches of God (Independent
          Holiness People)
        1225 East First Street
        Fort Scott, Kansas 66701

                 Church Advocate and Good Way

13309   Churches of God, Holiness
        170 Ashby Street, N.W.
        Atlanta, Georgia 30314

13101   Churches of God in North America
          (General Eldership)
        611 South 17th Street
        Harrisburg, Pennsylvania 17105

                 The Church Advocate (m)

17102   Churches of God in the British Isles
          and Overseas
        c/o Mr. V. Ramage
        44 Tweedsmuir Avenue
        Dudas
        Ontario, Canada

                 Needed Truth

14145   Churches of God of the Original
          Mountain Assembly
        Williamsburg, Kentucky 40769

21185   Churches of Spiritual Revelation
        c/o Bishop Edward M. Leighton
        1018 Washington Street
        Reading, Pennsylvania 19601

25290   Cimarron Zen Center
         2505 Cimarron Street
         Los Angeles, California   90018

21251   Circle of Inner Truth
         c/o Mr. Marshall N. Lever
         3784 Sacramento Street
         San Francisco, California   94118

                              Our News and Views (bi-m)

20144   The Colony
         Burnt Ranch, California   95527

23410   Commandment Keepers
         Congregation of the Living God
         c/o Rabbi Wentworth A. Matthews
         One West 123rd Street
         New York, New York 10027

23205   Community of Micah
         1808 Wyoming Avenue, N.W.
         Washington, D.C.   20009

                              Voice of Micah

14710   Concilio Olazabal de Iglesius
             Latino-Americano, Inc.
         Tabernaculo Bethesada
         1925 East First Street
         Los Angeles, California   90033

17340   Concordant Publishing Concern
         15570 West Knochaven Drive
         Saugus, California   91350

                              Unsearchable Riches (bi-m)

11027   Concordia Lutheran Conference
         c/o Rev. O.W. Schaeffer
         8630 West 163rd Street
         Orland Park, Illinois   60477

11034   Conference of Authentic Lutherans
         c/o Rev. Robert E. Yount, Secretary
         Christ the King Lutheran Church
         6541 Eastern Avenue
         Bell Gardens, California   90201

11906   Confraternity of Deists, Inc.
         Box 179
         Homosassa Springs, Florida   32647

22554   Congregation of Aten
        2809 South Trumbull Avenue
        Chicago, Illinois   60623

15114   Congregational Bible Church
        Marietta, Pennsylvania   17547

21965   Congregational Church of Practical
          Theology
        c/o Dr. E. Arthur Winkler
        211 North Pine Street
        Valley, Nebraska   68064

                    Success

14121   Congregational Holiness Church
        c/o Rev. Terry Crews
        Route 1
        Box 290
        Griffin, Georgia   30223

                        Gospel Messenger   (m)
                        701 Davis Street
                        Monroe, Georgia   30655

12310   Congregational Methodist Church
        906 Jefferson Boulevard
        Dallas, Texas   75208

                    The Congregational Methodist
                        Messenger   (w)

16127   Conservative Baptist Association
          of America
        P.O. Box 66
        25W560 Geneva Road
        Wheaton, Illinois   60187

                    C.B.A. Builder

                    The Challenge

11805   Conservative Congregational
          Christian Conference
        P.O. Box 171
        Hinsdale, Illinois   60521

                    Foresee   (q)

15304   Conservative Mennonite Conference
        c/o Ivan J. Miller
        Grantsville, Maryland   21536

                    The Missionary Bulletin
                    Hartville, Ohio   44632

15115   Conservative Mennonite Fellowship   (Non-conference)
         (no address available)

17403   Connyites
         (no address available)

21903   Coptic Fellowship of America
         c/o Mr. Hamid Bey
         2015 Beverly Boulevard
         Los Angeles, California   90057

10230   Coptic Orthodox Church,
             Diocese of North America
         186 Windermere Avenue
         Toronto
         Ontario, Canada

21255   Cosmerism
         P.O. Box 1389
         Winter Park, Florida   32789

                                 The Moon Monk

21237   Cosmic Awareness Communications
         c/o Paul Shockley
         P.O. Box 115
         Seattle, Washington   98507

21191   Cosmic Church of Life and Spiritual
             Science, Inc.
         c/o Rev. M. Russo
         660 Bush
         San Francisco, California   94116

21750   Cosmic Circle of Fellowship
         P.O. Box A3179
         Chicago, Illinois   60690

21761   Cosmic Communication Commune
         c/o Dr. W. John Weilgart, Director
         100 Elm Court
         Decorah, Iowa   52101

21713   Cosmic Science Research Center
         c/o Edward M. Palmer
         1646 S.E. Elliott Street
         Portland, Oregon   97214

21745   Cosmic Star Temple
         P.O. Box 1668
         Rosebury, Oregon   97470

                        123

22395   The Coven of the Mirror
        c/o Bob Clark
        1728 East 12th Street
        Des Moines, Iowa 60316

                              Revival Magazine (m)

11720   Covenant Presbytery
        c/o Ralph J. Schuler
        Faith Bible Presbyterian Church
        6901 Haycock Road
        Falls Church, Virginia 22043

30302   Crown of Life Fellowship
        Box 9048
        Spokane, Washington 99209

                          The Universal Message

11708   Cumberland Presbyterian Church
        c/o Cumberland Presbyterian Center
        Box 4149
        1978 Union Avenue
        Memphis, Tennessee 38104

                      The Cumberland Presbyterian (w)

                      The Missionary Messenger (m)

22305   Cymry Wicca, Association of
        c/o William
        P.O. Box 4236
        Campus Station
        Athens, Georgia 30601

14750   Damascus Christian Church
        c/o Rev. Enrique Melendez (Bp.)
        537 St. Lawrence Avenue
        Bronx, New York 10473

22511   Dancers of the Sacred Circle
        c/o Phyllis and Richard Stanewick
        1219 Spear Avenue
        Apartment 4
        Arcata, California 95521

18206   Davidian SDA Association
        Bashan Hill
        Exeter, Missouri 65647

                          The Symbolic Code

18416   Dawn Bible Students Association
        East Rutherford, New Jersey   07073

                    The Dawn (m)

24153   Dawn Horse Communion
        Star Route 2
        Middletown, California   95461

                    The Dawn Horse (m)

21978   Dawn of Truth
        c/o Mikkel Dahl
        1112 Drouillard Road
        Windsor
        Ontario, Canada

14720   Defenders of the Faith
        928 Linwood Boulevard
        Kansas City, Missouri   64109

                    The Defender (m)

22309   Delphic Coven
        230 Popo Agie Street
        Lander, Wyoming   82520

                    Medicine Wheel (s-a)

22537   Delphic Fellowship
        Box 668
        Baldwin Park, California   91706

                    The Julian Review

21219   Dena Foundation
        c/o Merta Mary Parkinson
        4117 N.W. Willow Drive
        Kansas City, Missouri   64116

25210   Diamond Sangha
        Maui Zendo
        R.R. 1
        Box 220
        Haiku, Hawaii   96708

                    Diamond Sangha (s-a)

22313   Dianic Wicca
        c/o Morgan McFarland
        P.O. Box 1646
        Dallas, Texas   75221

                    The New Broom (q)

                125

20538   Disciples of Faith
         P.O. Box 50322
         Nashville, Tennessee   37205

25589   Discordian Society
         P.O. Box 693
         Guerneville, California   95446

                          St. John's Bread

24214   Divine Light Mission
         P.O. Box 532
         Denver, Colorado   80201

                          And It Is Divine

20520   Divine Science Federation Interation
         1400 Williams Street
         Denver, Colorado   80218

                          Aspire (m)

21235   Divine Word Foundation, Inc.
         Warner Springs, California   92086

21992   Doctrine of Truth Foundation, Inc.
         P.O. Box 787
         Oceanside, California   92054

14127   Door of Faith Churches of Hawaii
         1161 Young Street
         P.O. Box 5362
         Honolulu, Hawaii 96814

16125   Duck River (and Kindred) Associations
             of Baptists
         Duck River Association:
         Mod. Elder Bryce Holder
         Route 1
         Tullahoma, Tennessee   37388

         OR

         General Association:
         Mod. Elder W.B. Kerbey
         Henagar, Alabama   35978

10177   Eastern Orthodox Catholic Church
       in America
       c/o Rev. Gregory R.P. Adair
       1914 Orlando Avenue
       Highway 17-92
       Fern Park, Florida 32730

                American Review of Eastern
                   Orthodoxy (m)
                   Box 725
                   Fern Park, Florida 32730

25350   Eastern States Buddhist Temple
       of America
       64 Mott Street
       New York, New York 10013

21949   Eckankar
       P.O. Box 5325
       Las Vegas, Nevada 89102

                ECK World News (m)

30415   Ecumenical Institute
       3444 West Congress Parkway
       Chicago, Illinois 60624

                I.E.

21161   Elesia Catolica Cristiana
       (no address available)

14224   Elim Missionary Assemblies
       Elim Bible Institute
       Lima, New York 14485

                Elim Herald

                World MAP Digest (bi-m)

21981   Embassy of the Gheez-Americans
       Mt. Helion Sanctuary
       Rock Valley Road
       Box 53
       Long Eddy, New York 12760

13115   Emmanuel Association
       West Cucharas at 27th Street
       Colorado Springs, Colorado 80904

14124   Emmanuel Holiness Church
         General Overseer, Rev. Clark Sorrow
         Social Circle, Georgia 30279

                        Emmanuel Holiness Messenger
                        Route 3
                        Anderson, South Carolina 29621

15509   Emmanuel's Fellowship
         c/o Rev. Paul Goodling
         Route 2
         Greencastle, Pennsylvania 17275

22352   Enchanted Moon Coven
         c/o Ernie Birdwell (Gwyn),
           High Priest
         2922 South Marvin Avenue
         Tucson, Arizona 85730

                        The Silver Ankh

18915   End Time Body-Christian Ministries
         c/o Christian Ministries Day School
         1305 State Street
         Lake Township
         Canton, Ohio

18411   Epiphany Bible Students Association
         1507 North Donnelly Avenue
         Mt. Dora, Florida 32757

                        Newsletter (m)

20155   Esoteric Fraternity
         Box 37
         Applegate, California 95703

                        Christian Esoteric

22133   Esoteric Traditions Research
           Academy
         5514 Blackstone
         Suite 326
         Chicago, Illinois 60637

22390   ESP Laboratory
         7559 Santa Monica Boulevard
         Los Angeles, California 90046

                        E.S.P. Laboratory Newsletter (m)

20540   ESP Picture Prayers, Inc.
         P.O. Box 4143
         Gary, Indiana 46404

                        128

21975   Essene Center
         c/o Rev. Walter Hagen
         1913 Central Avenue
         Hot Springs, Arkansas   71901

10163   Estonian Orthodox Church in Exile
         c/o The Very Rev. Sergius Samon
         5332 Fouintian Avenue
         Los Angeles, California   90029

21953   Etherian Religious Society of
           Universal Brotherhood
         P.O. Box 446
         San Marcos, California   92069

         Ethical Culture Society
           (See American Ethical Union)

10232   Ethiopian Orthodox Coptic Church,
           Diocese of North and South America
         c/o Most Rev. Abune Gabre Kristos Mikael
         1255 Bedford Avenue
         Brooklyn, New York   11216

10231   Ethiopian Orthodox Church in the
           United States of America
         140-142 West 176th Street
         P.O. Box 292
         Bronx, New York   10451

30210   Eucharistic Catholic Church
         c/o Church of the Beloved Disciple
         348 West 14th Street
         New York, New York   10011

14907   Evangelical Bible Church
           (Evangelical Church of the Gospel)
         2499 Washington Boulevard
         Baltimore, Maryland   21230

10182   Evangelical Catholic Communion
         c/o John Andrew, Bishop of Newbury
         Community of Saint Francis
         South Newbury, Vermont   05066

13214   Evangelical Church of North America
         8714 Johns Drive
         Indianapolis, Indiana   46234

                   The Evangelical Advocate (bi-m)
                   P.O. Box 232
                   Newberg, Oregon   97132

12373   Evangelical Congregational Church
         c/o Bishop H.D. Wittmaier
         3116 Octagon Avenue
         Sinking Springs, Pennsylvania 19608

                    The United Evangelical (bi-w)

12150   The Evangelical Covenant Church
             of America
         5101 North Francisco Avenue
         Chicago, Illinois 60625

                    Covenant Companion (s-m)

                    Covenant Quarterly (q)

30980   Evangelical Fellowship Chapels
         c/o Rev. Ludwig B. Amerding
         Evangelical Fellowship Deaconry
         Liberty Corner, New Jersey 07938

12151   The Evangelical Free Church
             of America
         1515 East 66th Street
         Minneapolis, Minnesota 55423

                    Evangelical Beacon (bi-m)

15740   Evangelical Friends Church
         Eastern Region
         Damascus, Ohio 44619

11029   Evangelical Lutheran Church
             in America (Eielsen Synod)
         c/o Rev. Thore Larson
         Jackson, Minnesota 56143

11028   The Evangelical Lutheran Synod
         c/o Bethany Lutheran College
         Mankato, Minnesota 56001

                    Lutheran Sentinel (bi-m)
                    206 North Second Avenue, W.
                    Lake Mills, Iowa 50450

                    Lutheran Synod Quarterly (q)

15203   Evangelical Mennonite Brethren
         5800 South 14th Street
         Omaha, Nebraska 68107

                    Gospel Tidings

                         130

15201   Evangelical Mennonite Church
         7237 Leo Road
         Ft. Wayne, Indiana 46825

                        Build (q)

12333   Evangelical Methodist Church
         3036 North Meridian
         Wichita, Kansas 67204

                   The Voice of Evangelical
                        Methodism (m)

12334   Evangelical Methodist Church
            in America
         P.O. Box 751
         Kingsport, Tennessee 37662

                   The Evangelical Methodist (m)
                   Street, Maryland 21154

17240   Evangelical Ministers & Churches
            International
         105 Madison Street
         Chicago, Illinois 60602

10332   Evangelical Orthodox Church
            in America (Non-Papal Catholic)
         c/o Most Rev. Frederick L. Pyman
         P.O. Box 982
         San Jose, California 95108

                        Together We Speak

13405   Evangelical Wesleyan Church
         Grand Island, Nebraska 68801

25420   Ewan Choden Tibetan Buddhist Center
         254 Cambridge Street
         Kensington, California 94707

13111   Faith Mission Church
         c/o Rev. Ray Snow
         1318 26th Street
         Bedford, Indiana 47421

20237   The Farm
         Summertown, Tennessee 38483

21221   The Father's House
         2656 Newhall Street, #43
         Santa Clara, California 95050

                   The Father's House Quarterly (q)

                        131

30457   Fellowship of Christian Men
        c/o Julius Rose, Secretary
        Box 188
        Richland, New Jersey 08350

30140   Fellowship of Christian Pilgrims
        133 Hualalai
        Kuilua
        Kona, Hawaii 96740

17219   Fellowship of Independent
          Evangelical Churches
        c/o Howard Boyll
        2311 Anderson Street
        Bristol, Tennessee 37620

22155   Fellowship of Kouretes
        The Pantheon
        P.O. Box 620
        Tujunga, California 91042

22127   Fellowship of Ma Ion
        (no address available)

22450   Fellowship of Pan
        c/o R. Dobey
        145 East Kenilworth Avenue
        Villa Park, Illinois 60181

11909   Fellowship of Religious Humanists
        105 West College Street
        Yellow Springs, Ohio 45387

21257   Fellowship of the Inner Light
        Box 206
        Virginia Beach, Virginia 23458

                    Reflections of the Inner Light
                    from the Rising Sun (m)

21231   Fellowship of Universal Guidance
        1674 Hillhurst Avenue
        Los Angeles, California 90027

22510   Fereferia
        P.O. Box 691
        Altadena, California 91001

                    Korythalia (q)

14217   Filipino Assemblies of the
          First Born, Inc.
        1229 Glenwood
        Delano, California 93215

12332   Filipino Community Churches
         in Hawaii
         838 Kanoa Street
         Honolulu, Hawaii   96827

10157   Finnish Orthodox Church
         c/o Fr. Denis Ericson
         P.O. Box 174
         Lansing, Michigan   48901

14508   Fire Baptized Holiness Church
         of God of the Americas
         556 Houston Street
         Atlanta, Georgia   30312

13142   Fire Baptized Holiness Church
         (Wesleyan)
         600 College Avenue
         Independence, Kansas   67301

                     The Flaming Sword (s-m)

                     John Three Sixteen (w)

21971   First Century Church
         c/o Rev. David Buber
         P.O. Box 4300
         Memphis, Tennessee   38104

                          Flaming Sword

20549   First Church of Divine Immanence
         2109 Broadway
         Apartment 8/144
         New York, New York   10023

12311   First Congregational Methodist
         Church of U.S.A.
         c/o Rev. Austin Watson
         Box 67
         Florence, Mississippi   39073

                          The Watchman

14309   First Deliverance Church
         65 Hardwick Street, S.E.
         Atlanta, Georgia   30315

14122   First International Christian Association
         Calvary Temple Holiness Church
         1061 Memorial Drive, S.E.
         Atlanta, Georgia   30316

22398   First Temple of the Craft
        of W.I.C.A.
        2735 Chicago Road
        South Chicago Heights, Illinois   60411

22326   First Wiccan Church of Minnesota
        476 Summit Avenue
        St. Paul, Minnesota   55702

25205   First Zen Institute of America, Inc.
        113 East 30th Street
        New York, New York   10016

                        Zen Notes (m)

24272   Fivefold Path, Inc.
        c/o Parama Dham
           (House of Almighty Father)
        R.F.D. 1
        Box 121-C
        Madison, Virginia   22727

                        Satsang (s-m)

30915   Followers of Christ
        c/o Elder Marion Morris
        Route 2
        Ringwood, Oklahoma   73768

21261   The Forum of Cosmic Awareness
        c/o Rev. Carol Bell
        4200-B Silver, S.E.
        Albuquerque, New Mexico   87108

22125   The Foundation, A Hermetic Society
        c/o W.E. Stone, Jr.
        P.O. Box 25298
        Houston, Texas   77005

21943   Foundation Church of the
           Millennium
        1147 First Avenue
        New York, New York   10021

                        Foundation (q)

                        The Founders (m)

21233   Foundation Church of the New Birth
        P.O. Box 996
        Benjamin Franklin Station
        Washington, D.C.   20044

                New Birth Christian Commentary
                   Quarterly Journal (q)

18224   Foundation for Biblical Research
        P.O. Box 928
        Pasadena, California   91102

                The Foundation Commentator (m)

21177   Foundation for the Science
           of Spiritual Law
        c/o Dr. Alfred Holmer
        Tonopah, Arizona   85354

                        Newsletter (bi-m)

24268   Foundation of Revelation
        59 Scott Street
        San Francisco, California   94117

18227   Fountain of Life Fellowship
        c/o James L. Porter
        Valley Center, Kansas   67147

                Fountain of Life Fellowship (m)

21994   Fransisters and Brothers
        2168 South Lafayette Street
        Denver, Colorado   80210

12354   Free Christian Zion Church
           of Christ
        1315 Hutchinson Street
        Nashville, Arizona   71852

                        Zion Trumpet

14503   Free Church of God in Christ
        (no address available)

14257   Free Gospel Church
        c/o Rev. Chester H. Heath
        P.O. Box 311
        Turtle Creek, Pennsylvania   15145

13120   Free Methodist Church of
           North America
        901 College Avenue
        Winona Lake, Indiana   46590

                        Light and Life (bi-w)

11605   Free and Old Christian Reformed Church
           of Canada and America
        c/o Jacob Tamminga
        950 Ball Avenue, N.E.
        Grand Rapids, Michigan   49503

                        135

10410   Free Protestant Episcopal Church
         c/o Very Rev. Albert J. Fuge,
           Bishop of New York
         80 Broad Street
         New York, New York   10005

11951   Free Thinkers of America, Inc.
         c/o Mr. Martin J. Martin
         Box 1812
         G.P.O.
         New York, New York   10001

14141   Free Will Baptist Church of the
           Pentecostal Faith
         P.O. Box 278
         Elgin, South Carolina   29045

                            The Advance

25525   Friends of Buddhism
         c/o Mr. Frank Baker
         211 Ward Avenue
         Staten Island, New York   10304

25520   Friends of Buddhism,
           Washington (D.C.)
         c/o Dr. Kurt F. Leidecker
         306 Caroline Street
         Fredericksburg, Virginia   22401

15710   Friends United Meeting
         101 Quaker Hill Drive
         Richmond, Indiana   47374

                         Quaker Life (m)

11961   Friendship Liberal League
         5233 North Fifth Street
         Philadelphia, Pennsylvania   19120

                         The Liberal (m)

14128   Full Gospel Church Association, Inc.
         P.O. Box 265
         Amarillo, Texas   79105

14910   Full Gospel Defenders Conference
           of America
         3311 Hartel Avenue
         Philadelphia, Pennsylvania   19152

14202   Full Gospel Evangelical Association
         106 North Pennsylvania Street
         Webb City, Missouri   64870

14301   Full Gospel Fellowship of
         Churches and Ministers,
         International
         Box 24910
         Dallas, Texas   75224

21353   Full Moon Meditation Groups of
         Southern California
         c/o Intergroup Committee for the
         Three Linked Festivals
         P.O. Box 5105
         Beverly Hills, California   90210

30917   Full Salvation Union
         51630 West Eight Mule Road
         Northville, Michigan   48167

16126   Fundamental Baptist Fellowship
         c/o Marquette Manor Baptist Church
         3255 Lowell Boulevard
         Chicago, Illinois   60641

                        Information Bulletin (bi-m)

16310   Fundamental Baptist Fellowship
         Association
         (no address available)

15507   Fundamental Brethren Church
         Mitchell County, North Carolina

12323   Fundamental Methodist Church, Inc.
         c/o Dr. Roy R. Keith
         27 West Pearl
         Aurora, Missouri   65605

                        The Evangelical Methodist (m)
                        Street, Maryland   21154

21972   Future Foundation
         Box 26
         Steinauer, Nebraska

                        Newsletter

22350   Gardnerian Wicca
         c/o Theos/Phoenix
         P.O. Box 56
         Commack
         Long Island, New York   11725

                   Gardnerian Aspects

                   The Hidden Path (8/yr)
                   c/o Modred
                   P.O. Box 17011
                   Louisville, Kentucky   40217

30220   Gay Synagogues
         (no central address)

         Contact: Congregation Or Chadash
                   c/o Second Unitarian Center
                   656 West Barry
                   Chicago, Illinois   60657

25107   Gedatsu Church of America
         2569 Clay Street
         San Francisco, California   94115

14236   General Assembly and Church of
           the First Born
         2719 Tindall Avenue
         Indianapolis, Indiana   46203

21105   General Assembly of Spiritualists
         c/o Rev. Rose Ann Erickson, Secretary
         237 West 72nd Street
         New York, New York   10023

16401   General Association of General
           Baptists
         Box 790
         Poplar Bluff, Missouri   63901

                   General Baptist Messenger (w)

16128   General Association of Regular
           Baptist Churches
         1800 Oakton Boulevard
         Des Plaines, Illinois   60018

                   Baptist Bulletin (m)

21011   General Church of the New Jerusalem
         Bryn Athyn, Pennsylvania   19009

                   New Church Life (m)

15204   General Conference Mennonite Church
         722 Main Street
         Newton, Kansas   67114

                        The Mennonite (w)
                        600 Shaftebury Boulevard
                        Winnipeg R3P OM4
                        Manitoba, Canada

18213   General Conference of the Church
           of God
         330 West 152nd Avenue
         P.O. Box 2370
         Denver, Colorado   80201

                        The Bible Advocate (m)

14142   General Conference of the Evangelical
           Baptist Church, Inc.
         Kevetter Building
         2400 East Ash Street
         Goldsboro, North Carolina   27530

                        The Evangelical Baptist

16411   General Conference of the Original
           Free Will Baptist Church
         Ayden, North Carolina   28513

                        The Free Will Baptist (w)
                        The Free Will Baptist Press
                          Foundation, Inc.
                        P.O. Box 158
                        Ayden, North Carolina   28513

21010   General Convention--
           The Swedenborgian Church
         48 Sargent Street
         Newton, Massachusetts   02158

                        The Messenger (m)
                        Box 2642
                        Station B
                        Kitchener N2H 6N2
                        Ontario, Canada

18215   General Council of the Churches
           of God
         302 East Gruber Avenue
         Meridian, Idaho   83642

                        The Fellowship Herald (m)

                        The Acts (bi-m)

                        139

16425   General Six-Principle Baptists
        Pennsylvania Association:
        President, Elder Daniel E. Carpenetti
        Nicholson, Pennsylvania 18546
        OR
        Rhode Island Conference:
        c/o Deacon Raymond L. Josefson
        146 Brunswick Drive
        Warwick, Rhode Island 02886

30979   German Apostolic Christian Church
        c/o Elder George Ift
        R.R. 3
        Fairbury, Illinois 61739

        OR

        c/o Elder Emil Hori
        200 Frye Avenue
        Peoria, Illinois 61600

14916   Glad Tidings Missionary Society
        3456 Fraser Street
        Vancouver, Washington 98665

11903   The Goddian Organization
        P.O. Box 4600
        Portland, Maine 04112

                        The Goddian News

14441   God's House of Prayer for
          All Nations, Inc.
        (no address available)

30335   God's Kingdom on Earth
        c/o Bishop David Zenor
        P.O. Box 233
        Melrose Park, Illinois 60160

13421   God's Missionary Church, Inc.
        c/o Rev. Paul Miller,
          General Superintendent
        Swengal, Pennsylvania 17880

14230   Gospel Assemblies (Sounders)
        c/o Rev. James W. Sowders
        1400 South Fourth Street
        Louisville, Kentucky 40208

14231   Gospel Assemblies (Mills)
        (no address available)

14232   Gospel Assemblies (Jolly)
         c/o Rev. Tom M. Jolly
         500 North Kings Highway
         St. Louis, Missouri   63108

14234   Gospel Assemblies (Tate)
         (no address available)

14235   Gospel Assemblies (Wallace)
         (no address available)

14814   Gospel Harvesters Evangelistic
            Association
         1710 De Foot Avenue, N.W.
         Atlanta, Georgia   30318

14815   Gospel Harvesters Evangelistic
            Association (Buffalo, New York)
         (no address available)

13206   Gospel Mission Corps.
         Box 175
         Highstown, New Jersey   08520

                         The Gospel Missionary (bi-m)
                         P.O. Box 16
                         Cranbury, New Jersey   08512

                         Loyalty to the Gospel (q)
                         P.O. Box 175
                         Highstown, New Jersey   08520

30935   The Gospel of Regeneration
         c/o Mr. and Mrs. Joseph Aidones
         Route 1
         Box 34
         Hope, Arizona   71801

13208   Grace and Hope Mission
         45 Guy
         Baltimore, Maryland   21202

14913   Grace Gospel Evangelistic
            Association International, Inc.
         c/o Rev. John D. Kennington, Chairman
         909 N.E. 30th Street
         Portland, Oregon   97232

17325   Grace Gospel Fellowship
         1001 Aldon Street, S.W.
         Grand Rapids, Michigan   49509

                         Truth (bi-m)
                         141

12501   Great I Am Movement
        176 West Washington Street
        Chicago, Illinois   60602

                        The Voice of the I Am

21564   Great White Brotherhood
        130 Southern
        P.O. Box 3274
        Corpus Christi, Texas   78404

                        The New Angelus for the New Age   (m)

10115   Greek Orthodox Archdiocese of
          North and South America
        c/o His Eminence Archbishop Iakovos
        8-10 East 79th Street
        New York, New York   10021

                        The Orthodox Observer   (bi-w)

10116   Greek Orthodox Archdiocese
          of Vasiloupolis
        47-61 47th Street
        Woodside
        Long Island, New York   11377

10118   Greek Orthodox Church of America
        c/o Dr. John A. Speropoulos
        6487 West Flagler Street
        Miami, Florida   33144

10117   Greek Orthodox Diocese of New York
        c/o Most Rev. Theoklitos
        37-14 Ditmars Boulevard
        Astoria
        Long Island, New York   11105

23825   Gurdjieff Foundation
        123 East 63rd Street
        New York, New York   10021

23870   Guru Baba Fellowship
        5820 Overbrook Avenue
        Philadelphia, Pennsylvania   19131

                        God's Light

23805   Habibiyya-Shadhiliyya Sufic Order
        3029 Benvenue
        Berkeley, California   94705

142

29183   Hakim International Meditation
         Society
         508 Sul Ross
         Houston, Texas   77098

14312   Hall Deliverance Foundation, Inc.
         2743 Rovey Avenue
         Box 11157
         Phoenix, Arizona   85061

Miracle Word (q)

21167   Hallowed Ground Fellowship of
         Spiritual Healing and Prayer
         c/o Rev. George Daisley
         629 San Ysidro Road
         Santa Barbara, California   93108

24252   Hanuman Foundation
         P.O. Box 4129
         Boulder, Colorado   80302

25540   Harmony Buddhist Mission
         c/o Rev. Frank Newton
         Clarksville, Arkansas   72830

30135   Harvest House Ministries
         116 Frederick, #45
         San Francisco, California   94117

23133   Hassidism-Amshinov
         (no address available)

23123   Hassidism-Bluzherer
         (no address available)

23121   Hassidism-Bobov
         c/o Rabbi Halberstam
         Yeshiva B'nai Zion
         1533 48th Street
         Brooklyn, New York   11219

23128   Hassidism-Boston
         c/o Rabbi Moshe L. Horowitz
         983 48th Street
         Brooklyn, New York   11219

23129   Hassidism-Boyan
         (no address available)

23113   Hassidism-Bratslav
         c/o Gedalia Fleer
         1738 East Fourth Street
         Brooklyn, New York   11225

143

23115   Hassidism-Cernobyl
         c/o Rabbi Israel Jacob Twersky
         1520 49th Street
         Brooklyn, New York   11232

23122   Hassidism-Klausenburg
         (no address available)

23131   Hassidism-Kosienice
         (no address available)

23135   Hassidism-Kopyczynce
         (no address available)

23137   Hassidism-Lisker
         (no address available)

23107   Hassidism-Lubavitch
         770 Eastern Parkway
         Brooklyn, New York   11213

                             Talks and Tales (m)
23105   Hassidism-Monostritsh
         (no address available)

23101   Hassidism-Novominsk
         c/o Rabbi Nahum Mordecai Perlow
         1620 46th Street
         Brooklyn, New York   11220

23125   Hassidism-Radzyn
         (no address available)

23110   Hassidism-Satmar
         c/o Congregation Yetew Lew D'Satmar
         152 Rodney
         Brooklyn, New York   11211

23109   Hassidism-Sighet
         (no address available)

23127   Hassidism-Spinka
         (no address available)

23117   Hassidism-Squira
         c/o New Squire, New York   10977

23103   Hassidism-Stolin
         c/o Yeshiva Karlin Stolin
         1818 54th Street
         Brooklyn, New York   11220

144

```
23119    Hassidism-Talnoye
         (no address available)

23139    Hassidism-Telem
         (no address available)

23141    Hassidism-Ziditshoiv
         c/o Chassidic Center of Ziditshoiv
         1519 57th Street
         Brooklyn, New York   11219

23203    Havurat Shalom
         113 College Avenue
         Boston, Massachusetts   02144

25915    Hawaii Ichizuchi Jinga
         2020 South King Street
         Honolulu, Hawaii   96814

25305    Hawaiian Chinese Buddhist Society
         1614 Nuuanu Avenue
         Honolulu, Hawaii   96817

24905    Healthy Happy Holy Organization
         1620 Preuss Road
         Los Angeles, California   90035

                              Beads of Truth (q)

10119    Hellenic Orthodox Church in America
         c/o Most Rev. Petros,
           Bishop of Astoria
         22-68 26th Street
         Astoria
         Long Island, New York   11105

22155    Hermetic Educational Institute
         c/o Allen A. Greenfield/Asherah
         1399 de Beers Drive, #6
         Tampa, Florida   33612

25121    Higashi Hongwangi Buddhist Church
         118 North Mott Street
         Los Angeles, California   90033

30305    Hilltop House Church
         c/o Mr. Ben F. Gay, Archbishop
         61 Bellevue Avenue
         P.O. Box 2125
         San Rafael, California   94901
```

24239   Himalayan International Institute
        of Yoga Science and Philosophy
        of the U.S.A.
        3061 North Lincoln Avenue
        Chicago, Illinois 60606

                        Newsletter (m)

16212   Hiwasee Primitive Baptist
        Association
        (no address available)

13147   Holiness Christian Church of the
        United States of America, Inc.
        Gibraltar, Pennsylvania 19524

13213   The Holiness Church of God, Inc.
        c/o Bishop B. McKinney
        602 East Elm Street
        Graham, North Carolina 27253

13209   Holiness Gospel Church
        Route 2
        Box 13
        Etters, Pennsylvania 17319

24155   Hohm, The Joyous Community
        Box 75
        Mt. Tabor, New Jersey 07878

                        At Hohm

22303   The Hollywood Coven--
        Celtic Traditional
        c/o Ms. Kitty Lessing
        P.O. Box 1179
        Hollywood, Florida 33020

                        The Enchanted Cauldron (q)

10190   Holy Catholic Apostolic Church
        Archdiocese of Albuquerque
        c/o Most Rev. Jerome Joachim
        St. Stephen Monastery
        Vequita, New Mexico 87062

21183   Holy Grail Foundation
        c/o Rev. Leona Richards
        1344 Pacific Avenue, #100
        Santa Cruz, California 95060

22379   Holy Order of Briget
        c/o Craftcast Farm
        Box 131-E, Route 1
        Weldona, Colorado 80653

                        146

21969   Holy Order of Ezekiel
         Box 1144
         Glendale, California   91209

21646   Holy Order of Mans
         20 Steiner
         San Francisco, California   94117

10174   Holy Orthodox Church in America
           (Eastern Catholic and Apostolic)
         c/o Archbishop Theodotus
         321 West 101st Street
         New York, New York   10025

                    Messenger of Holy Wisdom

21933   Holy Spirit Association for the
           Unification of World
           Christianity
           (The Unification Church)
         c/o Rev. Sun Myung Moon
         Four West 43rd Street
         New York, New York   10036

                    Way of the World (bi-m)

10152   Holy Ukrainian Autocephalic
           Orthodox Church in Exile
         Holy Trinity Cathedral Church
         c/o Very Rev. Serhij K. Pastukhiv
         185 South Fifth Street
         Brooklyn, New York   11211

                    Nasha Batkiwschyna

21759   Home Bible Study
         c/o Leo V. Bartsch
         744 South Fourth Street
         Coos Bay, Oregon   97420

25424   Home of the Dharma
         c/o Rev. Iru Price
         1450 Monterrey Boulevard
         San Francisco, California   94127

                    Aims of the Arya Maitreya Mandala

20532   Home of Truth
         175 Commonwealth Avenue
         Boston, Massachusetts   02116

25905   Honkyoku-Daijingu Temple
         61 Puiwa Road
         Honolulu, Hawaii 96817

                              147

30955   Hoomana Naauao O Hawaii
        Cooke Street
        Honolulu, Hawaii   96813

18820   House of David
        Box 1067
        Benton Harbor, Michigan   49022

14513   House of God, Which is the Church
        of the Living God, the Pillar
        and Ground of the Truth, Inc.
        c/o Bishop A.H. White
        6107 Cobbs Creek Parkway
        Philadelphia, Pennsylvania   19139

                    Spirit of Truth Magazine (m)
                    3943 Fairmont Avenue
                    Philadelphia, Pennsylvania   19104

14514   House of God, Which is the Church
        of the Living God, the Pillar
        and Ground of Truth Without
        Controversy
        (address not available)

23425   House of Judah
        720 West 69th Street
        Chicago, Illinois   60621

23201   House of Love and Prayer
        1456 Ninth Avenue
        San Francisco, California   94122

23910   House of Mankind
        c/o John Carre
        Yaqui Gulch Road
        P.O. Box 905
        Mariposa, California   95338

14509   House of the Lord
        (no address available)

30981   House of Prayer for All People
        c/o William L. Blessing
        P.O. Box 837
        Denver, Colorado   80201

                    "Showers of Blessing" (m)

21775   Human Individual Metamorphis (HIM)
        (no address available)

30401   Humanity Benefactor Foundation
        of Detroit
        University of Lawsonomy
        4529 Highway 41
        Sturtevant, Wisconsin 53177

21915   Huna Research Associates, Inc.
        126 Camellia Drive
        Cape Girardeau, Missouri   63701

22591   Huna International
        2617 Lincoln Boulevard
        Room 205
        Santa Monica, California   90405

11607   Hungarian Reformed Church
        in America
        c/o Rt. Rev. Dezso Abraham,
        Bishop
        771 Emmons Boulevard
        Lincoln Park, Michigan   48146

                        Magyar Egyhaz (m)
                        1657 Centerview Drive
                        Akron, Ohio   44321

20102   Hutterian Brethren-Dariusleut
        c/o Rev. Elias Walter
        Suprise Creek Colony
        Stanford, Montana   59479

20103   Hutterian Brethren-Lehraleut
        c/o Rev. Joseph Kleinsasser
        Milford Colony
        Wolf Creek, Montana   59648

20101   Hutterian Brethren-Schmiedeleut
        c/o Rev. David D. Decker
        Tachetter Colony
        Olivet, South Dakota   57052

14760   Iglesia Bando Evangelical Gedeon/
        Gilgal Evangelical International Church
        636 N.W. Second Street
        Miami, Florida   33128

                        El Mensa Jero

14212   Independent Assemblies of God
        c/o Fellowship Press
        657 West 18th Street
        Los Angeles, California   90015

                        Conviction

                        149

14211   Independent Assemblies of God,
         International
         c/o Rev. A.W. Rasmussen
         3840 Fifth Avenue
         San Diego, California   92103

21132   Independent Associated Spiritualists
         c/o Rev. Marion Owens
         124 West 72nd Street
         New York, New York   10023

16145   Independent Baptist Church of America
         President Elmer Erickson
         2646 Longfellow
         Minneapolis, Minnesota   55407

                    The Lighthouse

10183   Independent Catholic Church
         c/o Most Rev. Archbishop Edward C. Payne
         P.O. Box 261
         Wethersfield, Connecticut   06109

                    The Independent Catholic

17407   Independent Churches Affiliated
         c/o Rev. Robert Mayer
         317 East Chestnut
         Lebanon, Pennsylvania   17042

17210   Independent Fundamental Churches
            of America
         1860 Mannheim Road
         P.O. Box 242
         Westchester, Illinois   60153

                    The Voice (m)

17211   Independent Fundamentalist Bible Churches
         c/o Dr. M.H. Reynolds, Jr.
         205 North Union Avenue
         Los Angeles, California   90026

21111   Independent Spiritualist Association
            of America
         c/o Rev. Harry Hilborn
         5639 West Huron Street
         Chicago, Illinois   60644

20620   Infinite Way
         c/o Infinite Way Study Center
         157 First Avenue, N.
         St. Petersburg, Florida   33701

21937   Inner Light Foundation
         c/o Ms. Betty Berthards
         P.O. Box 761
         Novato, California   94947

21945   Inner Peace Movement
         c/o Rev. Francisco Coll
         5103 Connecticut Avenue, N.W.
         Washington, D.C.   20008

                    Expression (m)

23810   Institute for the Development
           of the Harmonious Human Being
         P.O. Box 1556
         Crestline, California   92325

                    Wud-Sha-Lo Newsletter (m)

23826   Institute for Religious Development
         Gurdjieff Students of William Nyland
         Chardavogne Barn
         Chardavogne Road
         Warwick, New York   19990

                    Newsletter

21921   Institute of Cosmic Wisdom
         c/o Clark Wilkerson
         1038 Enchanted Way
         Pacific Palisades, California   90252

18330   The Institute of Divine Metaphysical
           Research, Inc.
         P.O. Box 2701
         Hollywood, California   90028

20529   Institute of Esoteric
           Transcendentalism
         c/o Mr. Robert W.C. Burke
         3278 Wilshire Boulevard
         Los Angeles, California   90005

                    The Transcendentalist

21905   Institute of Mentalphysics
         P.O. Box 640
         Yucca Valley, California   92284

14504   Institutional Church of God
           in Christ
         c/o Rev. Carl E. Williams
         Cotillian Records
         1841 Broadway
         New York, New York   10025

                    151

24110   Integral Yoga Institute
         c/o Swami Satchidananda
         P.O. Box 108
         Pomfret Center, Connecticut   06259

                             Integral Yoga (q)

21552   Interdenominational Divine Order
         P.O. Box W
         Twin Falls, Idaho   83301

                             I DO

25275   International Buddhist Meditation
           Center
         928 South New Hampshire Avenue
         Los Angeles, California   90006

24246   International Center for
           Self Analysis
         102 David Drive
         North Syracuse, New York   13212

                             Self Analysis Bulletin (m)

14908   International Christian Churches
         2322-26 Kanealii Avenue
         Honolulu, Hawaii   96813

21990   International Church of Spiritual
           Vision
         P.O. Box 2627
         Reno, Nevada   89505

14215   International Church of the
           Foursquare Gospel
         Angelus Temple
         1100 Glendale Boulevard
         Los Angeles, California   90026

                             Foursquare World Advance (m)

30330   International Clergy Association
         469 Pacific Street
         Monterey, California   93940

21265   International Community of Christ
         100 North Arlington Avenue
         Reno, Nevada   89501

14303   International Deliverance Churches
        P.O. Box 353
        Dallas, Texas   75222

                    TVD--The Voice of Deliverance (bi-m)

14918   International Evangelism Crusades, Inc.
        7970 Woodman Avenue
        Van Nuys, California   91402

21103   International General Assembly
          of Spiritualists
        1809 East Bayview Boulevard
        Norfolk, Virginia   23503

21309   International Group of Theosophists
        551 South Oxford Avenue
        Los Angeles, California   90020

                    Theosophia

24234   International Kriya Babaji Yoga
          Sangam
        11305 Alondra Boulevard
        Norwalk, California   90650

21404   International Liberal Catholic Church
        c/o Most Rev. Edmund W. Sheehan
        840 Fairview Road
        Ojai, California   93023

24236   International Meditation Society
          (Transcendental Meditation)
        1015 Gayley Avenue
        Los Angeles, California   90024

20615   International Metaphysical
          Association, Inc.
        20 East 68th Street
        New York, New York   10021

14405   International Ministerial
          Association
        1312 North 67th Street
        Houston, Texas   77011

17235   International Ministerial
          Federation
        723 Clark Street
        Fresno, California   93701

21247   International Organization of
          Awareness
        1648 Alencastre Street
        Honolulu, Hawaii   96816

                    153

14135   International Pentecostal
         Assemblies
         892 Berne Street, S.E.
         Atlanta, Georgia   30316

                   The Bridegroom's Messenger (m)

24115   International School of Yoga
         and Vedanta
         6111 S.W. 74th Drive
         Miami, Florida   33143

                         Vision of Eternity (m)

24216   International Society of
         Krishna Consciousness
         38 North Beacon Street
         Boston, Massachusetts   02134

                            Back to Godhead (m)

21107   International Spiritualist Alliance
         c/o Rev. Beatrice Goulton Bishop
         3381 Findlay Street
         Vancouver
         British Columbia, Canada

                   International Spiritualist News
                         Review (bi-m)

23601   Islam, Orthodox
         Islamic Center
         2551 Massachusetts Avenue, N.W.
         Washington, D.C.   20008

18821   Israelite House of David as
         Reorganized by Mary Purnell
         P.O. Box 187
         Benton Harbor, Michigan   49022

                   The New Shiloh Messenger (m)

30918   JFK Memorial Temples
         (no address available)

24701   Jain Meditation International Center
         120 East 86th Street
         New York, New York   10028

18401   Jehovah's Witnesses
         124 Columbia Heights
         Brooklyn, New York   11201

                        The Watchtower (bi-w)

                        Awake! (bi-w)

25320   Jeng Sen Fut Do Yin Gow Wool
         (Jen Sen Association for the
         Examination of the Buddhist
         & Taoist Teachings)
         146 Waverly Place
         San Francisco, California   94108

14417   Jesus Church
         c/o Samuel E. Officer
         Box 362
         Cleveland, Tennessee   37311

                        Light of the World (q)

30110   Jesus People, International
         Box 1949
         Hollywood, California   90028

                        Hollywood Free Paper

30145   Jesus People, USA
         817 West Grace
         Chicago, Illinois   60613

                        Cornerstone (10/yr)

23020   Jewish Reconstructionist Foundation
         15 West 86th Street
         New York, New York   10024

                        Reconstructionist (10/yr)

23225   Jewish Science Society
         111 West 57th Street
         New York, New York   10019

25120   Jodo Mission
         1429 Makiki Street
         Honolulu, Hawaii   96822

         AND

         2003 West Jefferson Boulevard
         Los Angeles, California   90018

                              155

12329   John Wesley Fellowship and the
         Frances Asbury Society of
         Ministers
         P.O. Box 11585
         Atlanta, Georgia   30305

                        The Frances Asbury Society
                              Evangel (m)

30958   Ka Hale Haono Hou O Ke Akua
         Molokai, Hawaii

25190   Kailas Shugendo
         c/o Dr. Neville Warwick
         2362 Pine Street
         San Francisco, California   94115

22586   Kali Kong
         c/o Ms. Lily-Sabina
         P.O. Box 5032
         Santa Monica Shores, California   90405

25415   Karma Dzong Meditation Center
         1111 Pearl Street
         Boulder, Colorado   80302

                              Garuda

                              Loka (a)

20240   Katharsis
         P.O. Box 1330
         Nevada City, California   95959

14307   Kathrine Kuhlman Foundation
         603 Carlton House
         Pittsburgh, Pennsylvania   15219

30959   Kealaokalamalama Church
         1207 Prospect Street
         Honolulu, Hawaii   96822

13210   Kentucky Mountain Holiness Association
         c/o Lela G. McConnell
         Jackson, Kentucky   41339

20260   Kerista/Utopian Society
         c/o The Storefront Collective
         P.O. Box 1174
         San Francisco, California   94101

                        Utopian Eyes (q)

24232   Keshavashram International Order
          4601 Chesapeake Street, N.W.
          Washington, D.C. 20016

21205   Kethra E'da Foundation, Inc.
          931 26th Street
          San Diego, California   92102

21907   Kingdom of Yahweh
          c/o D.C. Joseph Jeffers
          P.O. Box 492
          St. James, Missouri   65559

                           Kingdom Voice (q)

13317   Kodesh Church of Immanuel
          c/o Rev. F.R. Killingsworth,
            Supervising Elder
          1509 S Street, N.W.
          Washington, D.C.   20009

20160   Koinonia Foundation
          c/o David Poist, Director
          P.O. Box 5744
          Baltimore, Maryland   21208

20140   Koinonia Partners
          Route 1
          Americus, Georgia   31709

25935   Konko-Kyo
          c/o The Reverend Alfred Y. Tsuyuki
          2924 East First Street
          Los Angeles, California   90033

20120   Koreshan Unity
          c/o Claude J. Rahn
          2012 28th Avenue
          Vero Beach, Florida

                      The American Eagle (m)
                      Estero, Florida   33928

25920   Kotohira Jinsha Temple
          1045 Kama Lane
          Honolulu, Hawaii   96817

24159   Kripalu Yoga Ashram
          Seven Walters Road
          Sumneytown, Pennsylvania   18084

                           Yoga Jyoti (q)

24230   Krishnamurti Foundation of America
         P.O. Box 216
         Ojai, California 93023

24256   Kundalini Research Foundation
         Ten East 39th Street
         New York, New York 10016

25920   Kwan Yin Temple
         170 North Vineyard Street
         Honolulu, Hawaii 96817

25280   Kwan Yin Zen Temple
         R.D. 2
         Temple Road
         Woodhull, New York 14898

Buddha World (q)

16112   Kyova Association of Regular
          Baptists
         (no address available)

25412   Labsum Shedrub Ling Malamist Buddhist
          Monastery of America
         c/o Venerable Geshe Wanyal, Abbot
         Route 3
         Box 140
         Farmingdale, New Jersey 07727

22555   Lady Sara's Coven
         P.O. Box 204
         Wolf Creek, Oregon 97497

15760   Lake Erie Association Yearly
          Meeting (Friends)
         c/o Ann Arbor Monthly Meeting
         1420 Hill Street
         Ann Arbor, Michigan 48104

20250   Lama Foundation
         Box 444
         San Cristobal, New Mexico 87564

14219   Lamb of God Church
         612 Isenberg Street
         Honolulu, Hawaii 96817

18412   Laodicean Home Missionary Movement
         7 Overbrook Lane
         Levittown, Pennsylvania 19055

The Present Truth of the
Apokalypsis (bi-m)

21755   Last Day Messengers
        Box 766
        Ft. Lauderdale, Florida   33302

17340   Last Day Messenger Assemblies
        Box 17056
        Portland, Oregon   97217

                      Last Day Messenger (bi-m)

14730   Latin American Council of the
        Pentecostal Church of God of
        New York, Inc.
        115 East 125th Street
        New York, New York   10035

14525   Latter House of the Lord for
        All People and the Church
        of the Mountain, Apostolic
        (no address available)

18410   Layman's Home Missionary Movement
        Chester Springs, Pennsylvania   19425

                      The Bible Standard and Herald
                      of Christ's Kingdom (m)

                      The Present Truth and Herald of
                      Christ's Epiphany (m)

21830   Lazy Nickels
        c/o Buffalo Ghost Dance Productions
        P.O. Box 39436
        Los Angeles, California 90039

                      The Black Dwarf

19110   LDS Scripture Researchers
        Salt Lake City, Utah

21616   Lectorium Rosicrucianum
        2509 Radience Drive
        Bakersfield, California   93304

21642   Lemurian Fellowship
        P.O. Box 397
        Ramona, California   92065

                      Lemurian Viewpoint

159

14305　　Leroy Jenkins Evangelistic
　　　　　Association
　　　　P.O. Box F
　　　　Deleware, Ohio　43015

　　　　　　　　　　Revival of America (bi-m)

21402　　Liberal Catholic Church
　　　　c/o Bishop Edward M. Matthews
　　　　P.O. Box 185
　　　　Bear Butte Road & U.S. Highway 101 Freeway
　　　　Miranda, California　95553

21401　　The Liberal Catholic Church,
　　　　　Province of the United
　　　　　States of America
　　　　c/o Rt. Rev. Gerrick Munnik,
　　　　　President
　　　　Box 62
　　　　Ojai, California　93022

30307　　Life Science Church
　　　　2207 Cardinal Drive
　　　　Rolling Meadows, Illinois　60008

20537　　Life Study Fellowship
　　　　Norton, Connecticut　06820

　　　　　　　　　　Faith (6/yr)

21722　　Light Affiliates
　　　　Box 431
　　　　Barnaby
　　　　British Columbia, Canada

21217　　Light of the Universe
　　　　161 North Sandusky Street
　　　　Tiffin, Ohio　44883

　　　　　　　　　　The L.O.T.U. (q)

22119　　Light of Truth Church
　　　　c/o Nelson White
　　　　P.O. Box 3125
　　　　Pasadena, California　91103

　　　　　　　　　　The White Light (q)

24258　　Light of Yoga Society
　　　　2404 Kenilworth
　　　　Cleveland, Ohio　44106

21572   The Lighted Way
         10929 Weyburn Avenue
         Los Angeles, California   90024

14901   Lighthouse Gospel Fellowship
         636 East Third Street
         Tulsa, Oklahoma   74120

23235   Little Synagogue
         27 East 20th Street
         New York, New York   10003

                    Kabbalah for Today (q)

17401   The (Local) Church
         P.O. Box 20755
         Los Angeles, California   90006

                    The Stream (q)

                    News of the Churches (m)

17715   Lord's Covenant Church
         c/o Pastor Sheldon Emry
         P.O. Box 5334
         Phoenix, Arizona   85010

                    America's Promise (bi-m)

21012   Lord's New Church Which Is
           Nova Hierosolyma
         c/o Rev. Philip M. Odhner
         Box 4
         Bryn Athyn, Pennsylvania   19009

21227   Lorain Association
         c/o David Spangler, President
         Box 941
         Belmont, California   94002

21181   Lotus Ashram
         128 N.E. 82nd Terrace
         Miami, Florida   33138

                    Lotus Leaves (bi-m)

21259   The Louis Foundation
         Orcas Island
         Eastsound, Washington   98245

21967   The Love Project
        4470 Orchard Avenue
        San Diego, California   92107

                        The Seeker Newsletter

13423   Lower Lights Church
        (no address available)

13201   Lumber River Annual Conference
        of the Holiness Methodist Church
        c/o Bishop C.N. Lowry, Secretary
        Rowland, North Carolina   28383

11001   Lutheran Church in America
        231 Madison Avenue
        New York, New York   10016

                        The Lutheran (bi-w)
                        2900 Queen Lane
                        Philadelphia, Pennsylvania   18129

11020   The Lutheran Church-
        Missouri Synod
        500 North Broadway
        St. Louis, Missouri   63102

                        The Lutheran Witness (m)
                        3558 South Jefferson Avenue
                        St. Louis, Missouri   63118

10142   Macedonian Orthodox Church
        c/o St. Peter & Paul Macedonian
        Orthodox Church
        Rev. Spiro Tanaskski
        51st & Virginia Streets
        Gary, Indiana   46409

26010   Macrobiotics--
        Order of the Universe
        Box 203
        Prudential Center Station
        Boston, Massachusetts   02199

                        Order of the Universe

20617   Margaret Laird Foundation
        Chicago Buildings
        13 White Chapel
        Liverpool 1, England

                        The Liverpool Newsletter

21701   Mark-Age Meta-Center
          327 N.E. 20th Terrace
          Miami, Florida   33137

                              Main/Mark-Age Inform-Nations (m)

21207   Martinist Institute of
            Spiritual Science
          c/o Grand Lodge
          15 Outlook Road
          Mattapan, Massachusetts   02126

21632   The Mayan Order
          P.O. Box 2710
          San Antonio, Texas   78299

                              Daily Meditations (bi-m)

16215   Mayo Primitive Baptist
            Association
          c/o Elder Robert C. Ashby
          Route 5
          Martinsdale, Virginia   24112

26050   Mazdaznan Association
          1159 South Norton Avenue
          Los Angeles, California   90019

                              Mazdaznan (bi-m)

24701   Meditation International Center
          120 East 86th Street
          New York, New York   10028

                              The Center In Formation (bi-m)

23152   Meditation Group for the
            New Age
          P.O. Box 566
          Ojai, California   93023

13215   Meggido Mission
          481 Thurston Road
          Rochester, New York   14619

                              Meggido Message (m)

17405   Members of "The Church Which Is
            Christ's Body"
          Box 1122
          Charlottesville, Virginia   22902

                              Sound Words

                        163

15206   Mennonite Brethren Church of
        North America
        Mennonite Brethren Publishing
        House
        Hillsboro, Kansas   67063

                Christian Leader (bi-w)

15116   Mennonite Christian Brotherhood
        c/o Bishop Paul Hollingshead
        Route 2
        Box 43
        Mt. Pleasant Mills, Pennsylvania   17583

15101   Mennonite Church
        528 East Madison Street
        Lombard, Illinois   60148

                Gospel Herald (w)
                616 Walnut Avenue
                Scottdale, Pennsylvania   15683

                Mennonite Quarterly Review (q)
                Goshen, Indiana   46526

22385   Mental Science Institute
        P.O. Box 16192
        Minneapolis, Minnesota   55416

12322   Methodist Protestant Church
        c/o Rev. F.E. Sellers
        Monticello, Minnesota   55362

13148   Metropolitan Church Association
        323 Broad Street
        Lake Geneva, Wisconsin   53147

                The Burning Bush (m)

30201   Metropolitan Community Churches,
        Universal Fellowship of
        1046 South Hull Street
        Hollywood, California   90015

                In Unity (m)

21145   Metropolitan Spiritual Churches
        of Christ
        4315 South Wabash
        Chicago, Illinois   60653

22378   Miami Pagan Grove
c/o John Ortiz and Mary Ann Herman
980 N.E. 170th Street, #218
North Miami Beach, Florida 33162

Wicca Times (q)

11803   Midwest Congregational Christian
      Fellowship
c/o Rev. Robert Schmitz
Route 1
Box 68
Union City, Indiana 47390

21715   Ministry of Universal Wisdom
P.O. Box 458
Yucca Valley, California 29284

16129   Minnesota Baptist Convention
5000 Golden Valley Road
Minneapolis, Minnesota 55422

The North Star Baptist (m)

14304   Miracle Life Revival, Inc.
P.O. Box 20707
Phoenix, Arizona 85036

Twentieth Century Life (bi-m)

14306   Miracle Revival Fellowship
Miracle Valley, Arizona 85645

Miracle Magazine

30316   Missionaries of the New Truth
P.O. Box 1393
Evanston, Illinois 60204

13162   Missionary and Soul Winning
      Fellowship
350 East Market Street
Long Beach, California 90805

14436   Missionary Body of Jesus Christ
(no address available)

13163   Missionary Church
3901 South Wayne Avenue
Fort Wayne, Indiana 46807

Emphasis (s-m)

18311   Missionary Dispensary Bible
          Research
        P.O. Box 5296
        Buena Park, California   90622

13113   Missionary Methodist Church
          of America
        c/o Rev. Dan S. Hardin
        Forest City Missionary
          Methodist Church
        Forest City, North Carolina   28043

15755   Missouri Valley Friends Conference
        c/o Anne Moore, Clerk
        1007 Alabama Street
        Lawrence, Kansas   66044

14311   Mita Movement
        Calle Duarte 235
        Hata Rey, Puerto Rico   00919

10111   Molokans
        (no address available)

10305   Moncado Foundation of America
        c/o Mario Moncado
        1534 Kulaepaa Drive
        Honolulu, Hawaii   96800

21707   The Monka Retreat
        c/o Samuel George Partridge
        Golden Sierra Printing
        116 Mercury Drive
        Grass Valley, California   95945

                          News from the Mountain Top

17221   Moody Church
        1630 North Clark Street
        Chicago, Illinois   60614

23710   Moorish Science Temple of America
        c/o Reynold N. El, President
        3810 South Wabash Avenue
        Chicago, Illinois   60653

30921   Moral Rearmament
        Suite 701
        124 East 40th Street
        New York, New York   10016

                          Pace
                          c/o Pace Publications
                          835 South Flower Street
                          Los Angeles, California   90017

166

12101   Moravian Church in America
        (Unitas Fratrum)
        69 West Church Street
        Bethlehem, Pennsylvania   18018

                        The North American Moravian (m)
                        Five West Market Street
                        Bethlehem, Pennsylvania 18018

21215   Morse Fellowship
        524 Sumit Drive
        Richardson, Texas   75080

13311   Mt. Calvary Holy Church of America
        9-15 Otisfield Street
        Boston, Massachusetts   02121

14516   Mt. Sinai Holy Church of America
        c/o Bishop Mary E. Jackson
        1601 Broad Street
        Philadelphia, Pennsylvania   19148

30923   Mt. Zion Sanctuary
        21 Dayton Street
        Elizabeth, New Jersey   07202

20616   Mountain Brook Studies
        c/o William Samuel
        P.O. Box 9206
        Mountain Brook, Alabama   35213

21951   Movement of Spiritual Inner
          Awareness
        P.O. Box 19458
        Los Angeles, California   90051

                        The Movement (m)
                        Hu-Man Enterprises
                        3500 West Adams Boulevard
                        Los Angeles, California   90018

20225   Mu Farm
        Route 1
        Box 143
        Yoncalla, Oregon   97499

24275   Narayanananda Universal Yoga
          Trust and Ashram in America
        9435 South 85th Court
        Apartment E-1
        Hickory Hills, Illinois   60457

11615   Narragansett Indian Church
         c/o Rev. Harold Mars
         61 Highland Avenue
         Wakefield, Rhode Island   02879

23716   Nation of Islam
         c/o Muhammed's Mosque #2
         2545 South Federal Street
         Chicago, Illinois   60616

                              Bilalian News (w)

11806   National Association of
           Congregational Christian
           Churches
         176 West Wisconsin Avenue
         Milwaukee, Wisconsin   53203

                      The Congregationalist (m)

16410   National Association of Free Will
           Baptists
         1134 Murfreesboro Road
         Box 1088
         Nashville, Tennessee   37202

                              Contact (m)

13425   National Association of Holiness
           Churches
         203 West Cherry Street
         Bickwell, Indiana   47512

16301   National Baptist Convention
           of America
         c/o Rev. Billy H. Wilson,
           Corresponding Secretary
         2620 South Marsallis Avenue
         Dallas, Texas   75216

16302   National Baptist Convention, USA, Inc.
         c/o President Rev. J.H. Jackson
         405 East 31st Street
         Chicago, Illinois   60616

                      National Baptist Voice (s-m)
                      902 North Good Street
                      Dallas, Texas   75204

16303   National Baptist Evangelical Life
          and Soul Saving Assembly of U.S.A.
          441-61 Monroe Avenue
          Detroit, Michigan 48226

                              The People's Soul Saving Radio
                              Magazine

21109   National Colored Spiritualist
          Association of the USA
          14228 Wisconsin
          Detroit, Michigan 48238

                              National Spiritualist Reporter (m)

14930   National David Spiritual Temple
          of Christ Church Union (Inc.), USA
          536 West 120th Street
          Los Angeles, California 90044

21127   National Federation of Spiritual
          Science Churches
          (no address available)

15503   National Fellowship of Brethren
          Churches
          Winona Lake, Indiana 46590

                              Brethren Missionary Herald (bi-w)

16205   National Primitive Baptist Convention
          of the U.S.A.
          P.O. Box 2355
          Tallahassee, Florida 32301

21147   National Spiritual Aid Association, Inc.
          5239 40th Street, North
          St. Petersburg, Florida   33714

21139   National Spiritual Alliance
          of the U.S.A.
          R.F.D. 1
          Keene, New Hampshire 03431

21125   National Spiritual Science Center
          5605 16th Street, N.W.
          Washington, D.C. 20011

                              Psychic Observer (m)

21101   National Spiritualist Association
         of Churches
         P.O. Box 128
         Cassadaga, Florida   32706

                          The National Spiritualist
                          4421 West Irving Road
                          Chicago, Illinois   60600
                          c/o William L. Clark, Editor

21810   Native American Church
         (no address available)

22533   Nemeton
         P.O. Box 13037
         Oakland, California   94661

                          Nemeton

21825   Neo-American Church
         c/o Arthur J. Kleps,
            Chief Boo Hoo
         Box 14
         Cristobal, New Mexico   87564

                          Divine Toad Sweat

25101   Neo-Dharma
         c/o Dr. Douglas Burns, M.D.
         2648 Graceland Avenue
         San Carlos, California   94070

22530   Neo-Dianic Faith
         c/o W. Holman Keith
         Contez Hotel
         375 Columbia Avenue
         Los Angeles, California   90017

22133   Neo-Pythagorean Gnostic Church
         c/o Michael P. Bertiaux
         Box 1554
         Chicago, Illinois   60637

11606   Netherlands Reformed Congregations
         c/o Rev. W.C. Lamain, Chairman
         2115 Romence Street, N.E.
         Grand Rapids, Michigan   49503

                          The Banner of Truth

14250   Neverdies
         (no address available)

170

21957   New Age Church of Truth
         Christ Light Community
         Star Route 2
         Box CLC
         Deming, New Mexico   88030

21780   New Age Foundation
         c/o Cathedral of the Stars
         5201 South I Street
         Tacoma, Washington   98408

                             Intelligent's Report

21935   New Age Samaritan Church
         c/o Rev. R. McWilliams
         Box 1172
         Everett, Washington   98201

21225   New Age Teachings
         P.O. Box 477
         Brookfield, Massachusetts   01506

                             Newsletter (m)

21564   New Angelus
            (Great White Brotherhood)
         130 Southern
         P.O. Box 3274
         Corpus Christi, Texas   78404

                             The New Angelus (m)

30976   New Apostolic Church of
            North America
         3753 North Troy Street
         Chicago, Illinois   60618

                             Word of Life (s-m)

                             New Apostolic Review (s-m)

14435   New Bethel Church of God
            in Christ (Pentecostal)
         c/o A.D. Bradley, Presiding Bishop
         First & Market Streets
         Richmond, California   94801

12312   New Congregational Methodist Church
         c/o Bishop Joe E. Kelley
         354 East Ninth Street
         Jacksonville, Florida   32206

                             171

17713   New Christian Crusade Church
         P.O. Box 3247
         Hollywood, California   90028

18406   New Creation Bible Students
         307 White Street
         Hartford, Connecticut   06106

                         The New Creation (m)

22301   New England Coven of Traditional
           Witches
         c/o Gwen Thompson, High Priestess
         P.O. Box 7185
         New Haven, Connecticut   06519

16106   New England Evangelical Baptist
           Fellowship
         c/o Dr. John Viall
         40 Bridge Street
         Newton, Massachusetts   02158

22129   New England Institute of
           Metaphysical Studies
         Box 171
         Methuen, Massachusetts   01844

21961   New Psychiana
         c/o Psychiana Study Center
         4069 Stephens Street
         San Diego, California   92103

22357   New Reformed Order of the
           Golden Dawn
         P.O. Box 23243
         Oakland, California   94623

                         The Witches Trine (8/yr)

16130   New Testament Association of
           Independent Baptist Churches
         1079 Westview Drive
         Rochelle, Illinois   61068

                         New Testament Testimonies

13105   New Testament Church of God
         c/o Rev. G.W. Pendleton
         307 Cockrell Hill Road
         Dallas, Texas   75211

                         The Seventh Trumpet

22310   New York Coven of Welch
        Traditional Witches
        c/o The Warlock Shop
        300 Henry Street
        Brooklyn, New York   11201

                    Earth Religious News (8/yr)

24248   New York Sacred Tantricks
        (no address available)

25115   Nichiren Mission
        3058 Pali Highway
        Honolulu, Hawaii   96817

25116   Nichiren Shoshu of America
        1351 Ocean Front Walk
        Santa Monica, California   90401

                    Seikyo Times
                    18 Shinano-machi
                    Shinjuku-ku
                    Tokyo, Japan

16140   North American Baptist
        General Conference
        7308 Madison Street
        Forest Park, Illinois   60130

                    The Baptist Herald (m)

10325   The North American Old Roman
        Catholic Church
        c/o The Most Rev. Archbishop
        Hubert A. Rogers
        Box 1647
        G.P.O.
        238 Wyona Street
        Brooklyn, New York   11202

                    The Augustinian (occ)

10335   North American Old Roman
        Catholic Church
        c/o Bishop Lane
        2820 North Lincoln
        Chicago, Illinois   60657

10342   North American Old Roman
        Catholic Church
        c/o Most Rev. John E. Schweikert
        4200 North Kedvale Avenue
        Chicago, Illinois 60641

10327   North American Old Roman Catholic
         Church Utrecht Succession
         c/o Most Rev. E.R. Verostek,
         Archbishop Presiding
         3519 Roosevelt Avenue
         Richmond, California 94805

                              Newsletter

15765   Northwest Yearly Meeting of
         Friends Church
         c/o Dorwin E. Smith, Clerk
         1001 West Pine
         Meridian, Idaho 83642

                     The Northwest Friend (m)

23730   Nubian Islamic Hebrew Mission
         833 St. John's Place
         Brooklyn, New York 11216

21566   Oasis Fellowship, Inc.
         c/o George and Alice White
         P.O. Box O
         Florence, Arizona 85232

22566   Odinist Movement
         P.O. Box 731
         Adelaide Street
         Toronto
         Ontario, Canada

                         The Runestone (q)

17212   Ohio Bible Fellowship
         c/o Rev. John Ashbrook
         5733 Hopkins Road
         Mentor, Ohio 44060

                     Ohio Bible Fellowship Visitor

10330   Old Catholic Church in America
         c/o Archbishop William Henry
            Francis Brothers
         Archdiocesan Chancery
         Box 433
         Woodstock, New York 12498

                              One Church

10345   Old Catholic Church in North
            America
         c/o Rev. Grant T. Billett
         P.O. Box 1252
         York, Pennsylvania 17405

                                174

10184   Old Catholic Order of Christ
         the King in Texas
         c/o Most Rev. Robert Williams,
         Provincial Bishop
         St. Hilarion Center
         1008 West Avenue
         Austin, Texas   78701

16217   Old Elkhorn Primitive Baptist
         Association
         (no address available)

10405   Old Episcopal Church
         c/o Rt. Rev. Jack C. Adam,
         Bishop of Arizona
         P.O. Box 2424
         Mesa, Arizona   85204

15504   Old German Baptist Brethren
         c/o Elder Lester Fisher,
         Writing Clerk
         4664 N Street
         Route 48
         Covington, Ohio   45318

                    The Vindicator (m)

15301   Old Order Amish Mennonite Church
         c/o Publication Board of the Amish
         Mennonite Publishing Association
         Kalona, Iowa 52247

                    Herold der Wahrheit

15109   Old Order (Hornung) Mennonite
         Church
         c/o Bishop Joseph O. Weaver
         Weaverland Meeting House
         New Holland, Pennsylvania   17557

15110   Old Order (Reidenbach) Mennonite
         Church
         c/o Bishop Amos M. Martin
         New Holland, Pennsylvania   17557

15107   Old Order (Wenger) Mennonite Church
         c/o Bishop Aaron Z. Sensenig
         Weaverland Meeting House
         New Holland, Pennsylvania   17557

15105   Old Order (Wisler) Mennonite Church
         c/o Henry W. Riehl
         Route 1
         Columbiana, Ohio   44408

175

15513   Old Order, or Yorker, River Brethren
         c/o Bishop Daniel M. Sipling
         356 East High Street
         Elizabethtown, Pennsylvania 17022

10344   Old Roman Catholic Church
         c/o Archbishop Earl Anglin James
         460 Danforth Avenue
         Toronto
         Ontario, Canada

10333   Old Roman Catholic Church
         c/o Most Rev. Richard A. Marchena
         348 West 14th Street
         New York, New York 10014

10347   Old Roman Catholic Church
            (Orthodox Orders)
         c/o His Holiness Claudius I,
            Patriarch (Guy F. Claude Hamel)
         P.O. Box 224
         Station J
         Toronto M4J 4Y1
         Ontario, Canada

                              C.S.P. News (m)

10334   Old Roman Catholic Church in
            the U.S.
         c/o Archbishop Joseph Damien Hough
         The Catholic Legation
         P.O. Box 269
         Venice, California 90291

30309   Omniume Church
         309 Breckenridge
         Texarkana, Texas 75501

25325   On Tsu To Lin Buddhist
            Lecture Hall
         1897 Sutter Street
         San Francisco, California 94115

21977   Only Fair Religion
         P.O. Box 57960
         Los Angeles, California 90057

10336   Ontario Old Roman Catholic Church
         c/o Most Rev. Nelson D. Hillyer,
            Archbishop
         Five Manor Road West
         Toronto
         Ontario, Canada

21913   Ontological Society
          P.O. Box 238
          Loveland, Colorado   80537

                         Ontological Thought (m)

14216   Open Bible Standard Churches, Inc.
          P.O. Box 1737
          Des Moines, Iowa   50306

                     The Message of the Open Bible (m)

22359   The Open Goddess
          142 Buckness Avenue
          Woodbridge, New Jersey   07095

21576   Open Way
          Route 2
          Box 217
          Celina, Tennessee   38551

21718   Orbit Family
          c/o E. Blanche Pritchett
          Route 4
          Arlington, Virginia   98223

                         MARCAP News

22330   Order of Osirus
          P.O. Box 654
          Kearney, Nebraska   68847

21405   Order of St. Germain
            Ecclesia Catholica Liberalis
          c/o James Matthews, Archbishop
          P.O. Box 5794
          San Francisco, California   94101

24230   Order of the Black Ram
            (Ordo Caperorum Nigra)
          P.O. Box 84
          Warren, Michigan   48092

                         Liber Venifica

25530   Order of the Circle Cross
         c/o Rev. Sister Ileena and
            Sister Myra
         P.O. Box 707
         Delta, Colorado   81415

                          Order of the Circle Cross

22131   Order of the Lily and the Eagle
         P.O. Box 398
         3330 South Broadway
         Englewood, Colorado   80710

                          EON

22415   Order of the Ram
         6546 Hollywood Boulevard
         Los Angeles, California   90028

22121   Order of Thelema
         4445 36th Street
         San Diego, California   92116

22112   Ordo Templi Orientis
         c/o Hymenaeus Alpha, Caliph
         P.O. Box 2043
         Dublin, California   94566

22110   Ordo Templi Orientis
         c/o D. Smith
         1566 Ixora
         North Fort Myers, Florida   33903

22111   Ordo Templi Orientis
         Roanoke, Virginia

22427   Ordo Templi Satanas
         c/o Temple of Moloch
         P.O. Box 8423
         Louisville, Kentucky   40208

21245   Organization of Awareness
         c/o Francis Marcx, President
         Federal Way, Washington   98002

21243   Organiation of Awareness
         c/o David DeMoulin, President
         P.O. Box 271
         Olympia, Washington   98507

13202   Oriental Missionary Society
         Holiness Conference
         c/o Rev. Akira Kuroda
         Los Angeles Holiness Church
         3660 South Gramercy
         Los Angeles, California   90018

13415   Original Allegheny Conference of
         the Wesleyan Methodist Church
         c/o Rev. C. Van Wormer
         413 East Main Street
         Titusville, Pennsylvania   16354

                          Allegheny Conference Messenger

13307   Original Church of God
         c/o Bishop Th. R. Jeffries
         653 Roscoe
         Akron, Ohio   14306

14102   The (Original) Church of God, Inc.
         P.O. Box 3086
         Chattanooga, Tennessee   37404

                          The Messenger (m)

23415   Original Hebrew Israelite Nation
         c/o A-Beta Hebrew Center
         4654 South Cottage Grove
         Chicago, Illinois 60653

14620   Original Pentecostal Church of God
         c/o Holiness Church
         2206 Andrew Jackson Way
         Huntsville, Alabama   35811

10172   Orthodox-Catholic Church of America
         c/o His Grace Bishop George A. Hyde,
            Archbishop
         P.O. Box 1273
         Anderson, South Carolina   29621

                          Ortho

10185   Orthodox Catholic Diocese of the
         Holy Spirit (See of Glorieta)
         c/o His Grace, Bishop Christopher Jones
         P.O. Box 432
         Las Vegas, New Mexico   87701

                          From the Bishop's Pad

179

10343   Orthodox Catholic Synod of the
      Syro-Chaldean Rite
      c/o Most Rev. Bashir Ahmed
      Oratory of St. Francis
      San Francisco, California 94109

10105   Orthodox Church in America
      c/o Serge Troubetz Koy,
        Secretary to the Metropolitan
      P.O. Box 675
      Syosset, New York 11791

               The Orthodox Church

30215   Orthodox Episcopal Church of God
      c/o Rev. Raymond L. Broshears
      St. Timothy's Church
      26 Seventh Avenue
      San Francisco, California 94118

10331   Orthodox Old Roman Catholic Church II
      c/o Most Rev. Mark I,
        Leo Christopher Skelton
      P.O. Box 38336
      Hollywood, California 90038

11702   Orthodox Presbyterian Church
      7401 Old York Road
      Philadelphia, Pennsylvania 19126

               Presbyterian Guardian (m)

11604   Orthodox Reformed Church
      3628 South Chestnut
      Grandville, Michigan 49418

               The Reformed Scope (m)

22410   Our Lady of Endor Coven
      808 West Central Avenue
      Toledo, Ohio 43610

15761   Pacific Yearly Meeting of Friends
      1430 East 27th Avenue
      Eugene, Oregon 97403

               Friends Bulletin

22525   Pagan Way
      P.O. Box 7712
      Philadelphia, Pennsylvania 19101

               The Crystal Well
               P.O. Box 18351
               Philadelphia, Pennsylvania 19120

180

25113   Palalo Kannondo Temple
        3326 Paalea Street
        Honolulu, Hawaii 96816

25440   Pansophic Institute
        P.O. Box 2971
        Reno, Nevada 89505

                    Clear Light (q)

18415   Pastoral Bible Institute
        P.O. Box 3252
        Chouteau Station
        St. Louis, Missouri 63110

                    The Herald of Christ's Kingdom
                    (bi-m)

30982   Peace Mission (Father Divine),
           Universal
        c/o New Day
        1600 Oxford Street
        Philadelphia, Pennsylvania 19121

                    The New Day

13165   Peniel Mission
        606 East Sixth Street
        Los Angeles, California 90021

14413   Pentecostal Assemblies of the
           World, Inc.
        3040 North Illinois Street
        Indianapolis, Indiana 46208

                    Christian Outlook (m)
                    228 South Orange Avenue
                    South Orange, New Jersey 07079

14101   Pentecostal Church of Christ
        Box 263
        London, Ohio 43140

                    Pentecostal Witness (m)
                    1600 Mill Road, S.W.
                    Canton, Ohio 44706

14220   Pentecostal Church of God
           of America
        Messenger Plaza
        221 Main Street
        Joplin, Missouri 64801

181

14221   Pentecostal Church of Zion, Inc.
c/o Zion College of Theology
P.O. Box 110
French Lick, Indiana 47432

The Word from Zion

14222   Pentecostal Evangelical Church
c/o Rev. Ernest Beroth
Box 4218
Spokane, Washington 99202

14123   Pentecostal Fire Baptized
Holiness Church
Toccoa, Georgia 30577

Faith and Truth (m)
Route 4
Commerce, Georgia 30529

14140   Pentecostal Free Will Baptist
Church, Inc.
c/o Rev. Herbert Carter,
General Superintendent
P.O. Box 1081
Dunn, North Carolina 28334

Promoter Pentecostal Free Will
Baptist News (bi-m)

14120   Pentecostal Holiness Church, Inc.
P.O. Box 12609
Oklahoma City, Oklahoma 73112

Pentecostal Holiness Advocate (bi-w)

20125   People of the Living God
2101 Prytania Street
New Orleans, Louisiana 70130

The Maturion (m)

18205   Peoples' Christian Church
c/o Mrs. Fred W. Loede, Secretary
451 Brook Avenue
Passaic, New Jersey 07055

Light
Box 2
Schenectady, New York 12306

30230   The People's Church Collective
        (Jesuene Ek-Klesia)
        c/o Bishop Mikhail F. Itkin
        716 North Irving Boulevard
        Studio 303
        Hollywood, California   90038

30410   People's Institute of Applied Religion
        Helena, Alabama   53080

12327   People's Methodist Church
        c/o John Wesley Bible School
        Greensboro, North Carolina

21929   People's Temple Christian
        (Disciples) Church
        P.O. Box 214
        Redwood City, California   95470

30923   Perfect Liberty Order
        700 South Adams Street
        Glendale, California   91205

                        Perfect Liberty

19245   Perfected Church of Jesus Christ
        of Immaculate Latter Day Saints
        c/o William C. Conway, D.D.
        Redondo Beach, California

15720   Philadelphia Yearly Meeting of
        the Religious Society of Friends
        1515 Cherry Street
        Philadelphia, Pennsylvania   19102

                Philadelphia Yearly Meeting News

18420   Philanthropic Assembly--
        The Church of the Kingdom
        of God
        709 74th Street
        North Bergen, New Jersey 07047

                        The Monitor of the Reign of
                        Justice (m)

21570   The Philo-Polytechnical Center
        c/o Mr. Ronald Clifton
        1905 Glendale Boulevard
        Los Angeles, California   90039

                        The Bodha Renaissance

21631   Philosophical Research Society
3910 Los Feliz Boulevard
Los Angeles, California 90027

PRS Journal (q)

25047   Phoenix Institute
2404 Broadway
San Diego, California 92102

Portal (q)

13409   Pilgrim Holiness Church of
New York State, Inc.
c/o Rev. Andrew J. Whitney,
President
32 Cadilas Avenue
Albany, New York 12205

13205   Pillar of Fire
1845 Champa Street
Denver, Colorado 80202

Pillar of Fire (w)
Zarephath, New Jersey 08890

17111   Plymouth Brethren (Exclusive):
Ames Brethren
c/o Christian Literature
Box 62
St. Paul, Minnesota 55102

17110   Plymouth Brethren (Exclusive):
Booth-Continental
c/o Erie Bible Truth Depot
112 West Eleventh Street
Erie, Pennsylvania 16512

Things Old and New (bi-m)

17113   Plymouth Brethren (Exclusive):
Ex-Taylor Brethren
(no address available)

17112   Plymouth Brethren (Exclusive):
Taylor Brethren
(no address available)

17115   Plymouth Brethren (Exclusive):
         Tunbridge Wells Brethren
         c/o Bible Truth Publishers
         239 Harrison Street
         Oak Park, Illinois 60304

                    Echoes of Grace (m)

            Christian Truth for the Household
                 of Faith (m)

17101   Plymouth Brethren (Open)
         c/o Stewards Foundation
         P.O. Box 294
         Wheaton, Illinois 60187

                 Letters of Interest (m)

10313   Polish Catholic Church
         c/o Rev. Francis I. Boryszewski
         91 Mercer Street
         Jersey City, New Jersey 07302

10312   Polish National Catholic Church
            of America
         529 East Locust Street
         Scranton, Pennsylvania 18505

            Rola Boza (God's Field) (bi-w)

10314   Polish Old Catholic Church
            in America
         c/o Rev. Felix Staruszewski
         48 Charles Street
         South River, New Jersey 08882

24055   Prema Dharmasala & Fellowship
            Association, Inc.
         c/o Vasudevadasji
         Route 4
         Box 265
         Bedford, Virginia 24523

                    Namaste

11711   Presbyterian Church in America
         c/o Rev. Erskine L. Jackson, Moderator
         P.O. Box 577
         Kosciusko, Mississippi 39090

11710   Presbyterian Church in the
         United States
         341 Ponce de Leon Avenue, N.E.
         Atlanta, Georgia   30308

                           Presbyterian Survey (m)

18112   Primitive Advent Christian Church
         c/o Elza Moss, President
         Sissonville, West Virginia   25185

16430   Primitive Baptist Conference of
         New Brunswick, Maine and
         Nova Scotia
         c/o St. John Valley Bible Camp
         Box 355
         Harland
         New Brunswick, Canada

                           The Gospel Standard (m)

16202   Primitive Baptists--
         Absolute Predestination
         (no central address)

                           Signs of the Times
                           c/o Elder David V. Spangler
                           Route 1
                           Box 539
                           Beechwood Lane
                           Danville, Virginia   24541

                           Zion's Landmark
                           117 North Goldsboro Street
                           Wilson, North Carolina   27893

16204   Primitive Baptists--Black
         (no central address)

         Contact: Elder W.J. Berry
         Primitive Baptist Library
         Route 2
         Elon College, North Carolina   27244

16703   Primitive Baptists Progressive
         (no central address)

                           Banner Herald (m)
                           Box 4168
                           Martinez, Georgia   31601

16201   Primitive Baptists--Regulars
         (no central address)

                              Old Faith Contender (q)
                              Route 2
                              Elon College, North Carolina 27244

                              Primitive Baptist Library Quarterly
                              Route 2
                              Elon College, North Carolina 27244

                              Primitive Baptist (m)
                              Five Second Street
                              Thornton, Arkansas 71766

                              Baptist Witness (m)
                              Box 17032
                              Cincinnati, Ohio 45217

19921   Primitive Church of Jesus Christ
         c/o Frederick L. Dias
         4103 Niagara Place
         Lawrence Park
         Erie, Pennsylvania 16511

12391   Primitive Methodist Church, USA
         c/o Rev. J. Fred Parkyn
         300 Morris Road
         Exton, Pennsylvania 19341

                              The Primitive Methodist Journal (m)
                              2874-J Monnier Street
                              Portage, Indiana 56368

22552   Pristine Orthodox Egyptian Church
         5017-15 North Clark Street
         Chicago, Illinois 60640

21941   The Process
         c/o Ken Humpherys
         Three Eleanor Street
         Stratford, Connecticut 06497

                              Processeans

16304   Progressive National Baptist
             Convention, Inc.
         (no central address)

                              Baptist Progress (q)
                              6300 Hartford Avenue
                              Detroit, Michigan 48210

                              187

21137   Progressive Spiritualist Church
         (no address available)

17703   Prophetic Herald Ministry
         P.O. Box 7
         Spokane, Washington 92210

                   Prophetic Herald (m)

23830   The Prosperos
         1441 Fourth Street
         Santa Monica, California 90401

                   The Prosperos Newsletter

11031   Protestant Conference (Lutheran)
         c/o Pastor Gerald Hinz
         Shiocton, Wisconsin 54170

                   Faith-Life (bi-m)
                   728 North Ninth Street
                   Manitowoc, Wisconsin 54220

10401   Protestant Episcopal Church
         815 Second Avenue
         New York, New York 10017

                   The Living Church
                   407 East Michigan Street
                   Milwaukee, Wisconsin 53202

11603   Protestant Reformed Churches
            of America
         16515 South Park Avenue
         South Holland, Illinois 60473

                   The Standard Bearer (s-m)
                   Reformed Free Publishing
                      Association
                   1842 Plymouth Terrace, S.E.
                   Grand Rapids, Michigan 44506

                   The Reformed Messenger
                   c/o Oak Lawn Protestant Reformed
                   Church
                   9536 South Minnick Avenue
                   Oak Lawn, Illinois 60453

25281   Providence Zen Center
         48 Hope Street
         Providence, Rhode Island 02906

                   Newsletter (m)

                   188

22585   Psychedelic Venus Church
        c/o Rev. Headstone
        Box 4163
        Sather Gate Station
        Berkeley, California 94704

                    The Nelly Heathen

21961   Psychiana Study Center
        4069 Stephens Street
        San Diego, California 92103

21151   Pyramid Church of Truth
          and Light
        c/o Rev. Steele M. Goodman
        2426 G Street
        Sacramento, California 95816

25285   Pyramid Zen Society
        Box 16021
        Pittsburgh, Pennsylvania 15242

21919   Quimby Center
        c/o Dr. Neva Dell Hunter
        Box 453
        Alamagordo, New Mexico 88310

                    Newsletter (q)

25335   Quong Ming Buddhism and Taoism
          Society
        17 Jason Court
        San Francisco, California 94133

23015   The Rabbinical Assembly
        3080 Broadway
        New York, New York 10027

                United Synagogue Review (q)

23011   Rabbinical Council of America
        220 Park Avenue
        New York, New York 10027

                    Tradition (q)

24910   Radha Soami Spiritual Science
          Foundation
        c/o Roland G. DeVries
        2922 Los Flores Avenue
        Riverside, California 92503

                    R.S. Greetings

21249   Radiant School of the Seekers
         and Servers
         624 South Mt. Shasta Boulevard
         Mt. Shasta, California 96667

20265   Rainbow Family of Living Light
         Box 5577
         Eugene, Oregon 97405

                    Rainbow Family Newsletter

24264   Rajneesh Foundation
         c/o Rajneesh Meditation Center
         Blackmore Lane
         P.O. Box 143
         East Islip, New York 11730

                    Sannyas

11952   The Rationalist Association
         Box 1742
         St. Louis, Missouri 63199

                    The American Rationalist (bi-m)

21784   Reach Out (Hodan)
         c/o Ray and Sally Serbert
         239 Barkley Place
         Columbus, Ohio 43213

24255   Real Yoga Society
         c/o Swami Shiva
         47 Harrison Street
         Oak Park, Illinois 60304

20210   Reba Place Fellowship and
         Associated Communities
         727 Reba Place
         Evanston, Illinois 60202

10355   Reformed Catholic Church
         (Utrecht Confession),
         Province of North America
         c/o Primate, Most Rev. W.W. Flynn
         P.O. Box 2421
         Los Angeles, California 90053

11601   Reformed Church in America
         475 Riverside Drive
         New York, New York 10027

                    The Church Herald (w)
                    146 Division Street, North
                    Grand Rapids, Michigan 49502

11608   Reformed Church in the United States
         c/o Rev. N.C. Hoeflunger
         124 22nd Street, S.W.
         Minot, South Dakota 58701

                        The Reformed Herald (m)
                        Box 233
                        Sutton, Nebraska 68979

22535   Reformed Druids of North America
         c/o P.E.I. Bonewits
         Box 9398
         Berkeley, California 94709

10404   Reformed Episcopal Church
         c/o Rev. D. Ellsworth Raudenbush
         560 Fountain Street
         Havre de Grace, Maryland 21078

                        Episcopal Recorder (m)
                        25 South 43rd Street
                        Philadelphia, Pennsylvania 19104

15103   Reformed Mennonite Church
         c/o Bishop J. Henry Fisher
         35 Greenfield Road
         Lancaster, Pennsylvania 17602

12351   Reformed Methodist Union
            Episcopal Church
         c/o Rt. Rev. Eddie Ogden Gibbs
         Route 17
         Box 1057
         Seaside Lane
         Charleston, South Carolina 29407

11705   Reformed Presbyterian Church,
            Evangelical Synod
         12330 Conway Road
         St. Louis, Missouri 63141

                        Mandate (tri-w)
                        415 Krupski Loop
                        Lookout Mountain, Tennessee 37350

                        NPM (m)
                        12330 Conway Road
                        St. Louis, Missouri 63141

191

11707   Reformed Presbyterian Church of
         North America (Old School)
         c/o Rev. E. Clark Copeland
         5205 Fawn Haven Drive
         Gibsonia, Pennsylvania 15044

                        The Covenanter Witness (bi-w)
                        800 Wood Street
                        Pittsburgh, Pennsylvania 15221

12352   Reformed Zion Union Apostolic Church
         c/o F.M. Pegram
         411 B.N. Main Street
         Lawrenceville, Virginia 23868

                        Union Searchlight
                        South Hill, Virginia 23970

16216   Regular Baptist Association
         (no address available)

16110   Regular Baptists (Calvinist/Arminian)
         (no central address)

                        Regular Baptist
                        c/o Tom Marshall
                        7223 Little River Turnpike
                        Annandale, Virginia 22003

                        Regular Baptist Messenger
                        c/o Elder Sherman Essex
                        Route 1
                        Box 246A
                        Pittsboro, Indiana 46167

16111   Regular Baptists (Predestinarian)
         (no address available)

18207   Religious Liberty and Temperance
           Association
         Route 2
         Box 128
         Clarksville, Arkansas 72830

22205   Religious Order of Witchcraft
         521 St. Phillip Street
         New Orleans, Louisiana 70116

20516   Religious Science International
         885 East Telegraph Road
         Fillmore, California   93015

                        Creative Thought

15715   Religious Society of Friends
           (Conservatives)
         c/o Lewis Mott
         R.R. 3
         Indianaola, Iowa   50125

15720   Religious Society of Friends
           (General Conference)
         1520 Race Street
         Philadelphia, Pennsylvania   19102

                        FGC Quarterly (q)

15730   Religious Society of Friends,
           Kansas Yearly Meeting
         c/o President Clerk Warren E. Stanfield
         Haviland, Kansas   67059

18901   Remnant Church
         P.O. Box 9527
         Rochester, New York   14607

17711   Remnant of Israel
         11303 East Seventh Avenue
         Opportunity, Washington   99206

10360   Renovated Church of Christ
         c/o The Apostles of Infinite Love
         Monastery of the Apostles
         P.O. Box 308
         Saint Jovite JOT 2HO
         Quebec, Canada

                        Magnificat (m)

19401   Reorganized Church of Jesus Christ
           of Latter-Day Saints
         The Auditorium
         Independence, Missouri   64051

                        Saints' Herald (m)

                        Restoration Witness (m)

25117   Rissho Kosai Kai
         2280 Auhuhu Street
         Honolulu, Hawaii   90000

                              193

21229   Robin's Return
        1008 Lamberton Street, S.E.
        Grand Rapids, Michigan 49505

Newsletter (m)

15725   Rocky Mountain Yearly Meeting of
        the Friends Church
        2610 East Bijou Street
        Colorado Springs, Colorado 80909

10301   The Roman Catholic Church
        National Conference of Catholic Bishops
        1312 Massachusetts Avenue, N.W.
        Washington, D.C. 20005

14904   Romanian Apostolic Pentecostal Church
        of God of North America
        c/o Rev. Petru Tivadan, Sr.
        7794 Rosemont
        Detroit, Michigan 48228

11036   Romanian Orthodox Church in America
        c/o Rt. Rev. Bishop Victorin (Ursache)
        19959 Riopelle
        Detroit, Michigan 48203

Credinta--The Faith (m)

10135   The Romanian Orthodox Episcopate
        of America
        2522 Grey Tower Road
        R.F.D. 7
        Jackson, Michigan   49201

SOLIA, Roumanian News (m)
11341 Woodward Avenue
Detroit, Michigan 48202

21155   Roosevelt Spiritual Memorial
        Benevolent Association
        P.O. Box 38-825
        Miami, Florida 33138

21614   Rosicrucian Fellowship
        P.O. Box 713
        Oceanside, California 92054

Rays from the Rose Cross (m)

16211   Roundlick Primitive Baptist
         Association
         c/o Charles L. West
         Route 1
         Carthage, Tennessee   37030

21524   "Ruby Focus" of Magnificent
         Consummation
         c/o Revs. Garland and Evangeline
         Van Polen
         P.O. Drawer 1188
         Sedona, Arizona   86336

                        Open Letter

24911   Ruhani Satsang
         Divine Science of the Soul
         211 West Broadway
         Anaheim, California   92803

22564   Runic Society
         c/o Honorable N.J. Templin
         P.O. Box 2811
         Milwaukee, Wisconsin   53219

                        Einherjar (3/yr)

10107   Russian Orthodox Church in
           the USA
         St. Nicholas Patriarchial Cathedral
         15 East 97th Street
         New York, New York   10029

                 Journal of the Moscow
                   Patriarchate (m)

                 One Church (bi-m)
                 P.O. Box 363
                 East Lansing, Michigan   48823

10106   The Russian Orthodox Church
           Outside Russia
         75 East 93rd Street
         New York, New York   10028

                 Orthodox Life (bi-m)

10110   Russian Orthodox (Old Believers)
         Nikolaevsk, Alaska

16150   Russian/Ukrainian Evangelical
       Union of the U.S.A., Inc.
       c/o Dr. Ivan A. Kmeta, President
       Roosevelt Boulevard & Seventh Street
       Philadelphia, Pennsylvania 19120

"A Herald of Good Tidings" (q)

22580   Sabaen Religious Order of Am'n
       2447 North Halsted
       Chicago, Illinois 60614

Isis (q)

21648   Sabian Assembly
       c/o Marc Edmund Jones
       Stanwood, Washington 98292

21510   Sacred Society of the Eth, Inc.
       P.O. Box 3
       Forks of Salmon, California 96031

24218   Sai Baba Movement
       "Sai Nilayam" Retreat
       Tecate, California 92080

21171   St. Paul's Church of Aquarian Science
       1220 16th Street, North
       St. Petersburg, Florida 33705

21175   St. Timothy's Abbey Church
       c/o Rev. Kingdom L. Brown
       6508 East Cactus Road
       Scottsdale, Arizona 85254

New Age Forum

20215   Salem Acres
       R.R. 1
       Box 175A
       Rock City, Illinois 61070

13130   Salvation Army
       120-30 West 14th Street
       New York, New York 10011

War Cry (w)
346 Avenue of the Americas
New York, New York 10011

13213   Sanctified Church of Christ
       2715 18th Avenue
       Columbus, Georgia 31901

21520   Sanctuary of the Master's Presence
         c/o Mrs. Mary Myneta
         Two Lakin Road
         Scarsdale, New York   10583

                            Mentor (bi-m)

24253   Sanatana Dharma Foundation
         c/o Yogeshwar Muni
         1135 Oxford Street
         Berkeley, California   94707

                         Vishvamitra

16214   Sandlick/Spencer Primitive
            Baptist Associations
         (no address available)

25111   Sasana Yeiktha Meditation Center--
            The Buddhist Society
         5184 Scranton Court
         Denver, Colorado   80239

22425   Satanic Church of America
         c/o Anton Szander LaVey
         6114 California Street
         San Francisco, Claifornia   94121

                          The Cloven Hoof

21976   Savitria
         2405 Ruscombe
         Baltimore, Maryland   21209

21351   School for Esoteric Studies
         Suite 1903
         40 East 49th Street
         New York, New York   10017

20527   School of Esoteric Christianity
         130 East Girard
         Englewood, Colorado   80110

                         The Esoterian News

21356   School of Light and Regeneration
            (SOLAR)
         Route 1
         Box 72
         Suttons Bay, Michigan   49682

21203   School of Natural Science
         25355 Spanish Ranch Road
         Los Gatos, California   95030

197

20562   School of Truth
        75 Malaya Cove Plaza
        Palos Verdes Estates, California   90274

15910   Schwenkfelder Church
        Pennsburg, Pennsylvania   18073

                The Schwenkfeldian   (q)

21923   Scientology, Church of
        2125 S Street, N.W.
        Washington, D.C.   20008

                Ability

                The Auditor
                c/o David Gates
                American Saint Hill Organization
                2723 West Temple Street
                Los Angeles, California   90026

18303   Scripture Research Association
        c/o A.B. Traina
        Route C
        Box 128
        Big Rapids, Michigan   49307

22380   Seax Wicca
        c/o Dr. Raymond Buckland
        P.O. Box 238
        Weirs Beach, New Hampshire   03246

                Seax-Wicca Voys

11712   Second Cumberland Presbyterian Church
          in the USA & Africa
        226 Church Street
        Huntsville, Alabama   35801

                Cumberland Flag
                545 Vanderhorst Drive
                Nashville, Tennessee   37209

20536   Seicho-No-Ie
        14527 Vermont Avenue
        Gardena, California   90247

                Seicho-No-Ie   News   (m)

24050   Self-Realization Fellowship
        3880 San Rafael Avenue
        Los Angeles, California   90065

                Self Realization   (q)

198

24051   Self-Revelation Church of
         Absolute Monism
         Golden Lotus Temple
         4748 Western Avenue, N.W.
         Washington, D.C. 20016

16113   Separate Baptists in Christ
         c/o Rev. Roger Popplewell, Moderator
         Route 6
         Russell Springs, Kentucky 42642

10140   Serbian Eastern Orthodox Church
         in the U.S.A. and Canada
         c/o Rt. Rev. Bishop Firmilian
         5701 North Redwood Drive
         Chicago, Illinois 60656

                         Serbian Orthodox Church Herald

10141   Serbian Orthodox Diocese for the
         United States and Canada
         c/o Rt. Rev. Bishop Dionisji
         St. Sava Monastary
         Libertyville, Illinois 60048

                         The Diocesan Observer (w)
                         Box 417
                         Libertyville, Illinois 60048

21239   Servants of Awareness
         c/o David Worchester
         4403 Fourth Avenue, N.E.
         Seattle, Washington 98105

18201   Seventh-Day Adventist Church
         6840 Eastern Avenue, N.W.
         Washington, D.C.   20012

                         Review and Herald (w)

                         Signs of the Times (m)
                         Pacific Press Publishing
                         Association
                         Mountain View, California 94040

                         These Times (m)
                         P.O. Box 59
                         Nashville, Tennessee 37202

18202   SDA Reform Movement
         3031 Franklin Boulevard
         Sacramento, California 95817

16601   Seventh Day Baptist General Conference
         Seventh Day Baptist Building
         510 Watchung Avenue
         Plainfield, New Jersey 07061

                              Sabbath Recorder (m)

16610   Seventh Day Baptist (German)
         c/o President Crist M. King
         238 South Aiken Street
         Pittsburgh, Pennsylvania 15206

                              Church News

18211   Seventh Day Christian Conference
         252 West 138th Street
         New York, New York 10030

18216   The Seventh Day Church of God
         c/o Elder M.L. Ogren
         Box 804
         Caldwell, Idaho 83605

                              Herald of Truth (m)

14223   Seventh Day Pentecostal Church of
            the Living God
         1143 South Euclid Avenue
         Washington, D.C. 20009

18902   Shiloh True Light Church of Christ
         c/o James Rommie Purser, Elder
         4001 Sheridan Drive
         Charlotte, North Carolina 28205

18903   Shiloh True Light Church of Christ
         c/o Elder H. Flake Braswell
         Monroe, North Carolina 28110

20130   Shiloh Trust
         c/o Rev. James Janisch
         Sulphur Springs, Arkansas 72768

25105   Shingon Mission
         915 Sheridan Street
         Honolulu, Hawaii 96810

25109   Shinnyo-En
         c/o Bishop J. Kuriyama
         2348 South Beretania Street
         Honolulu, Hawaii 96814

25940   Shinrei-Kyo
         c/o Mr. Kameo Kiyota
         310C Uulani Street
         Hilo, Hawaii 96720

25550   Shivapuram
         (no address available)

24152   Shree Gurudev Rudrananda Yogashram
         88 East Tenth Street
         New York, New York 10003

24151   Shree Gurudev Siddha Yoga Ashram
         27 Highland Avenue
         Piedmont, California 94611

22123   Shrine of Sothis
         P.O. Box 14096
         San Francisco, California 94114

24901   Sikh Foundation
         P.O. Box 727
         Redwood City, California 94064

                         The Sikh Sansar (q)

25315   Sino-American Buddhist Association
         1731 15th Street
         San Francisco, California 94103

                         Vajra Bodhi Sea (m)

24114   Sivananda Conservatory of Yoga
           One Science
         R.D. 3
         Box 400
         Stroudsburg, Pennsylvania 18360

                         Yoga Newsletter

30929   Smithvenner
         (no address available)

15901   Social Brethren
         c/o Rev. Harry E. Carr
         Moderator of General Assembly
         54 Hudson Avenue
         Pontiac, Michigan 48058

21612   Societas Rosicruciana in America
         321 West 101st Street
         New York, New York 10025

21947   Society for the Teaching of the Inner Christ
        2333 Albatross Street
        San Diego, California   92101

20104   Society of Brothers
        Rifton, New York 12471

21189   Society of Christ, Inc.
        c/o Bishop Dan B. Boughan, S.C.D.D.
        229-1/2 North Western Avenue
        Los Angeles, California   90004

20526   Society of Pragmatic Mysticism
        140 West 58th Street, Apt. S-E
        New York, New York   10019

23220   Society of the Bible in the Hands of Its Creators
        342 Madison Avenue
        New York, New York   10017

22150   Society of the Magians
        Box 46
        Cathedral City, California   92234

21515   Sologa, Inc.
        Box 759
        Melbourne, Florida   32901
                              Solograph (m)

21735   Solar Light Center
        c/o Miss Alieuti Francesca
        Route 2, Box 572-J
        7700 Avenue of the Sun
        Central Point, Oregon   97501
                              Starcraft Journal (q)

24238   Sonorama Society
        P.O. Box 17007
        Los Angeles, California   90017

14505   Sought Out Church of God in Christ and Spiritual
           House of Prayer, Inc.
        Brunswick, Georgia   31520

21638   Soulcraft Fellowship, Inc.
        Box 192
        Noblesville, Indiana   46060

16132   South Carolina Baptist Fellowship
        c/o Rev. John Water
        1607 Greenwood Road
        Laurens, South Carolina   29360

15745   Southeastern Yearly Meeting
        (Friends)
        c/o James O. Bond
        1705 North Oregon Circle
        Tampa, Florida   33612

15750   Southern Appalachian Association
        of Friends
        c/o Lucretia Evans
        301 Hayes Street
        Crossville, Tennessee   38555

16102   Southern Baptist Convention
        460 James Robertson Parkway
        Nashville, Tennessee   37219

                    Home Missions (m)

                    The Baptist Program (m)

10402   Southern Episcopal Church
        c/o Presiding Bishop B.H. Webster
        420 Mid-State Medical Center
        Nashville, Tennessee   37203

12325   Southern Methodist Church
        P.O. Box 132
        Orangeburg, South Carolina   29115

                    The Southern Methodist (m)
                    P.O. Drawer A
                    Orangeburg, South Carolina   29115

16131   Southwide Baptist Fellowship
        c/o Rev. John R. Waters
        Faith Baptist Church
        1607 Greenwood Road
        Laurens, South Carolina   29360

16122   Sovereign Grace Baptist Movement
        (no central address)

                    Baptist Reformation Review (q)
                    c/o Norbert Ward
                    Box 40161
                    Nashville, Tennessee   37204

                    Sovereign Grace Message (m)
                    c/o E.W. Johnson, Pastor
                    Calvary Baptist Church
                    P.O. Box 7464
                    Pine Bluff, Arkansas   71611

21149   Spiritual Prayer Home, Inc.
         c/o Rev. Norman C. Fredrikson,
            President
         144 East Baseline Road
         San Dimas, California 91773

21223   Spiritual Research Society
         740 Hubbard Street, N.E.
         Grand Rapids, Michigan 49505

21123   Spiritual Science Mother Church, Inc.
         c/o Rev. Glenn Argal
         Studio 1010
         Carnegie Hall
         56th Street & Seventh Avenue
         New York, New York 10019

21115   Spiritualist Episcopal Church
         c/o Rev. Ivey M. Hooper
         727 North Capitol Avenue
         Lansing, Michigan 48906

                    Golden Rays

24220   Sri Aurobindo Centers
         c/o Matagiri
         Mt. Tremper, New York 12457

                    Collaboration (q)

24228   Sri Chinmoy Centers
         85-45 149th Street
         Jamaica Hills, New York 11435

24259   Sri Ram Ashram
         P.O. Drawer AR
         Benson, Arizona 85602

24262   Sri Sri Ma Ananda Mati Ashram
         c/o Swami Nirmalananda Giri
         1835 N.W. 16th Street
         Oklahoma City, Oklahoma 73106

                    Ananda Jyoti (m)

13114   Standard Churches of America
         Brockville
         Ontario, Canada

21710   Star Light Fellowship
         P.O. Box 74
         Cooper Station
         New York, New York 10003

                    The Star Light Messenger
                    204

21996   Star of Truth Foundation
         118 West Sparks Street
         Galena, Kansas   66739

                    The Sparkler (bi-m)

15111   Stauffer Mennonite Church
         c/o Bishop Jacob S. Stauffer
         Route 3
         Ephrata, Pennsylvania   17522

21644   Stelle Group
         P.O. Box 5900
         Chicago, Illinois   60680

                    The Lemuria Builder (m)

25111   Stillpoint Institutes
         c/o Howard Elrod, Secretary
         5184 Scranton Court
         Denver, Colorado   80239

24210   Subramuniya Yoga Order
         108 Mill Street
         Virginia City, Nevada   89440

23835   Subud Committee
         P.O. Box 1766
         Old Chelsea Station
         New York, New York   10011

23801   Sufi Order
         c/o Pir Vilayat Khan
         P.O. Box 96
         New Lebanon, New York   12125

                    The Message (m)

23820   Sufism Reoriented, Inc.
         1290 Sutter Street
         San Francisco, California   94109

21505   Summit Lighthouse
         Church Universal and Triumphant
         P.O. Box 7018
         Pasadena, California   91102

                    Pearls of Wisdom   (w)

23723   Sunni Muslims (Hanafi Movement)
         (no address available)

21143   Superet Light Center
        2512-16 West Third Street
        Los Angeles, California   90059

                        Newsletter (m)

22315   Susan B. Anthony Coven
          (Feminist Wicca)
        c/o Lady Meolou (Z. Budapest)
        442 Lincoln Boulevard
        Venice, California   90291

24254   Swami Kuvalayananda Yoga Foundation
        Ten South Front Street
        Philadelphia, Pennsylvania   19106

                        Skylight (q)

11021   Synod of Evangelical Lutheran Churches
        c/o Rev. John Kovac
        4126 Blow Street
        St. Louis, Missouri   63116

                        The Lutheran Beacon

10220   Syrian Orthodox Church of Antioch
          (Archdiocese of the USA and Canada)
        c/o Archbisohp Mar Athanasius Y. Samuel
        293 Hamilton Place
        Hackensack, New Jersey   07601

10221   Syrian Orthodox Church of Malabar
        c/o Dr. K.M. Simon
        Union Theological Seminary
        Broadway & 120th Street
        New York, New York   10027

25910   Taishakyo-Hawaii Izumo Taisho
        215 North Kukui Street
        Honolulu, Hawaii   96817

26005   Taoist Sanctuary
        P.O. Box 5018
        Beverly Hills, California   91210

                        Tao and Change (q)

21526   The Teachings of the Angelic Host
          Within the Kingdom of Heaven
        c/o Mary L. Myers
        3427 Denson Place
        Charlotte, North Carolina   28215

                        The Teachings for the New Age by
                        the Ascended Masters of the White
                        Brotherhood
        206

24052   Temple of Kriya Yoga
505 North Michigan Avenue
Chicago, Illinois 60611

The Current

21121   Temple of Universal Law, First
5030 North Drake
Chicago, Illinois 60625

20116   Temple Society
c/o Gertrude Paulas Reno
423-B East Sola Street
Santa Barbara, California 93101

OR

c/o Dr. Richard Hoffman, Director
152 Tucker Road
Bentleigh 3204
Victoria, Australia

25930   Tenrikyo (Teaching of Divine Wisdom)
2727 East First Street
Los Angeles, California 90033

25925   Tensho--Kotai--Jingu-Kyo
253 Margarita Avenue
Palo Alto, California 94306

Voice from Heaven (bi-m)

22562   Teutonic Temple
P.O. Box 681
The Dalles, Oregon 97058

22436   Thee Satanic Church
P.O. Box 1123
Melrose Park, Illinois 60160

22435   Thee Satanic Church of Nethilum Rites
c/o Terry Taylor, High Priest
3109 North Central Avenue
Chicago, Illinois 60634

21931   Theocentric Foundation
3341 East Cambridge Avenue
Phoenix, Arizona 85008

21301   The Theosophical Society
P.O. Bin C
Pasadena, California 91109

Sun Rise

21303   Theosophical Society (Hartley)
          Altadena, California   91001

21305   Theosophical Society of America
          1926 North Main Street
          Wheaton, Illinois   60187

                         The American Theosophist (m)

25945   Third Civilization
          P.O. Box 2506
          Santa Fe, New Mexico   87501

                         Third Civilization Monthly (m)

17402   This Testimony
          c/o Atlantic States Christian Convention
          c/o Ernest L. Chase
          1370 Ray Street
          Norfolk, Virginia   23502

          OR

          MORE
          c/o Dean Baker
          Box 68505
          Indianapolis, Indiana   46286

25410   Tibetan Nyingmapa Meditation Center
          2425 Hillside Avenue
          Berkeley, California   94704

                         Crystal Mirror (a)

17335   Timely Messenger Fellowship
          c/o R.B. Shiflet
          P.O. Box 473
          Mineral Wells, Texas   76067

16738   Tioga River Christian Conference
          c/o Rev. George Kyrk
          Bible School Park, New York   16837

25103   Todaiji Hawaii Bekkaku Honzan
          c/o Bishop Tatsucho Hirai
          426 Luakini Street
          Honolulu, Hawaii   98617

20511   Today Church
          c/o Bud and Carmen Moshier
          5002 West Lovers Lane
          Dallas, Texas   75209

                         For You (w)

21169   T.O.M. Religious Foundation
Box 52
Chimayo, New Mexico 87522

10324   Traditional Christian Catholic Church
in Europe and North America
c/o Dr. Thomas Fehervary,
Metropolitan-Archbishop
2399 Orleans
Montreal
Quebec, Canada

13313   Triumph the Church and Kingdom of
God in Christ
213 Farrington Avenue, S.E.
Atlanta, Georgia 30315

17709   True Church
5644 Fauntleroy
Seattle, Washington 98116

21979   True Church of Christ, International
P.O. Box 2
Station G
Buffalo, New York 14213

19901   True Church of Jesus Christ
(Cutlerite)
Clitherall, Missouri 56524

14528   True Fellowship Pentecostal
Church of America, Inc.
c/o Rt. Rev. Charles E. Waters
4238 Pimlico Road
Baltimore, Maryland 21215

14523   True Grace Memorial House of Prayer
205 V Street, N.W.
Washington, D.C. 20001

24112   True World Order
5178 St. Lawrence Boulevard
Montreal
Quebec, Canada

Yoga Life International

17310   Truth for Today
Route 2
Warsaw, Indiana 46580

Truth for Today (m)

209

10164   Turkish Orthodox Church in America
         Patriarchal Exarchate
         Exarchal Chancery and Residence
         I.C.N.P. Building
         784 Grand Street
         Jersey City, New Jersey 07304

                      Orthodoks Mustakil (q)

18221   Twentieth Century Church of God
         P.O. Box 129
         Vacaville, California 95688

                           Newsletter (m)

17403   Two-by-Twos
         (no address available)

16218   Two-Seed-In-The-Spirit
         Predestinarian Baptist
         (no address available)

11713   Ukrainian Evangelical Alliance of
         North America
         c/o Rev. W. Borosky, Executive
         Secretary
         5610 Trowbridge Drive
         Dunwoody, Georgia 30338

                      Evangelical Morning

16151   Ukrainian Evangelical Baptist Convention
         c/o Rev. O.R. Harbuziuk
         690 Berkeley Avenue
         Elmhurst, Illinois 60126

10150   Ukrainian Orthodox Church in
         the U.S.A.
         c/o Most Rev. Mstyslav S. Skrypnyk,
         Metropolitan
         P.O. Box 595
         South Bound Brook, New Jersey 08880

                      Ukrainian Orthodox Word

10151   Ukrainian Orthodox Church of America
         (Ecumenical Patriarchate)
         c/o Most Rev. Bishop Andrei Kuschak
         St. Andrew's Ukrainian Orthodox Diocese
         90-34 139th Street
         Jamaica, New York 11435

                      Ukrainian Orthodox Herald (q)

21740   Unarius--Science of Life
P.O. Box 1042
El Cajon, California 92022

13112   Undenominational Church of the Lord
c/o Pastor Robert Wallace
P.O. Box 291
Placentia, California 92779

21725   Understanding, Inc.
P.O. Box 206
Merlin, Oregon 97532

Understanding (m)

18210   Unification Association of
Christian Sabbath Keepers
145-151 Central Park North
New York, New York 10026

Unification Leader (m)

Unification Church
(See Holy Spirit Association for the
Unification of World Christianity)

12556   Union American Methodist Episcopal
Church
c/o Rt. Rev. David McClellan Harmon
774 Pine Street
Camden, New Jersey 08103

23010   Union of Orthodox Rabbis of the
United States and Canada
116 East 27th Street
New York, New York 10016

Jewish Life (q)

11901   Unitarian-Universalist Association
25 Beacon Street
Boston, Massachusetts 02108

UU World (s-m)
Journal of the Liberal Ministry
Box 485
Oak Ridge, Tennessee 37830

16405   United Baptists
c/o Omer E. Baker, Corresponding
Secretary
8640 Brazil Road
Jacksonville, Florida 32208

12372   United Brethren in Christ
United Brethren Building
48 East Franklin Street
Room 401
Huntington, Indiana 46750

The United Brethren (m)

12371   United Christian Church
c/o Moderator, Elder Henry C. Heagy
Lebanon R.D. 4
Lebanon County, Pennsylvania 17042

30931   United Christian Church
c/o Rev. Herbert J. Elliot
117 Rose Lane
New Hyde Park, New York 11040

14919   United Christian Ministerial
Association
Box 754
Cleveland, Tennessee 37311

The Shield of Faith (bi-m)

20515   United Church and Science of
Living Institute
c/o Dr. Frederick J. Eikerenkoetten II
Box 1000
Boston, Massachusetts 02103

Action (m)

11803   United Church of Christ
297 Park Avenue, South
New York, New York 10010

A.D. (m)

20515   United Church of Religious Science
3251 West Sixth Street
Los Angeles, California 90005

Science of Mind (m)

10411   United Episcopal Church
         c/o Bishop Russell G. Fry
         Schwenksville, Pennsylvania   19473

14917   United Evangelical Churches
         Box 28
         Monrovia, California   91016

                    Koinonia

16415   The United Free Will Baptist Church
         Kinston College
         1000 University Street
         Kinston, North Carolina   28501

                    Free Will Baptist Advocate (s-m)

14259   United Fundamentalist Church
         c/o Rev. Paul Kopp
         3236 Larga Avenue
         Los Angeles, California   90039

23420   United Hebrew Congregation
         c/o Rabbi Naphtali Ben Israel
         131 West 74th Street
         Chicago, Illinois 60621

13427   United Holiness Church
         Cedar Springs, Michigan   49319

                    United Holiness Sentinel

14526   United Holy Church of America, Inc.
         159 West Coulter Street
         Philadelphia, Pennsylvania   19144

                    The Holiness Union (m)

14518   United House of Prayer for
             All People
         c/o Bishop McColloch
         1721-1/2 Seventh Street, N.W.
         Washington, D.C.   20001

23220   United Israel World Union
         507 Fifth Avenue
         New York, New York   10017

                    United Israel Bulletin (3/yr)

21307   United Lodge of Theosophists
         347 East 72nd Street
         New York, New York 10021

12301   United Methodist Church
         The Program Council
         601 Riverview Avenue, West
         Dayton, Ohio 45406

                     Newscope (w)
                     1661 North Northwest Highway
                     Park Ridge, Illinois 60068

14437   United Pentecostal Church, International
         8855 Dunn Road
         Hazelwood, Missouri 63042

                     The Pentecostal Herald (m)

11701   The United Presbyterian Church In
            The United States Of America
         475 Riverside Drive
         New York, New York 10027

                     A.D. (m)

11959   United Secularists of America, Inc.
         P.O. Box 5146
         Los Angeles, California 90055

                     The Progressive World (m)

18223   United Seventh Day Brethren
         c/o President Myrtle Ortiz
         Box 225
         Enid, Oklahoma 73701

                     The Vision (bi-m)
                     2401 Third Avenue
                     Marion, Iowa 53203

20115   United Society of Believers
         Sabbath Lake, Maine

         OR

         Canterbury, New Hampshire 03224

21119   United Spiritualist Church
         813 West 165th Place
         Gardena, California 90247

12312   United Wesleyan Methodist Church
        Of America
        c/o Rev. David S. Bruno, President
        270 West 126th Street
        New York, New York 10037

                    The Herald

15515   United Zion Church
        c/o Bishop Brinser Heistand
        R.D. 3
        Elizabethtown, Pennsylvania 17022

12102   Unity of the Brethren
        c/o Marvin Chlapek
        2513 Revere
        Pasadena, Texas 77502

                    Brethren Journal (m)
                    5905 Carleen Drive
                    Austin, Texas 78731

20510   Unity School of Christianity
        Unity Village, Missouri 64065

                    Unity (m)

                    The Word   (m)

21980   Universal Brotherhood
        P.O. Box 366
        Grand Central Station
        New York, New York 10017

                    The Light Beyond (bi-m)

25544   Universal Buddhist Fellowship
        c/o Venerable Harold Halsey (Tissa)
          Priebe, President
        Box 1079
        Ojai, California 93023

                    Western Bodhi

21179   Universal Christ Church, Inc.
          (School of Spiritualism)
        1704 West Venice Boulevard
        Los Angeles, California 90006

10356   Universal Christian Apostolic Church
         c/o Patriarch William Franklin Wolsey,
         Primate
         Gilpin Street & Deer Lake Avenue
         Burnaby
         British Columbia, Canada

30933   Universal Christian Churches
         of America
         8648 Oakleigh Road
         Baltimore, Maryland   21234

10350   Universal Christian International
         Catholic Church
         c/o His Holiness, M. Zidones Hamatheite,
         Presiding Archpatriarche
         30 Malta Street
         Brooklyn, New York   11207

14921   Universal Church, Mystical
         Body of Christ
         c/o Bishop R.O. Fraser
         P.O. Box 874
         Saginaw, Michigan   48605

                       The Light of Life Herald

21193   Universal Church of Psychic
         Science, Inc.
         4740 Taconey Street
         Philadelphia, Pennsylvania   19124

25030   Universal Church of Scientific Truth
         1250 Indiana Street
         Birmingham, Alabama   35224

                       Divine Scientific Truth Journal

21133   Universal Church of the Master
         399 West San Carlos Street
         P.O. Box 692
         San Jose, California   95106

                       UCM Quarterly (q)

21201   Universal Faithists of Kosmon
         c/o Kosmon Service Center
         P.O. Box 392
         Vernal, Utah   84078

                       The Faithist Journal (bi-m)
                       2324 Suffock Avenue
                       Kingman, Arizona   86401

                       Esprit De Corps! (q)
                       216

30311   Universal Free Life Church
         1503 South State Road
         Hollywood, Florida   33023

30970   Universal Great Brotherhood
         Box 9154
         St. Louis, Missouri   63117

                      Ta-Khaze
                      6004 Pershing Avenue
                      St. Louis, Missouri   63117

21131   Universal Harmony Association
         216 23rd Avenue, N.E.
         St. Petersburg, Florida   33704

20245   Universal Industrial Church of the
           New World Comforter
           (One World Family)
         P.O. Box 704
         Berkeley, California   94704

30301   Universal Life Church
         601 Third Street
         Modesto, California   95351

                      Universal Life

21129   Universal Religion of America
         976 Sorozon Drive
         Rockledge, Florida   32955

10178   Universal Shrine of Divine Guidance
         c/o Archbishop Mark Athanasios C. Karras
         P.O. Box 31
         Miami, Florida   33145

21117   Universal Spiritualist Association
         c/o Pauline Swann
         P.O. Box 158
         Chesterfield, Indiana   46017

                      The Universal Spiritualist (q)
                      217 Eastern Drive
                      Chesterfield, Indiana   46017

14920   (Universal) World Church
         123 North Lake Street
         Los Angeles, California   90026

                           217

21711   Universariun Foundation, Inc.
        3600 S.E. 84th Avenue
        Portland, Oregon 97266

                        The Voice of Universarius (m)

21157   University of Life Church
        c/o Rev. Richard Ireland
        5600 South Sixth Street
        Phoenix, Arizona 85040

11709   Upper Cumberland Presbyterian Church
        c/o Roaring River U.C.P.C.
        Gainesboro, Tennessee 38562

21211   Urantia Foundation
        533 Diversey Parkway
        Chicago, Illinois 60614

                        The Urantian (q)

22526   Uranus Temple
        1125 West Wellington
        Chicago, Illinois 60657

21240   USA Communications
        c/o Fred Anthony Warren
        P.O. Box 900
        Royal Oak, Michigan 48068

24001   Vedanta Society
        34 West 71st Street
        New York, New York 10023

                        Vedanta and the West (bi-m)
                        c/o Vedanta Press
                        1946 Vedanta Place
                        Hollywood, California 90028

22560   Viking Brotherhood
        Box 2552
        Wichita Falls, Texas 76301

                        The Runestone (q)
                        c/o Stephen A. McNallen
                        A. Co. 1 Bn. 39th Inf.
                        APO New York, New York 09034

30125   Voice of Elijah
        c/o Carl Parke
        Box 3455
        Spokane, Washington 99220

                        Truth (8/yr)

218

13407   Voice of The Nazarene
         Association of Churches, Inc.
         Box 1
         Finelyville, Pennsylvania   15332

                    The Voice of the Nazarene (m)

                    The Universal Challenger (m)

13132   Volunteers of America
         340 West 85th Street
         New York, New York   10024

                    The Volunteer (m)

30120   Way Biblical Research Center
         Box 328
         New Knoxville, Ohio   45871

                    The Way

30410   Way of Righteousness
         c/o Rev. Claude Williams
         Route 1
         Box 905
         Helena, Alabama   35080

14510   Way of the Cross Church
         19th & D Streets, N.E.
         Washington, D.C.   20000

15112   Weaver Mennonites
         c/o Pike Meetinghouse
         New Holland, Pennsylvania   17557

13110   Wesleyan Church
         P.O. Box 2000
         Marion, Indiana   46952

                    The Wesleyan Advocate (bi-w)

13419   Wesleyan Holiness Association
            of Churches
         726 West 13th Street
         Tempe, Arizona   85281

                    Eleventh Hour Messenger (m)

13207   Wesleyan Tabernacle Association
         626 Elliott Avenue
         Cincinnati, Ohio   45215

18407   Western Bible Students
        12739 26th Avenue, N.E.
        Seattle, Washington 98125

11704   Westminster Biblical Fellowship
        c/o Rev. Earl Pinckney
        205 Orchard Drive
        Bristol, Tennessee 37620

21720   White Star
        P.O. Box 307
        Joshua Tree, California 92252

11030   Wisconsin Evangelical Lutheran Synod
        c/o Rev. Oscar Naumann
        3512 West North Avenue
        Milwaukee, Wisconsin 53208

                        Northwestern Lutheran (bi-w)
                        3624 West North Avenue
                        Milwaukee, Wisconsin 53208

20531   Wisdom Institute of Spiritual
          Education (WISE)
        1236 South Marlborough
        Dallas, Texas 75208

22243   Witchcraft and Pagan Institute
        c/o Phyllis Ammirati
        69 Strathmore Village Drive
        South Setauket, New York 11720

22320   Witches International Craft Associates
        153 West 80th Street
        Suite 1B
        New York, New York 10024

                        WICA Newsletter/Psychic Eye (m)

20135   W.K.F.L. Fountain of the World
        Box 61
        Route 5
        Canoga Park, California 91305

21209   The Word Foundation, Inc.
        Seven West 44th Street
        New York, New York 10036

16133   World Baptist Fellowship
        P.O. Box 1345
        Arlington, Texas 76010

21982   World Catalyst Church
        P.O. Box 282
        Rosewell, New Mexico   88201

23143   Work of the Chariot
        P.O. Box 2226
        Hollywood, California   90028

18314   Workers Together with Elohim
        P.O. Box 14411
        Jerusalem, Israel

                    The Jerusalem Reporter (m)

30105   World Christian Liberation Front
        2736 Dwight Way
        Berkeley, California   94703

18229   World Insight International
        P.O. Box 35
        Pasadena, California   91102

                    World Insight

14905   World Renewal, Inc.
        P.O. Box 775
        Richland, Missouri   65556

                    Life in the Spirit (bi-m)

18220   Worldwide Church of God
        Box 111
        Pasadena, California   91123

                    The Plain Truth (m)

                    Good News (m)

19225   Yahshua's Army
        3937 Randell Road
        Columbus, Ohio   43228

24117   Yasodhara Ashram Society
        Box 9
        Kootenay Bay   VOB 1X0
        British Columbia, Canada

                    Ascent (q)

24226   Yoganta Meditation Center
        Netherland, Colorado   80466

                    221

24224   Yogi Gupta Association
        127 East 56th Street
        New York, New York 10022

24222   Yogiraj (Swami Swanandashram) Sect
        c/o Arnold Ralph
        606 McCarthy Street
        Easton, Pennsylvania 18042

22201   Yoruba (Orisha) Religion
        Oyo-Tienji
        Beaufort County, South Carolina 29902

17716   Your Heritage
        c/o Pastor Bertrand L. Comparet
        Box 5486
        San Diego, California 92105

25287   Zen Buddhist Temple of Chicago
        2230 North Halsted Street
        Chicago, Illinois 60614

                        Chicago Zen Notes (bi-m)

25260   Zen Center of San Francisco
        300 Page Street
        San Francisco, California 94102

                        Wind Bell (q)

25283   Zen Center of Los Angeles
        927 South Normandie Avenue
        Los Angeles, California 90006

                        Zen Writings (bi-a)

25215   Zen Meditation Center
        Arnold Park
        Rochester, New York 14607

                        Zen Bow (q)

25265   Zen Mission Society
        Shasta Abbey
        Box 577
        R.R. 1
        Mt. Shasta, California 96067

                        Journal of the Zen Mission
                            Society (m)

25225   Zen Studies Society, Inc.
         223 East 67th Street
         New York, New York   10021

                           Dharma Seasons (q)

25255   Zen Shuji Soto Mission
         123 South Hewitt Street
         Los Angeles, California   90012

18240   Zion Church of God International
         Box 133
         Monument, Oregon   97864

                           Voice of Zion

18245   Zion's Gate
         P.O. Box 1433
         Jerusalem, Israel

19105   Zion's Order of the Sons of Levi
         c/o William A. Hilles, Secretary
         Mansfield, Missouri   65704

CHAPTER IV

FAMILY GROUPS OF THE RELIGIOUS ESTABLISHMENT

Of the eighteen family groups, eleven are included
within the "Christian" establishment. Three families are
questionable as to their relation to the establishment.
The Liberal group is included within the establishment, in
spite of its deviation from the allegiance to the Christian
symbols, for several reasons:

1) Its influential member, the Unitarian-Universalist
Church, has remained in friendly dialogue with
Protestantism and its members have been active in
ecumenical endeavors;

2) The Liberal tradition is still largely involved
in a polemic on the Christian symbols and membership in a group is primarily defined by its acceptance of the problem rather than the answer;

3) The Liberals, because of their base in the university, the major legitimizer of ideas in contemporary America, have remained a definite member
of current religious dialogue;

4) And finally, Liberal views (from Unitarianism to
the death of God) have found a home within the
larger Protestant bodies.

The Communal groups include many groups such as the
Hutterites, the Reba Place Fellowship, and the Church of
the Savior which are definitely part of the religious establishment. Yet the major thrust of the new Communal ideal
which has produced the majority of communes since 1960
offers an alternative to Christianity--a one-world spiritual
monism drawn from an eclecticism of Eastern religion. They
are also running counter to a major American cultural theme--
individualism. Finally, Judaism, particularly of the
Reformed variety, is often seen as part of the Protestant/
Catholic/Jewish American religious structure. Yet in the
main, Judaism is and will remain the faith of a minority
group whose role will be determined by the tolerance level
of the establishment and the continuing vocal demands of
the Jewish leadership.

Below will be presented a picture of each family group
along with a brief description of its heritage, life style

224

and thought world. Influential members will be designated by
an asterisk. Intra-family ecumenical structures will be cited
since they are further delineators of the group itself. Several ecumenical bodies draw from across family lines along a
liberal/conservative/fundamentalist-separatist spectrum; as

National Council of Churches of Christ in the
   United States of America
475 Riverside Drive
New York, New York 10027

National Association of Evangelicals
3505 Main Place, P.O. Box 28
Wheaton, Illinois 60187

American Council of Christian Churches
P.O. Box 816
Valley Forge, Pennsylvania 19482

American Christian Council
c/o Dr. Carl McIntire
756 Haddon Avenue
Collingswood, New Jersey 08101

The Liturgical Family

The Liturgical Family is defined by the central role of
liturgy in its life, combined with a strong attachment to various creedal documents of the Patristic Church and a claim to
apostolic succession through an episcopal lineage.[1] Only the
Lutheran family and the Magical Family place as much emphasis
on liturgy as does the Liturgical Family, and any study of individual members will quickly encounter their liturgy as a
main document of their faith and life.

During the third, fourth and fifth centuries, the classical Christian creedal statements were formulated. The acceptance or non-acceptance of the bodies (the ecumenical councils)
which formulated certain creeds is the major issue which di-
vides the Liturgical Family into sub-families. The East accepts no more than seven ecumenical councils while the West
has held many more.[2] Reaction to the Reformation, the Council
of Trent, and the First Vatican Council (1870) divided the
Western Liturgical Church.[3]

Common to all Liturgical churches and distinguishing
them from most other Christian groups is their attachment to
an apostolic succession. They believe that their priests have
a direct connection with the apostles of Christ by the passing of authority through an unbroken line of bishops reaching
back to the first century. Each sub-family, in most cases,
will trace its authority to a different apostle and each
bishop will most likely be able to recite his line to antiquity.

In America the manifestation of the Liturgical tradition has been largely determined by immigration. The Roman
Catholic Church, with over 40,000,000 members, claims almost
twenty percent of the United States' population and is the

225

dominant Western Liturgical church, while the Greek Orthodox
Archdiocese of North and South America, with 2,000,000 mem-
bers, is the dominant Eastern church. The smaller Protestant
Episcopal Church, however, because of its ambiguous position
between Rome and Wittenburg and its relationship to
Methodism, is probably more influential with the total
American Christian communion than either. It is also in
communion with some of the Old Catholics.

Ecumenical developments within the Liturgical Family
have been slight and on the Standing Conference includes only a
significant number of bodies. The independent Catholic and
Orthodox jurisdictions have had difficulty forming stable
ecumenical structures.

Standing Conference of Canonical Orthodox Bishops
   in the Americas
8-10 East 79th Street
New York, New York 10021

National Conference of Independent Catholic and
   Orthodox Jurisdictions
c/o Chancery Office
Most Rev. Jerome Joachim, National Chancellor
805 Tijeras, Northwest
Albuquerque, New Mexico

Anglican Episcopal Council
P.O. Box 52702
Atlanta, Georgia 30305

Eastern Orthodoxy

(Accepts only the authority of seven of the ecumenical
councils and rejects the filioque clause in the Roman
version of Chalcedonian-Niceno Creed.)

10105	Orthodox Church in America	1970
10106	Russian Orthodox Church Outside of Russia	1920
10107	Russian Orthodox Church in the U.S.A.,	
	Patriarchal Parishes	1970
10108	American Carpatho-Russian Orthodox Greek	
	Catholic Church	1938
10110	Russian Orthodox (Old Believers)	1963
10111	Molokans	1905
10115	Greek Orthodox Archdiocese of North and	
	South America	1922
10116	Greek Orthodox Archdiocese of Vasiloupolis	1964
10117	Greek Orthodox Diocese of New York	1971
10118	Greek Orthodox Church of America	1971
10119	Hellenic Orthodox Church in America	1964
10125	Albanian Orthodox Archdiocese in America	1908
10126	Albanian Orthodox Diocese in America	1950
10130	Bulgarian Eastern Orthodox Church	1909

10131	Bulgarian Eastern Orthodox Church,	
	Diocese of the U.S.A. and Canada	1947
10135	Romanian Orthodox Episcopate of America	1929
10136	Romanian Orthodox Church in America	1950
10140	Serbian Eastern Orthodox Church in the	
	United States of America and Canada	1964
10141	Serbian Orthodox Diocese for the United	
	States and Canada	1921
10142	Macedonian Orthodox Church	1961
10145	Antiochean Orthodox Christian Archdiocese	
	of All North America	1975
10150	Ukrainian Orthodox Church of America	1919
10151	Ukrainian Orthodox Church of America	
	(Ecumenical Patriarchate)	1928
10152	Holy Ukrainian Autocephalic Orthodox	
	Church in Exile	1951
10155	Autocephalous Slavonic Orthodox Catholic	
	Church (In Exile)	1969
10157	Finnish Orthodox Church	1955
10160	Byelorussian Autocephalic Orthodox Church	
	in the U.S.A.	1958
10161	Byelorussian Orthodox Church	19__
10163	Estonian Orthodox Church in Exile	1949
10164	Turkish Orthodox Church in America,	
	Patriarchal Exarchate	1966
10169	African Orthodox Church	1929
10170	American Catholic Church, Archdio. of New York	1927
10172	Orthodox-Catholic Church of America	
10174	Holy Orthodox Church in America (Eastern	
	Catholic and Apostolic) (De Witow)	1934
10175	American Orthodox Catholic Church,	
	Archdiocese of New York	1961
10176	American World Patriarchs, Inc. (Ryzy-Ryski)	196_
10177	Eastern Orthodox Catholic Church in	
	America (Adair)	1927
10178	Universal Shrine of Divine Guidance	
	(Karras)	1966
10179	American Orthodox Church	
10180	Archdiocese of the American Orthodox	
	Catholic Church in the United States of	
	America and Canada (Zaborowski)	
10182	Evangelical Catholic Communion	
10183	Independent Catholic Church	
10184	Old Catholic Order of Christ the King	
	in Texas	
10185	Orthodox Catholic Diocese of the Holy	
	Spirit (Cris Jones)	
10187	American Orthodox Catholic Church,	
	Diocese of Wisconsin	
10190	Holy Catholic Apostolic Church--	
	Archdiocese of Albuquerque	

Non-Chalcedonian Orthodox Churches

(Accept the authority of only four ecumenical councils.)

10210	Church of the East in America	1911
10215	Armenian Apostolic Church in America	1933
10216	Armenian Church of North America, Diocese of the	1889
10220	Assyrian Orthodox Church (Archdiocese of the Syrian Church of Antioch)	1924
10221	Syrian Orthodox Church of Malabar	196_
10230	Coptic Orthodox Church--Diocese of North America	1964
10231	Ethiopian Orthodox Church in the United States of America	1959
10232	Ethiopian Orthodox Coptic Church, Diocese of North and South America	196_

Western Roman Tradition

(Accepts the authority of both the seven ecumenical councils and the later Roman councils and has inserted the filioque clause in the creed. Differences in the group have occurred over the rejection by some of Vatican I or Vatican II.)

10301	Roman Catholic Church	1634
10305	Moncado Foundation of America	1924
10310	American Catholic Church	1915
10311	American Catholic Church (Syro-Antiochean)	1915
10312	Polish National Catholic Church of America	1904
10313	Polish Catholic Church	1930
10314	Polish Old Catholic Church in America	1960
10320	Christ Orthodox Catholic Exarchate of Americas and Eastern Hemisphere	1937
10321	Christ Catholic Church	1968
10322	American Orthodox Catholic Church	1962
10324	Traditional Christian Catholic Church in Europe and North America	1962
10325	North American Old Roman Catholic Church	1916
10326	Archdiocese of the Old Catholic Church in America	1941
10327	North American Old Roman Catholic Church Utrecht Succession	
10330	Old Catholic Church in America	1917
10331	Orthodox Old Roman Catholic Church, II	1969
10332	Evangelical Orthodox Church in America (Non-Papal Catholic)	1953
10333	Old Roman Catholic Church	1958
10334	Old Roman Catholic Church in the U.S.	1966
10335	North American Old Roman Catholic Church (Burns)	1962
10336	Ontario Old Roman Catholic Church	1962
10340	Catholic Life Church	1971

10342	North American Old Roman Catholic Church	
10343	Orthodox Catholic Synod of the Syro-Chaldean Rite	1970
10344	Old Roman Catholic Church	1945
10345	Old Catholic Church in North America	1950
10347	Old Roman Catholic Church (Orthodox Orders)	1966
10350	Universal Christian International Catholic Church	196_
10355	Reformed Catholic Church (Utrecht Confession)	
10356	Universal Christian Apostolic Church	1947
10360	Renovated Church of Christ	196_

Anglican Tradition

(Accepts the Roman tradition only to 1540.)

10401	Protestant Episcopal Church	1789
10402	Southern Episcopal Church	1953
10403	Apostolic Episcopal Church	1932
10404	Reformed Episcopal Church	1873
10405	Old Episcopal Church	
10406	Anglican Orthodox Church	1964
10407	Anglican Church of America	1968
10408	American Episcopal Church	1969
10409	American Eastern Orthodox Church	193_
10410	Free Protestant Episcopal Church	1958
10411	United Episcopal Church	1973
10412	Anglican Episcopal Church	197_

The Lutheran Family

The Lutheran Family is a liturgical group whose member churches are oriented on a heritage that dates to the symbolic act of nailing the Ninety-Five Theses by Martin Luther to the church door at Wittenburg, and the more substantive act of their distribution throughout the Holy Roman Empire. They differ from the Liturgical Family in their rejection of apostolic succession through an episcopacy and are governed by a synodical system. Although they do not reject the Patristic Creeds, their doctrinal statements of central importance are to be found in the Book of Concord of 1580 which contains six items produced between 1529 and 1577, most notably the Augsburg Confession of 1530 and Luther's Catechisms of 1529. Doctrine is for Lutherans an important concern.[4]

The Lutherans are one of three major families to derive from the sixteenth-century turmoil known as the Reformation. The Lutheran Family is distinct from the others because of its liturgical heritage. It is distinguished from the Reformed Church by its polity and its understanding of the sacraments. It is distinguished from the Free Church Family at almost every point.

The Lutheran bodies have not been active in ecumenical structures such as the National Council of Churches (of which only one is a member) and the National Association of Evangelicals (of which none is a member). Intra-family ecumenics have been predominant and have resulted in the amalgamation of the numerous nineteenth-century separate Lutheran bodies into the twenty-one there are today. Intra-family expressions are found in the Lutheran World Federation and the Lutheran Council in the U.S.A. (which has three members). There are no sub-families distinguishable. Intra-family expressions include:

U.S.A. National Committee of the Lutheran World
Federation
Suite 1910
315 Park Avenue, South
New York, New York 10010

Lutheran Council in the U.S.A.
315 Park Avenue, South
New York, New York 10010

Lutherans

11001	Lutheran Church in America	1962
11010	American Lutheran Church	1961
11020	Lutheran Church--Missouri Synod	1847
11021	Synod of Evangelical Lutheran Churches	1902
11024	Association of Free Lutheran Congregations	1962
11025	Church of the Lutheran Brethren in America	1900
11026	Church of the Lutheran Confession	1960
11027	Concordia Lutheran Conference	1956
11028	Evangelical Lutheran Synod	1918
11029	Evangelical Lutheran Church in America	1846
11030	Wisconsin Evangelical Lutheran Synod	1850
11031	Protestant Conference	1927
11032	Lutheran Churches of the Reformation	1964
11034	Conference of Authentic Lutherans	1971
11035	Association of Evangelical Lutheran Churches	1976
11040	Apostolic Lutheran Church	1872
11041	Apostolic Lutherans (Church of the First Born)	1897
11042	Apostolic Lutherans (The New Awakening)	1910
11043	Apostolic Lutherans (Evangelicals #1)	1890
11044	Apostolic Lutherans (Evangelicals #2)	1940
11045	Apostolic Lutherans (Heidemans)	1921-1922

The Reformed-Presbyterian Family

The Reformed-Presbyterian Family has a heritage that began with the work of Ulrich Zwingli (1484-1531) and of John Calvin (1509-1564) in Switzerland in the 1500s. Calvin, in particular, is the focus of the heritage because of his

authorship of The Institutes of the Christian Religion, a
primal literary expression of the family's belief and polity.
Calvin's ideas quickly spread from the continent to the
British Isles. The particular European source of American
groups becomes a major factor in delineating sub-families.

The Reformed-Presbyterian Family could be seen as
the first major Christian community to leave a sacred (liturgical) life style for a secular one. Ethical concerns became dominant, and in later years the format of activity
would be labeled the "Protestant work ethic." Worship is
orderly but varies widely.[5]

The Reformed theological tradition of Calvin is given
confessional expression in the Heidelberg Catechism and the
Westminster Confession of Faith, which provide the major
doctrinal focus for the family, besides Calvin's Institutes.

The Presbyterian form of government, which received
its definitive statement in Calvin's Institutes, is the
second major attribute of the family. It is a government
based on the joint authority of teaching (pastoral) elders
(presbyters) and ruling (lay) elders. These elders gather
in judicatories from the local congregational sessions to the
General Synod or Assembly which legislates for the whole
church.

The Congregationalists are family members who kept
Calvin's ethic and doctrine but deviated on church polity.
The divergence is due in part to the peculiar British Puritan
situation as opposed to the Continental one. On the continent episcopal authority was banished from those countries
dominated by the Reformed churches. In England, where no
such banishment occurred, a continual struggle with episcopal
ecclesiology led some Puritans to abandon presbyterial forms
for an even looser authority structure--Congregationalism.[6]

The Reformed-Presbyterian Family has been a leader
in ecumenical endeavors both within and outside of the family.
The main intra-family expressions are the World Alliance of
Reformed Churches (Presbyterian and Congregational) and the
World Calvinist Fellowship. There are twenty-three members
in three sub-families. Intra-family expressions are:

World Alliance of Reformed Churches (Presbyterian
    and Congregational)
1501 Route de Ferney
1211 Geneva 20, Switzerland

Reformed Ecumenical Synod
1677 Gentian, S.E.
Grand Rapids, Michigan 49508

231

Reformed-Presbyterian Tradition

11601	Reformed Church in America	1628
11602	Christian Reformed Church	1857
11603	Protestant Reformed Churches of America	1936
11604	Orthodox Reformed Church (Unaffiliated)	1971
11605	Free and Old Christian Reformed Church of Canada and America	1926
11606	Netherlands Reformed Congregations	1907
11607	Hungarian Reformed Church in America	1922
11608	Reformed Church in the United States	1934
11609	Church of the Golden Rule	1939
11615	Narragansett Indian Church	16__

Presbyterian Churches (originated in England and Scotland)

11701	United Presbyterian Church of the United States	1958
11702	Orthodox Presbyterian Church	1936
11703	Bible Presbyterian Church	1956
11704	Westminister Biblical Fellowship	1970
11705	Reformed Presbyterian Church (Evangelical Synod)	1965
11706	Associate Reformed Presbyterian Church (General Synod)	1858
11707	Reformed Presbyterian Church of North America	1798
11708	Cumberland Presbyterian Church	1906
11709	Upper Cumberland Presbyterian Church	1954
11710	Presbyterian Church in the United States	1861
11711	Presbyterian Church in America	1973
11712	Second Cumberland Presbyterian Church in the United States and Africa	1869
11713	Ukrainian Evangelical Alliance of North America	1922

Congregational Churches (have a non-Presbyterian church polity)

11801	United Church of Christ	1961
11803	Midwest Congregational Christian Church	
11805	Conservative Congregational Christian Conference	1947
11806	National Association of Congregational Christian Churches	1955

The Liberal Family

The Liberal tradition dates from the Socinian Movement in the sixteenth century and comes through the Deists of the eighteenth. At its source, the family's major expressions are protest movements against certain dogmatic expressions of orthodox Christianity, particularly the Trinity. The tradition climaxed in the nineteenth century in the free-thought movement that challenged the whole theistic approach to life.[7]

232

In the twentieth century, while protest of Christian dogma and assertion of anti-Christian themes are still present, a religion centered upon ethics has risen to dominance. A positive humanistic philosophy, as represented in the Humanist Manifestos, has emerged.[8] Generally an intellectual, rational approach is dominant, and "emotional" forms of religious expression are looked upon with some disdain.

No sub-families are recognized for this smallest family of only twelve members. The range is from the more traditional liberal religion of the Unitarian-Universalists to the militant atheism of Madelyn Murray O'Hair's American Atheists, Inc.

The Liberal Family has been so small in numerical size that there has been little need of formal ecumenical structures and only one has arisen:

International Humanist and Ethical Union
P.O. Box 114
Utrecht, Netherlands

Liberal

11901	Unitarian Universalist Association	1960
11902	Christian Universalist Churches of America	1964
11903	Goddian Organization	1965
11904	Church of the Humanitarian God	1967
11905	American Ethical Union	1876
11906	Confraternity of Deists	1970
11907	American Humanist Association	1941
11950	American Association for the Advancement of Atheism	1925
11951	Freethinkers of America, Inc.	1940
11952	Rationalist Association	1955
11953	American Atheists, Inc.	1970
11954	Americans First, Inc.	1969
11959	United Secularists of America	
11961	Friendship Liberal League	
11969	Fellowship of Religious Humanists	

The Pietist Family

The Pietist Family dates to the great worldwide revival that swept the Protestant world in the early eighteenth century. In America it was called the Great Awakening but produced no lasting schismatic forms, as it was absorbed by the existing churches. On the European continent, it was termed the Pietist Movement.[9] The continental phase was one of the original sources of the American and British phases and thus properly gives its name to them. It dates to the ministry of Philip Jakob Spener (1635-1705) and August Hermann Francke (1663-1727). The British phase was called the Evangelical Revival and centered upon the ministry

233

of John Wesley. Wesley founded the Methodist societies which
eventually became the dominant embodiment of the Movement,
particularly in America. The Methodists also became the
parents of two other families, the Holiness and Pentecostal.

Christian life and experience were the emphases that
distinguished Pietism from those churches out of which it
emerged. Given the context of the Lutheran Church and post-
Elizabethan Anglicanism, Pietists emphasized the life of
faith--the witness of the Spirit, sanctification, perfect
love, and growth in grace. Pietists accepted the Reformation-
Protestant tradition and added an evangelical zeal.

Part of the subtle distinction that the Pietist position made in reference to the major traditions that sur-
rounded it was in its loss of the feeling of being at home
in the "Christian" culture. Pietists challenged the immed-
iate environment in terms of a New Testament standard and
from that challenge the movement to missions in non-Christian
lands was begun.[10]

American Pietists are divided into two basic groups;
those with Continental origins which were shaped by the debate with Lutheranism, and those out of the British Isles
shaped by the debate with the Anglicans. In the New World
growth of the continental bodies was largely limited by the
language barrier, while the Methodists became the dominant
Protestant religious group. The family is largely structured by its relation to the United Methodist Church whose
ten million members make up over half of the membership of
the family. Sub-families among the Methodists formed over
rejections of episcopacy, language and race.

Because of the contemporary non-doctrinal emphasis,
Pietists have been leaders in ecumenical endeavors and are
found prominently on the NCC, NAE and ACCC. Intra-family
structures include:

World Methodist Council
Lake Junaluska, North Carolina 28745

Pietism

Continental Bodies

12101	Moravian Church in America	1735
12102	Unity of the Brethren	1919
12150	Evangelical Covenant Church in America	1885
12151	Evangelical Free Church in America	1950

Methodism

12301	United Methodist Church	1968

234

Non-Episcopal Methodism

12310	Congregational Methodist Church	1852
12311	First Congregational Methodist Church of the U.S.A.	1937
12312	New Congregational Methodist Church	1881
12321	Bible Protestant Church	1940
12322	Methodist Protestant Church (1939-)	1939
12323	Fundamental Methodist Church	1942
12324	Apostolic Methodist Church	1932
12325	Southern Methodist Church	1939
12327	People's Methodist Church	1939
12328	Church of Daniel's Bond	1893
12329	John Wesley Fellowship and the Francis Asbury Society of Ministers	1971
12330	Asbury Bible Churches	1971
12331	Association of Independent Methodist Churches	1965
12332	Filipino Community Churches	1927
12333	Evangelical Methodist Church	1946
12334	Evangelical Methodist Church in America	1952

Black Methodism

12350	African Methodist Episcopal Church	1816
12351	Reformed Methodist Union Episcopal Church	1885
12352	Reformed Zion Union Apostolic Church	1882
12353	African Methodist Episcopal Zion Church	1821
12354	Free Christian Zion Church of Christ	1906
12355	African Union First Colored Methodist	1866
12556	Union American Methodist Episcopal Church	1850
12357	Christian Methodist Episcopal Church	1870

German-Speaking Methodism

12371	United Christian Church	1878
12372	United Brethren in Christ (Old Constitution)	1889
12373	Evangelical Congregational Church	1922

Methodism (never connected with the United Methodist Church)

12391	Primitive Methodist Church	1829
12392	United Wesleyan Methodist Church of America	1905

The Holiness Family

No line of distinction between families is so difficult to draw as that between the Pietists and the Holiness Family. The emphasis on the holy life and sanctification that characterizes the Holiness churches grades into the Pietist emphasis on Christian experience. In fact, many groups bearing the name "Methodist" are Holiness bodies.

235

What distinguishes the Holiness Family is a concentration on the doctrine of Christian holiness or perfection
or sanctification to the point that it becomes the major
theme around which other doctrinal work is built and the
major subject of literature and polemics.

The Holiness churches share a heritage that began in
the post-Civil War period in the Methodist Episcopal Church.
Holiness people within the Methodist Episcopal Church formed
associations that soon attracted non-Methodists. The doctrinal unity of Methodism was lost and only the consensus
on holiness remained. Methodist leaders began to attack
unbalanced presentations of Holiness themes. Schisms began
to occur and independent Holiness churches formed. Other
Methodist groups found a kinship and moved into the Holiness
emphasis.[11]

Today the members of the Holiness Family have a
strong sense of belonging to a specific family group. This
image of oneness is focused in the Christian Holiness
Association, its main intra-family ecumenical body. Within
the Holiness movement are a range of groups, from those which
still keep informal ties with the United Methodist Church
(Wesleyans, Free Methodists) all the way over to groups like
the Church of God of the Mountain Assembly, which has Baptist
origins.

Two sub-family groups have been distinguished: the
black Holiness bodies are distinguished on the basis of race.
In the 1950s and 1960s a conservative Holiness wing which
protested the laxity of the larger Holiness bodies developed
around Glenn Griffith, a Church of the Nazarene minister.[12]
The division into nineteenth and twentieth century groups
is for convenience only. The two ecumenical organizations
serve the more liberal (CHA) and conservative (IHC) wings
of the Holiness movement, and are:

Christian Holiness Association
21 Beachway Drive
Indianapolis, Indiana 46224

Inter-denominational Holiness Convention
375 West State Street
Salem, Ohio 44460

Holiness Bodies

(Originated in the nineteenth century and their children.)

13101	Churches of God in North America	
	(General Eldership)	1825
13102	Church of God (Anderson, Indiana)	1880
13103	Association of Fundamental Ministers and	
	Churches	1931

13104	Church of God (Guthrie, Oklahoma)	1911
13105	New Testament Church of God	1942
13110	Wesleyan Church	1968
13111	Faith Mission Church	1958
13112	Undenominational Church of the Lord	1918
13113	Missionary Methodist Church of America	1913
13114	Standard Churches of America	1919
13115	Emmanuel Association	1942
13120	Free Methodist Church of North America	1860
13130	Salvation Army	1880
13131	American Rescue Workers	1896
13132	Volunteers of America	1896
13140	Christ's Sanctified Holiness Church (S.C.)	1892
13141	Christ's Sanctified Holiness Church (La.)	1903
13142	Fire Baptized Holiness Church (Wesleyan)	1890
13143	Church of God (Holiness)	1883
13145	Churches of God (Independent Holiness People)	1922
13146	Church of the Nazarene	1907
13147	Holiness Christian Church of the United States of America	1882
13148	Metropolitan Church Association	1894
13160	Christian and Missionary Alliance	1887
13161	Christian Nation Church, U.S.A.	1895-1896
13162	Missionary and Soul Winning Fellowship	1957
13163	The Missionary Church	1969
13164	Bible Fellowship Church	1947
13165	Peniel Mission	189_

Holiness Bodies which Originated in the Twentieth Century

13201	Lumber River Annual Conference of the Holiness Methodist Church	1900
13202	Oriental Missionary Society Holiness Conference	1901
13203	Churches of Christ in Christian Union	1909
13204	Church of the Gospel	1911
13205	Pillar of Fire	1901
13206	Gospel Mission Corps	1962
13207	Wesleyan Tabernacle Association	1936
13208	Grace and Hope Mission	1914
13209	Holiness Gospel Church	1945
13210	Kentucky Mountain Holiness Association	1925
13211	Christian Pilgrim Church	1937
13212	Sanctified Church of Christ	1937
13213	Holiness Church of God, Inc.	1920
13214	Evangelical Church of North America	1968
13215	Meggido Mission	1901
13216	Calvary Holiness Church	1934
13217	Christian Kingdom Centers	

Black Holiness Churches

13301	Church of Christ (Holiness) USA	1894
13303	Associated Churches of Christ Holiness	1947
13305	Church of God (Sanctified Church)	1906
13307	Original Church of God	1927
13309	Churches of God, Holiness	1914
13311	Mt. Calvary Holy Church of America	
13313	Triumph the Church and the Kingdom of God in Christ	1902
13315	The Church of Universal Triumph/The Dominion of God	1938
13317	Kodesh Church of Immanuel	1929

Glenn Griffith Movement

13401	Bible Missionary Church	1955
13403	Church of the Bible Covenant	1967
13405	Evangelical Wesleyan Church	1963
13407	Voice of the Nazarene Association of Churches	1961
13409	Pilgrim Holiness Church of New York State, Inc.	
13411	Bible Methodist Connection of Tennessee	1967
13413	Original Allegheny Wesleyan Methodist Connection	1966
13415	Bible Holiness Church	1968
13417	Bible Methodist Church	1967
13419	Wesleyan Holiness Association of Churches	1960
13421	God's Missionary Church	1935
13423	Lower Lights Church	1940
13425	National Association of Holiness Churches	197_
13427	United Holiness Church	1955̄

The Pentecostal Family

The Pentecostal Family is one of the easiest of the family groups to define as it is characterized by the central place given to the gifts of the Spirit mentioned by Paul in I Corinthians 12:4-11, particularly one gift--speaking in tongues. While the tongues experience was present in Christian bodies prior to the Pentecostal movement, and still is present in non-Christian religious bodies, the distinctive features of Pentecostalism are: 1) their focus on tongues as a desirable gift; 2) their equation of it with the Baptism of the Holy Spirit; and 3) their intentionally seeking it as a normative experience.[13] Such "seeking" activity creates a new gestalt of religious life; and, while Pentecostals have been basically Protestant in their theology, they have found this new gestalt a major barrier to integration in the larger Christian community. Structurally, then, life style is the most distinguishing feature of the Pentecostals whose worship is geared to a specific religious experience. The possession of the Baptism

238

of the Holy Spirit defines the movement clearly and precisely. Their experience-oriented life style is the reason for their close resemblance to the Psychic Family.

Pentecostalism dates from 1901 when students at Charles Parham's Bible College in Topeka, Kansas, began to seek for and receive what they believed to be a New Testament charism. As the movement grew, based on reception of the experience, theological issues and racial issues came to the fore and splintered it. The basic doctrinal controversy was between the former Methodist-Holiness people and the non-Methodist-Holiness people. Methodists tended to believe that holiness was a precondition for reception of the gifts in their true form. Others felt that a Christian was always ready to receive. A third group of anti-Trinitarians, actually monotheists of the second person, arose to form the "Apostolic" or "Jesus Only" movement.[14] Most of the "Oneness" churches are black. Other issues that have led to splintering and the development of new sub-families are an emphasis on healing (the Deliverance Movement),[15] race (black Pentecostal bodies),[16] signs indicative of God's protective power (snake handling and poison drinking),[17] and language (Spanish-speaking).[18]

In the last half of the 1960s there developed what has been termed the Charismatic or Neo-Pentecostal Movement. It is made up of members of the Roman Catholic Church and larger Protestant Church bodies who have accepted the Pentecostal experience. As of 1974 there are organized Roman Catholic, Presbyterian, Lutheran, United Methodist, and Episcopal charismatic fellowships, not to mention the Neo-Pentecostal Full Gospel Business Men's Fellowship International. Several groups, such as the United Evangelical Church and the World Renewal, Incorporated, are products of this movement. These organizations may well be the sources of future primary religious bodies.

Pentecostals have attempted to be ecumenical outside of their family group but were largely rebuffed until the late 1960s. Some openness to Pentecostal bodies within ecumenical circles has come about largely through the efforts of David DuPlessis.[19] Pentecostals have succeeded on a limited scale to form intra-family ecumenical organizations:

Pentecostal Fellowship of North America
c/o P.F.N.A. News (q)
Dr. Ray H. Hughs, Editor
Keith at 25th Street, N.W.
Cleveland, Tennessee 37311

World Conference of Pentecostal Churches
c/o Reverend P.S. Brewster
The City Temple
Cowbridge Road, Cardiff
England

Pentecostal Bodies

White Pentecostal Bodies (Trinitarian, Holiness)

14101	Church of God (Cleveland, Tennessee)	1886
14102	(Original) Church of God	1917
14103	Church of God of Prophecy	1923
14104	Church of God (World Headquarters)	1943
14105	Church of God (Jerusalem Acres)	1957
14106	Church of God, The House of Prayer	1939
14110	Pentecostal Church of Christ	1917
14120	Pentecostal Holiness Church	1899
14121	Congregational Holiness Church	1921
14122	First Interdenominational Christian Association	1946
14123	Pentecostal Fire Baptized Holiness Church	1918
14124	Emmanuel Holiness Church	1953
14125	Apostolic Faith (Oregon)	1906
14126	Carolina Evangelistic Association	1930
14127	Door of Faith Churches of Hawaii	1936
14128	Full Gospel Church Association, Inc.	1952
14129	Church of God of the Apostolic Faith	1914
14130	Association of International Gospel Assemblies	
14140	Pentecostal Free Will Baptist Church	1959
14141	Free Will Baptist Church of the Pentecostal Faith	1959
14142	General Conference of the Evangelical Baptist Church	1935
14143	Church of God of the Mountain Assembly	1906
14144	Church of God of the Union Assembly	1921
14145	Church of God of the Original Mountain Assembly	1944

White Pentecostal Bodies (Trinitarian)

14201	Apostolic Faith (Kansas)	1901
14202	Full Gospel Evangelical Association	1952
14210	Assemblies of God	1914
14211	Independent Assemblies of God, International	1948
14212	Independent Assemblies of God (Unincorporated)	1922
14215	International Church of the Foursquare Gospel	1921
14216	Open Bible Standard Churches, Inc.	1935
14217	Filippino Assemblies of the First Born	1933
14218	Calvary Pentecostal Church	1931
14219	Lamb of God Church	1942
14220	Pentecostal Church of God of America	1919
14221	Pentecostal Church of Zion	1956
14222	Pentecostal Evangelical Church of God, National and International, Inc.	1936

14223	Seventh-Day Pentecostal Church of the Living God	
14224	Elim Missionary Assemblies	1933
14230	Gospel Assemblies (Sowders)	1907
14231	Gospel Assemblies (Mills)	1962
14232	Gospel Assemblies (Jolly)	1962
14234	Gospel Assemblies (Tate)	196_
14235	Gospel Assemblies (Wallace)	196_
14236	General Assembly and Church of the First Born	1907
14240	Anchor Bay Evangelistic Association	1940
14241	Christian Church of North America	1948
14250	The Neverdies	
14255	Apostolic Church	1920
14256	Bethel Temple	1914
14257	Free Gospel Church, Inc.	1916
14258	American Indian Evangelical Church	1956
14259	United Fundamental Church	1939

The Deliverance Movement

14301	Full Gospel Fellowship of Churches and Ministers International	1962
14303	International Deliverance Churches	
14304	Miracle Life Revival, Inc.	1967
14305	Leroy Jenkins Evangelistic Association	196_
14306	Miracle Revival Fellowship	1951
14307	Katherine Kuhlman Foundation	1947
14309	First Deliverance Church of Atlanta	1956
14311	Mita Movement	1940
14312	Hall Deliverance Foundation	1965

Apostolic (Oneness) Movement

14401	Church of God (Apostolic)	1897
14403	Apostolic Church of Jesus	1936
14405	International Ministerial Association	1954
14407	Apostolic Faith (Hawaii)	1925
14409	Associated Brotherhood of Christians	1933
14411	Assemblies of the Lord Jesus Christ, Inc.	1952
14413	Pentecostal Assemblies of the World	1914
14415	Apostolic Church of Jesus Christ	
14417	Jesus Church	1955
14419	Apostolic Overcoming Holy Church of God	1916
14421	Church of Our Lord Jesus Christ of the Apostolic Faith	1919
14422	Church of the Lord Jesus Christ of the Apostolic Faith	1968
14433	Bible Way Church of Our Lord Jesus World Wide, Inc.	1951
14435	New Bethel Church of God in Christ (Pentecostal)	1945
14436	Missionary Body of Jesus Christ	
14437	United Pentecostal Church, International	1945

14439	Apostolic Gospel Church of Jesus Christ	1963
14440	Apostolic Evangelistic Association	
14441	God's House of Prayer for All Nations, Inc.	1964
14443	Bethel Ministerial Association	1934

Black Trinitarian Pentecostals

14501	Church of God in Christ	1895
14502	Church of God in Christ, Congregational	1932
14503	Free Church of God in Christ	1925
14504	Institutional Church of God in Christ	
14505	Sought Out Church of God in Christ	1947
14506	Church of God in Christ, International	1969
14508	Fire Baptized Holiness Church of God of the Americas	1908
14509	House of the Lord	1925
14510	Way of the Cross Church	
14512	Church of the Living God (Christian Workers for Fellowship)	1889
14513	House of God Which Is the Church of the Living God The Pillar and Ground of Truth	1925
14514	House of God Which Is the Church of the Living God The Pillar and Ground of Truth, Without Controversy	
14516	Mt. Sinai Holy Church	1924
14518	United House of Prayer for All People	1926
14523	True Grace Memorial House of Prayer	1960
14525	Latter House of the Lord for All People and the Church of the Mountain, Apostolic Faith	1936
14526	United Holy Church in America	1894
14527	Alpha and Omega Christian Church of America, Inc.	1944
14528	True Fellowship Pentecostal Church of America	1964
14529	African Universal Church	1927

Signs' People (Snake Handlers)

| 14610 | Church of God with Signs Following | 1909 |
| 14620 | Original Pentecostal Church of God | 1900 |

Spanish-Speaking Pentecostals

14710	Concilio Olazabal de Iglesias Latino Americano	1923
14720	Defenders of the Faith	1923
14730	Latin American Council of the Pentecostal Church of New York, Inc.	1951
14740	Assembly of Christian Churches, Inc.	1939
14750	Damascus Christian Church	
14760	Iglesia Bando Evangelical Gedeon/Gilgal Evangelistic International Church	195_

Miscellaneous

14901	Lighthouse Gospel Fellowship	1958
14902	Church of the Little Children	1916
14903	Association of Seventh-Day Pentecostal Assemblies	1967
14904	Roumanian Apostolic Pentecostal Church of God of North America	
14905	World Renewal, Incorporated	1963
14906	Alpha and Omega Christian Church	1962
14907	Evangelical Bible Church	1947
14908	The Body of Christ Movement	196_
14909	International Christian Churches	1943̄
14910	Full Gospel Defenders Conference of America	
14911	American Evangelistic Association	1954
14912	Church of God by Faith	1918
14913	Grace Gospel Evangelistic Association International, Inc.	193_
14814	Gospel Harvesters Evangelistic Association (Atlanta)	1961
14915	Gospel Harvesters Evangelistic Association (Buffalo)	1962
14916	Glad Tidings Missionary Society	1970
14917	United Evangelical Churches	1967
14918	International Evangelism Crusades	1959
14919	United Christian Ministerial Association	1956
14920	(Universal) World Church	1952
14921	Universal Church, Mystical Body of Christ	
14922	Christ's Faith Mission	1908
14923	Church of God in the Lord Jesus Christ	
14925	Churches of Christ (Non-Instrumental-Charismatic)	
14930	National David Spiritual Temple of Christ Church Union (Inc.), U.S.A.	

The European Free Church Family

The European Free Church Family represents churches from a variety of backgrounds which are descendants of what Troeltsch called the classic "sects." Their heritage, though quite diverse, does share a common attempt to find alternatives to: 1) a state church; 2) a clerical orientation; and 3) a feeling of being at home in the world. They share a history of persecution in Europe which most brought with them into eastern Pennsylvania in the seventeenth and eighteenth centuries. Since that time they have been able increasingly to think of themselves as "free church" people.

Their common thought world includes: non-liturgical worship; a non-creedal, Bible-oriented theology; a social ethic tending toward isolation from social structures (often expressed as pacifism); and a congregational polity.

243

Within the Free Churches are a variety of theologies which derive from reaction to differing state churches (Lutheran, Reformed, Anglican and Roman Catholic) and from the variety of experiences of the founders. George Fox was a mystic/psychic/medium. Menno Simons was a scholar.

The questionable member of this family is the Quakers. While the other bodies have a direct organizational tie to each other, due to their common origin on the Continent, the Quakers are from Britain and do not share so obviously in the common pool of ideas. Until recently the connection was a common assumption of the Quaker scholarship, dominated as it was by Rufus Jones. However, in the last twenty years, some scholars have challenged the connection of Quaker ties to Anabaptism and have asserted instead the Puritan nature of the Friends. The arguments have, however, proved unconvincing, and the Quakers have emerged much closer in their characteristics to the Mennonites and Brethren than the Puritans.

A key to understanding the Quakers is the Pennsylvania experiment. In seeking colonists to populate his new colony, Penn turned to the Continent and sought out the Mennonites and Brethren especially, and all three groups had their major strength within a hundred-mile radius of Philadelphia. Out of that experience has come a mutual designation as the "historical peace churches." Though the custom was largely abandoned later, at one time they shared an attachment for "plain clothes." Quaker theology is more closely related to the mystical/spiritual aspect of the Radical Reformation (including such men as Caspar Schwenckfeld) than the Anabaptists.

Among the Mennonites are three groups: those who migrated to America directly from Europe; those who followed the lead of Jacob Amman; and those who came to America after having settled in Russia. The latter group is located primarily in the states west of the Mississippi River.

Ecumenical endeavors among the European Free Churches are numerous and include service agencies such as the Mennonite Central Committee and the American Friends Service Committee. More formal structures are:

Mennonite World Conference
3003 Benham Avenue
Elkhart, Indiana   46514

Friends World Committee for Consultation
American Section and Fellowship Council
152-A North 15th Street
Philadelphia, Pennsylvania   19102

OR:

203 South East Street
Plainfield, Indiana   46168

Friends General Conference
1520 Race Street
Philadelphia, Pennsylvania   19102

European Free Church Bodies

The Mennonites

(Anabaptists deriving from the work of Menno Simons.)

15101	The Mennonite Church	1683
15103	Reformed Mennonite Church	1812
15105	Old Order (Wisler) Mennonite Church	1870
15107	Old Order (Wenger) Mennonites	193_
15109	Old Order (Hornung or Black Bumper) Mennonites	19__
15110	Old Order (Reidenbach) Mennonites	194‾
15111	Stauffer Mennonite Church	1846‾
15112	Weaver Mennonites	1916
15113	Church of God in Christ (Mennonite)	1858
15114	Congregational Bible Church	1951
15115	Conservative Mennonite Fellowship (Non-conference)	1956
15116	Mennonite Christian Brotherhood	1960
15150	Bethesda Mennonite Colony Conference	

Russian Mennonites

15201	Evangelical Mennonite Church (Kleine Gemeinde)	187_
15203	Evangelical Mennonite Brethren	187‾3
15204	General Conference Mennonite Church	1860
15206	Mennonite Brethren Church of North America	1874

Amish

15301	Old Order Amish Mennonite Church	1862
15304	Conservative Mennonite Conference	1910
15305	Beachy Amish Mennonite Churches	1923

The Brethren

15501	Church of the Brethren	1919
15502	Brethren Church (Ashland, Ohio)	1882
15503	National Fellowship of Brethren Churches	1939
15504	Old German Baptist Brethren	1881
15505	Association of Fundamental Gospel Churches	1954
15507	Fundamental Brethren Church	1962
15509	Emmanuel's Fellowship	1966

15511	Brethren in Christ	1778
15513	Old Order or Yorker River Brethren	1843
15515	United Zion Church	1855

Quakers

15710	Friends United Meeting	1902
15715	Religious Society of Friends (Conservative)	1845
15720	Religious Society of Friends (General Conference)	1827
15725	Rocky Mountain Yearly Meeting	1957
15730	Religious Society of Friends (Kansas), Yearly Meeting	1937
15735	Central Yearly Meeting of Friends	1926
15740	Evangelical Friends Church, Eastern Division	1813
15745	Southeastern Yearly Meeting	1962
15750	Southern Appalachian Association of Friends	1959
15755	Missouri Valley Friends Conference	1962
15760	Lake Erie Association Yearly Meeting	1963
15765	Oregon Yearly Meeting of Friends	1893
15766	Pacific Yearly Meeting of Friends	1947

Miscellaneous

| 15901 | Social Brethren | 1867 |
| 15910 | Schwenkfelder Church in America | 1782 |

The Baptist Family

The Baptists share with the Free Churches many characteristics: non-creedal, Bible-oriented theology; a non-liturgical worship; and a history of persecution in Europe. But they differ from Continental Free Churches by their adoption of the revivalist camp meeting techniques in the early 1880s. Led by an intense evangelical zeal coupled with a freedom from the obstacles that hindered the growth of the other Free Churches (foreign languages, unpopular moral beliefs, such as pacifism and antislavery sentiment), they soon grew into a national body. [20]

Doctrinally, they place an emphasis on adult believers' baptism by immersion, a belief shared with most other Free Churches. They have developed a corollary belief in an apostolic succession passed from generation to generation by congregations of properly baptized believers.

History is a problem for Baptists. While a clear lineage to seventeenth-century England is shared, there is argument about a further lineage through Anabaptists, Waldensians, and various medieval heretical movements all the way to the first century. The English phase was definitive, however, as Baptists developed allegiance to Reformed thinking--the Calvinist (Predestinarian) and Arminian (Free

246

Will) theologies--and eventually divided into two theological camps. Any hope of further doctrinal unanimity was blocked by an adoption of a strong congregational polity.

In America to the Calvinist-Arminian schisms were added schisms concerned with missionary societies (which infringed on local church sovereignty) and race. Local church sovereignty has also limited ecumenical endeavors.[21] There is, however, an intra-family structure:

> World Baptist Alliance
> 1628 Sixteenth Street, N.W.
> Washington, D.C. 20009

Definitely part of the Baptist family are a group collectively called the Restorationists. Their theology, as set by Barton Stone and Thomas and Alexander Campbell, was thoroughly "Baptist" in its actual history and its adoption of a non-creedal, Bible-oriented, non-liturgical form of Christianity. The main point on which they differed was ecclesiology.[22]

The idea of Restoration rejected the several forms of apostolic succession for a view of history that negated all activity between 100 A.D. and the careers of Stone and the Campbells. The true church died at some point early in Christian history and was being restored de novo in the nineteenth century.

Baptist Family Groups

Calvinistic Missionary Baptists

16101	American Baptist Churches in the USA	1707
16102	Southern Baptist Convention	1845
16105	Association of Evangelicals for Missions	1899
16106	New England Evangelical Baptist Fellowship	
16110	Regular Baptists (Calvinist/Arminian)	1890
16111	Regular Baptists (Predestinarian)	1890
16112	Kyova Association of Regular Baptists	1945
16113	Separate Baptists in Christ	1912
16120	American Baptist Association	1905
16121	Baptist Bible Fellowship International	1950
16122	Sovereign Grace Baptist Movement	1966
16123	Baptist Missionary Association of America	1905
16124	Christian Unity Baptist Association	1934
16125	Duck River (and Kindred) Association of Baptists	1825
16126	Fundamental Baptist Fellowship	1920
16127	Conservative Baptist Association	1947
16128	General Association of Regular Baptist Churches	1932
16129	Minnesota Baptist Convention	1947

247

16130	New Testament Association of Independent Baptist Churches	1965
16131	Southwide Baptist Fellowship	1956
16132	South Carolina Baptist	1954
16133	World Baptist Fellowship	
16140	North American Baptist General Conference	1851
16145	Independent Baptist Church of America	1927
16150	Russian/Ukrainian Evangelical Union of the U.S.A., Inc.	1901
16151	Ukrainian Evangelical Baptist Convention	1945

Calvinistic Anti-Missionary Baptists

16201	Primitive Baptists-Regulars	1827
16202	Primitive Baptists-Absolute Predestinarians	
16203	Primitive Baptists-Progressive	
16204	Primitive Baptists-Black	1869
16205	National Primitive Baptist Convention	1907
16210	Central District Primitive Baptist Association	1956
16211	Roundlick Primitive Baptist Association	
16212	Hiwasee Primitive Baptist Association	
16213	Buffalo River Primitive Baptist Association	
16214	Sandlick/Spencer Primitive Baptist Association	
16215	Mayo Primitive Baptist Association	
16216	Regular Baptist Association	
16217	Old Elkhorn Primitive Baptist Association	
16218	Two-Seed-in-the-Spirit Predestinarian Baptists	1833

Black Baptists (Calvinistic Missionary)

16301	National Baptist Convention of America	1915
16302	National Baptist Convention, U.S.A.	1880
16303	National Baptist Evangelical Life and Soul Saving Assembly of the U.S.A.	1921
16304	Progressive National Baptist Convention, Inc.	1961
16310	Fundamental Baptist Fellowship Association	1962

General Baptists (Arminian)

16401	General Association of General Baptists	1824
16405	United Baptists	1786
16410	National Association of Free Will Baptists	1727
16411	General Conference of the Original Free Will Baptist Church	1962
16415	United Free Will Baptist Church	1870
16420	Baptist General Conference	1879
16425	General Six-Principle Baptists	1652
16430	Primitive Baptist Conference of New Brunswick, Maine and Nova Scotia	1870

Seventh-Day Baptists

| 16601 | Seventh-Day Baptist General Conference | 1664 |
| 16610 | Seventh-Day Baptists (German) | 1728 |

The Restoration

16701	The Christian Church (Disciples of Christ)	1809
16710	Christian Churches-Independent	1967
16720	Churches of Christ (Non-instrumental)	1906
16722	Churches of Christ (Non-instrumental Conservative)	
16724	Churches of Christ (Non-instrumental Non-Sunday School)	
16726	Churches of Christ (Non-instrumental One Cup)	
16728	Churches of Christ (Non-instrumental Open)	
16730	Churches of Christ (Premillennialist)	
16735	The Christian Congregation	
16738	Tioga River Christian Conference	
16750	Christadelphians-Unamended	1844
16755	Christadelphians-Amended	1890

The Independent Fundamentalist Family

John Nelson Darby, founder of the Plymouth Brethren, is one of several unheralded nineteenth-century thinkers who have widely influenced the Christian Church in the twentieth century. So ahistorical are many students of his theology that they do not even know his name although they follow his thought as popularized by some of this theological converts, like Dwight L. Moody or C.I. Scofield.

Integral to Darby's followers was the focus on Bible study, exposition, and application. The crux of Darby's thought was a new principle of Biblical interpretation, dispensationalism.[23] The Bible's history was seen as divided into seven periods (the number varied with different people). Biblical passages were assigned to each period with an understanding that they were more relevant to this dispensation than to other times. "Present truth," meaning those scriptures of particular relevance to the present dispensation, is a popular phrase among dispensationalists.

The widespread circulation of Bibles, coupled with a growing literacy, aided the Plymouth Brethren in developing a practical Biblical theology which found expression in lay Bible study groups, as a focus of group meeting, and the Bible reading, a sermon-like presentation which usually involved the tracing of a single word or idea through a series of otherwise disconnected Biblical passages.

The growth of Darby's following in late nineteenth-century North America was the major force in producing Fundamentalism. Darby's followers had influenced the authors of the major dispensational texts, Jesus is Coming[24] and the

Scofield Reference Bible,[25] and two Plymouth Brethren oil
men underwrote the cost of The Fundamentals: A Testimony
of Truth.

Darby also preached a particular type of ecclesiology
which centered on local assemblies of believers very loosely
affiliated with other like-minded assemblies. There would
be no central office or other formal denominational structure. Periodicals would be unofficial, private enterprises
which would serve the brethren as they proved useful.

The ecclesiology has kept the large following of
Darby practically invisible. Even astute observers have
difficulty in defining structures. Emphasis on like-
mindedness and lack of formal structure make ecumenical
efforts difficult. Even intra-family communion is difficult.
Structures are defined by mutual polemics.

In the United States, Darby's main ideas became freed
from his total theology and one or the other would often be
rejected by fundamentalist Bible students. On the American
scene, various forms of dispensationalism became an issue in
fundamentalist theological circles.[26] Sub-families are
based on acceptance of one or more of Darby's ideas and disagreement on the exact nature and number of dispensations.
There have also arisen groups of Bible study oriented people,
possessing quite unorthodox views of the Bible.[27]

Independent Fundamentalist

Plymouth Brethren (accept Darby's dispensationalism and
ecclesiology)

17101	Plymouth Brethren (Open)	1870
17102	Churches of God in the British Isles and Overseas (Needed Truth)	
17110	Plymouth Brethren (Exclusive): Booth-Continental Brethren	1928
17111	Plymouth Brethren (Exclusive): Ames Brethren	1928
17112	Plymouth Brethren (Exclusive): Taylor Brethren	1890
17113	Plymouth Brethren (Exclusive): Ex-Taylor Brethren	1960
17115	Plymouth Brethren (Exclusive): Tunbridge Wells Brethren	1926

Fundamentalism (accepts Darby's dispensationalism)

17210	Independent Fundamental Churches of America	193_
17211	Independent Fundamentalist Bible Churches	1968
17212	Ohio Bible Fellowship	1968
17215	Associated Gospel Churches	1939

17217	Bethany Bible Church and Related Independent Bible Churches of the Phoenix (Arizona) Area	195_
17219	Fellowship of Independent Evangelical Churches	1949
17221	Moody Church	1864
17223	American Evangelical Christian Churches	1945
17225	Cathedral of Tomorrow	1958
17230	Church of Christian Liberty	1964
17235	International Ministerial Federation	1935
17240	Evangelical Ministers and Churches, International, Inc.	1956
17245	Berean Fundamental Churches	1934

Grace Gospel Movement (accept the ultra-dispensationalism of Elbert Bullinger and deny contemporary relevance of baptism and the Lord's Supper)

17310	Truth for Today	1948
17315	Bible Churches (Classics Expositor)	
17320	Berean Bible Fellowship	
17325	Grace Gospel Fellowship	1939
17330	Berean Bible Society (Illinois)	1969
17335	Timely Messenger Fellowship	1939
17340	Last Day Messenger Assemblies	
17345	Concordant Publishing Concern	1909

Miscellaneous Bible Student Bodies

17401	The (Local) Church	1909
17402	This Testimony	192_
17403	Two-by-Twos (Cooneyites)	1903
17405	Members of "The Church which is Christ's Body"	1927
17407	Independent Churches Affiliated	

British-Israelites

17701	Anglo-Saxon Federation of America	1928
17703	Prophetic Herald Ministry	1933
17705	Christian Research, Inc.	1964
17707	Calvary Fellowships, Inc.	196_
17709	The True Church	1903
17711	Remnant of Israel	
17713	New Christian Crusade Church	
17715	Lord's Covenant Church	
17716	Your Heritage	

The Adventist Family

The Adventists might best be described as Baptists for whom eschatology had become the issue of first priority. The context for the eschatological emphasis can be traced to Baptist sources--the non-creedal, Bible-oriented theology, immersion, and non-liturgical worship. Interaction with the Dispensationalists did occur as the movement progressed.

The history of Adventism began with William Miller, who is usually seen in Adventist thinking as an eschatological figure. Popular among Adventists is Restorationism, a view traceable to the Disciples of Christ. The Restoration is a prelude to the end of time.

A prominent theological process is date-setting and disappointment. Setting specific dates for an imminent cosmic end-time event was and is still a constant occurrence among Adventists. The date is chosen by an examination of Biblical chronology and prophecy in the light of historical events. Ezekiel 4:4,5 is an essential Biblical text allowing Biblical days to be treated as years. The continual disappointment creates a syndrome, well described in sociological literature.[28] Disappointment can and has led to concentration on other topics, such as sabbatarianism.

The basic cleavage among Adventists revolves around those who recognize the tradition begun by William Miller and those who recognize the ministry of Charles Taze Russell, a second generation Adventist.[29] Miller's followers have separated over the issue of Saturday sabbath and the use of transliterations of Hebrew names for the deity and Jesus. This later movement is termed the Sacred Name.

While American Adventism has been primarily related to the tradition begun by Miller, other groups have arisen. Joana Southcott was a popular British apocalypticist of the late eighteenth century. Of the many groups which she spawned, two are located in the United States. Other minor prophets of the end time come and go.

Adventists have been the prime force in the Bible Sabbath Association, Fairview, Oklahoma, 73737, even though the directory lists some Mormon, Baptist and Pentecostal bodies.

Adventist Family

Adventists--First-Day (worship on Sunday)

18110	Advent Christian Church	1861
18112	Primitive Advent Christian Church	1920
18120	Church of God (Abrahamic Faith)	1888

Adventist-Sabbatarians (worship on Saturday)

18201	Seventh-Day Adventist Church	1863
18202	SDA Reform Movement	1925
18203	Branch SDAs	1929
18204	Bible Holiness Mission	1949

```
18205    People's Christian Church                             1916
18206    Davidian SDA Association
18207    Religious Liberty and Temperance Association
18210    Unification Association of Christian
           Sabbath Keepers                                     1957
18211    Seventh-Day Christian Conference                      1934
18213    General Conference of the Church of God               1865
18214    Church of God (Seventh Day)                           1949
18215    General Council of the Churches of God                1950
18216    Seventh-Day Church of God
18217    Church of God, Sabbatarian
18218    Bible Church of God
18219    Church of God, Bible Beacon
18220    World Wide Church of God                              1934
18221    Twentieth Century Church of God                       1974
18222    A Candle                                              196_
18223    United Seventh-Day Brethren                           1947
18224    Foundation for Biblical Research                      1975
18225    Church of God, The Eternal                            1976
18226    Associated Churches of God                            1975
18227    Fountain of Life Fellowship
18228    Church of God Seventh Era                             1976
18229    World Light, International                            1976
18230    Church of God, Body of Christ
18235    Church of God at Cleveland
18240    Zion Church of God-International
18245    Zion's Gate

Sacred Name Movement

18301    Assembly of Yahweh (Michigan)                         1937
18303    Scripture Research Association                        194_
18305    Assembly of Yahvah                                    1949
18307    Assemblies of Yahweh (Oregon)
18309    Assemblies of Yahweh (Pennsylvania)                   1966
18311    Missionary Dispensary Bible Research
18313    Church of God (Jerusalem)                             1955
18315    Assemblies of the Called Out Ones of Yah

Bible Students of Charles Taze Russell

18401    Jehovah's Witnesses                                   1874
18405    Christian Believers Conference                        1909
18406    New Creation Bible Students                           1940
18407    Western Bible Students Association
18410    Laymen's Home Missionary Movement                     1918
18411    Epiphany Bible Students Association                   1955
18412    Laodicean Home Missionary Movement                    1955
18415    Pastoral Bible Institute                              1918
18416    Dawn Bible Students                                   1939
18417    Christian Bible Students Association                  1969
18420    Philanthropic Assembly                                192_
18425    Back to the Bible Way                                 1952
```

Southcottites

18810	Christian Israelite Church	1844
18820	House of David	1903
18821	Israelite House of David as Reorganized by Mary Parnell	193_

Miscellaneous Adventist Traditions

18901	Remnant Church	1957
18902	Shiloh True Light Church of Christ	1870
18903	Shiloh True Light Church of Christ (Braswell faction)	1970
18910	Star of Truth Foundation	
18915	End Time Body--Christian Ministries	196_

CHAPTER V

FAMILY GROUPS OUTSIDE OF THE

RELIGIOUS ESTABLISHMENT

The family groups discussed in this chapter are so grouped because their ideas and religious life are significantly different from the American Christian religious consensus. Because of these differences, they are and will remain minority faiths for the foreseeable future even though individual groups may have a momentary growth spectacular enough to attract the attention of the mass media, such as in the past decade the International Society of Krishna Consciousness (Hare Krishna), Divine Light Mission (headed by a teenage guru), and the psychedelic drug groups.

These groups move the church historian and sociologist into the realm of world religions and into the wide variety of ideas actually held by different religious practitioners. As a whole, when examined in depth, these groups offer a viable alternative to the dominant faith, and often includes both a sophisticated theology and a new way to think theologically.

The Latter-Day Saints Family

While drawing on a number of sources, the Latter-Day Saints are people united by a belief in the new revelations of Joseph Smith.[1] His revelations were eventually collected into a set of books which function as scripture in addition to the Bible. The most famous item in the new canon is the Book of Mormon from which the Saints are often labeled Mormons. Other scripture includes the Doctrines and Covenants and the Pearl of Great Price.[2] Beginning as a cultic movement built around the charisma of Joseph Smith, the Mormons shifted to a more bureaucratic format of collective leadership after his death.

Central to Mormon belief is the idea of the Restoration. True Christianity was re-established in Joseph Smith's ordination and ministry. Zion, an earthly visible home for the saints, was a major goal of the Restoration. Old Testament polygamy was restored also as a part of this new life.[3]

Schism[4] among the Mormons began in the struggle for power after Smith's murder in 1845. Those who did not follow Brigham Young to Utah splintered and founded one set

255

of churches.[5] In Utah other schisms occurred; one set of
them was the continuing polygamists.[6] The largest group
who did not go to Utah settled near Kansas City, Missouri,
and became the source for still another set of groups. A
final cause of schism is new prophets receiving new revelations.

Latter-Day Saints

Utah Mormons

19101	Church of Jesus Christ of Latter-Day Saints	1830
19105	Zion's Order of the Sons of Levi	1951
19110	L.D.S. Scripture Researchers	1942
19115	Aaronic Order	1942

Polygamous Fundamentalists

19210	Church of the First Born of the Fullness of Time	1956
19211	Church of the First Born	1956
19220	Church of Jesus Christ of Latter-Day Saints (Leroy Johnson)	
19225	Church of Jesus Christ (Allred)	
19229	Church of Jesus Christ (Musser)	
19235	Church of Jesus Christ of Latter-Day Saints (Kingston)	193_
19240	Church of Jesus Christ (Goldman)	
19245	Perfected Church of Jesus Christ Immaculate Latter-Day Saints	1955

Missouri Mormons

19401	Reorganized Church of Jesus Christ of Latter-Day Saints	1860
19410	Church of Christ (Temple Lot)	1857
19411	Church of Christ (Bronson)	1929
19412	Church of Christ with the Elijah Message (Dravesite)	1940
19415	Church of Christ (Bible and Book of Mormon Teaching)	1946

Miscellaneous (never associated with either the Missouri or
Utah churches and centered upon separate revelations)

19901	True Church of Jesus Christ (Cutlerite)	1853
19905	Church of Jesus Christ (Cutlerite)	1969
19910	Church of Jesus Christ (Strangite)	1844
19920	Church of Jesus Christ (Bickertonite)	1856
19921	Primitive Church of Jesus Christ (Bickertonite)	1914
19225	Yahshua's Army	

The Communal Family

The communal imperative has appeared frequently in the Western religious tradition but rarely leaves surviving forms to carry on a tradition from generation to generation. A renewal of perfectionism, utopianism or Biblical literalism (Acts 2) is required to bring on a new set of communal experiments. The 1960s witnessed such a renewal which has resulted in the establishment of communes which have drawn from a number of religious and secular sources for their peculiar thinking and life forms. Yet, whenever a commune comes into being, the desire for the common, shared life is the determining force which animates the spirit of the group. The communal imperative gives groups a bond of attachment to each other which makes secondary any previous theological history.[7]

There have been several attempts to form a network of communication, including Communities, a periodical published bi-monthly by Twin Oak Community at Louisa, Virginia. Beyond the several periodicals, ecumenical structures have mainly been informal and short-lived. Currently both religious and non-religious communes stay in touch through magazines such as Communities (Box 426, Louisa, Virginia, 23093) and Utopian Eyes (Box 1174, San Francisco, California, 94101). Both publish communal directories and provide services for people wishing to locate a commune in which they can join. A Communal Living Clearing House has recently been created by Family Synergy (P.O. Box 30103, Terminal Annex, Los Angeles, California, 90030).

Any attempt at distinguishing sub-families would be artificial. Those formed prior to the contemporary wave of communalism have shown a remarkable stability and, with two exceptions (the Koreshan Unity and the Esoteric Fraternity) are mainline Christian in their orientation. Even these two groups possess a Christian veneer. Those formed after 1960 are mostly non-Christian.

Communal Groups

Before 1960

20101	Hutterites--Schmiedleut	1874
20102	Hutterites--Dariusleut	1874
20103	Hutterites--Lehrerleut	1877
20104	Society of Brothers	1954
20105	Church of the Brotherhood	
20110	Amana Community of Inspirationists	1842
20115	United Society of Believers in Christ's Second Appearing	1776
20116	Temple Society	1866
20120	Koreshan Unity	1886
20125	People of the Living God	1962

257

20130	Shiloh Trust	1952
20135	WFLK Fountain of the World	1948
20140	Koinonia Partners	1942
20145	Church of the Savior	1946
20149	The Colony	1941
20155	The Esoteric Fraternity	1887
20160	Koinonia Foundation	1951

After 1960

20210	Reba Place Fellowship and Association Communities	1966
20215	Salem Acres	196_
20220	Aquarian Research Foundation	1969
20225	Mu Farm	1966
20230	Brotherhood of the Spirit	1968
20235	Brotherhood of the Sun	1971
20236	Church of Armageddon	1969
20237	The Farm	1970
20240	Katharsis	1971
20245	Universal Industrial Church of the New World Comforter (One World Family)	1966
20250	Lama Foundation	1967
20255	Lorian Association	196_
20260	Kerista/Utopian Society	196_
20265	Rainbow Family of Living Light	196_

The New Thought Metaphysical Family

New Thought is an eclectic movement combining elements of mesmerism, New England transcendentalism, and a basic drive for applied religion. The founder of the movement was Phineas Parkhurst Quimby, a clockmaker and amateur mesmerist (magnetic healer) in Maine. Success in his healing work led to the development of a monistic philosophy which served as a rational metaphysics for the healing work.[8]

Basic to Quimby's healing method was the patient's mental change to a healthy perspective on life. Metaphysically, healthiness, the good, was the only reality of Mind, God. Health was gained by "tuning-in" to God. Emphasis was placed on "demonstration" of the powers of Mind within the movement. The gaining of health, wealth, and happiness by mental processes was the single main topic of conversation.

New Thought has had an impact upon liberal Christianity through ministers who have accepted it but choose to remain in mainline churches. Such names as Lewis Dunnington (Methodist), Norman Vincent Peale (Reformed), and Vincent Sheen (Roman Catholic) are well-known in Christian churches. Jewish exponents, such as Rabbi Joshua Leibman, also became popular.

258

Soon after Quimby's death disagreement arose among his students over their rights to his ideas, the primal role of one student (Mary Baker Eddy) and the structure that would carry the movement. Mrs. Eddy believed that she had priority in all matters and created the Church of Christ, Scientist, as a personal cult.[9] Other students created more loosely affiliated New Thought centers. After Mrs. Eddy's death, splintering led to the emergence of a Christian Science sub-family of groups. The various bodies created by Quimby's other students have come together in:

The International New Thought Alliance
6922 Hollywood Boulevard
Suite 811
Hollywood, California   90028

New Thought Bodies

20510	Unity School of Christianity	1889
20511	Today Church	197_
20515	United Church of Religious Science	1927
20516	Religious Science International	1949
20520	Divine Science Federation International	1898
20525	Christ Truth League	1934
20526	Society of Pragmatic Mysticism	1951
20527	School of Esoteric Christianity	19__
20528	Church of the Truth	1922
20529	Institute of Esoteric Transcendentalism	1965
20530	Universal Church of Scientific Truth	1943
20531	Wisdom Institute of Spiritual Education (Wise)	
20532	Home of Truth	1891
20533	Church of the Trinity (Invisible Ministry)	1966
20534	Christian Assembly	1900
20535	United Church and Science of Living Institute	1966
20536	Seicho-No-Ie	1938
20537	Life Study Fellowship	1939
20538	Disciples of Faith	
20540	ESP Picture Prayers	
20541	Church of the Fuller Concept	
20545	American School of Mentalvivology	196_
20546	Psychophysics Foundation	
20547	Phoenix Institute	1967
20548	Calvary Missionary Church	1943
20549	First Church of Divine Immanence	1922
20550	Church of the Science of Religion	1922
20555	Antioch Association of Metaphysical Science	1932
20560	Church of Inner Wisdom	1968
20561	Inner Powers Society	
20562	School of Truth	1959

Christian Science Bodies

20610	Church of Christ, Scientist	1879
20615	International Metaphysical Association	1963
20616	Mountain Brook Studies	1963
20617	Margaret Laird Foundation	1959
20620	Infinite Way	1946

The Psychical Family

The Psychical Family can be said to share a non-history, as they are the most ahistorical of all the religious families. Geoffrey Nelson[10] has shown their shared characteristic to be a relation to science which includes belief that psychic phenomena demonstrate "scientifically" their religious perspective. While parapsychology has become a recognized scientific discipline and the Parapsychological Association has been admitted to the American Association for the Advancement of Science, practitioners have, as a whole, an attitude which could be termed scientism. Scientism is a religious world view based on a love of science coupled with little or no appreciation of what science or scientific methodology is.

Historically, the psychic community dates from the Swedish seer, Emmanuel Swedenborg, and the arrival in the United States of the disciples of Franz Anton Mesmer in the early nineteenth century.[11] Spiritualism emerges out of these two movements.[12] Andrew Jackson Davis, Spiritualism's great prophet, while under a mesmeric trance, began to communicate with Galen, the Greek physician, and Swedenborg. Other names include the Fox sisters, Madame Blavatsky, William James, and Josiah Royce.[13] The psychic component in religious experience has always brought clergymen from establishment bodies into the psychic realm. Such ministers as Wesleyan Methodist mesmerist LaRoy Sunderland have provided a bridge between the psychic and the mainline religious community.[14] On the other hand, the fear by many people of psychic/occult phenomena, accompanied by heavy antipsychic polemics by some segments of the Pentecostal and Baptist communities,[15] has helped to form the psychic family into a distinct entity.

Differences in the psychic community have been formed by: 1) variant revelations including the relation to several outstanding teachers like Blavatsky, Swedenborg, Alice Bailey[16] and Frank Ballard;[17] 2) levels of openness to the Christian establishment; and 3) the active participation in psychic development and the use of psychic gifts. Unidentified flying objects[18] and drugs[19] have also created their own sub-families. Like the Pentecostals, the family group in the establishment to which the Psychical Family is closest, the psychics emphasize subjective experience, which has led to a tremendous splintering. There are more psychic groups than any other family.

260

The Psychical Family has tried to form many cooperative bodies, only a few of which ever attained any degree of stability. One that has is:

International Cooperation Council
17819 Roscoe Boulevard
Northridge, California 91324

The Psychic Groups

Swedenborgian (accepts the mediumistic revelation of Emmanuel Swedenborg and does not encourage development)

21010	General Convention - The Swedenborgian Church	1792
21011	General Church of the New Jerusalem	1890
21012	Lord's New Church which is Nova Hierosolyma	1951

Spiritualism (believes in the centrality of mediumship as a demonstration of survival of bodily death; development is encouraged but phenomena remains focused in the mediums)

21101	National Spiritualist Association of Churches	1893
21103	International General Assembly of Spiritualists	1936
21105	General Assembly of Spiritualists	1931
21107	International Spiritualist Alliance	
21109	National Colored Spiritualist Association of Churches	1922
21111	Independent Spiritualist Association	1924
21113	Church of Revelation	1930
21115	Spiritualist Episcopal Church	1941
21117	Universal Spiritualist Association	1956
21119	United Spiritualist Church	1967
21121	Temple of Universal Law	1936
21123	Spiritual Science Mother Church	
21125	National Spiritual Science Center	196_
21127	National Federation of Spiritual Science Churches	
21129	Universal Religion of America	1958
21131	Universal Harmony Association	1942
21132	Independent Associated Spiritualists	1925
21133	Universal Church of the Master	1931
21135	Aquarian Fellowship Church	1969
21137	Progressive Spiritualist Church	1907
21139	National Spiritual Alliance of the USA	1913
21141	Church of the Four Leaf Clover	1925
21143	Superet Light Center	1925
21145	Metropolitan Spiritual Churches of Christ, Inc.	1925
21147	National Spiritual Aid Association, Inc.	1937
21149	Spiritual Prayer Home, Inc.	1939
21151	Pyramid Church of Truth and Light	1937
21153	Agasha Temple of Wisdom	1943

21155	Roosevelt Spiritual Memorial Benevolent	
	Association	1949
21157	University of Life Church	1959
21159	Church of Tzaddi	1962
21161	Eclesia Catolica Cristiana	1956
21163	Church of Metaphysical Christianity	1958
21165	Church of Cosmic Science	
21167	Hallowed Ground of Fellowship of Healing	
	and Prayer	1961
21169	T.O.M. Religious Foundation	196_
21171	St. Paul's Church of Aquarian Science	196_
21173	The Church of Ageless Wisdom	1954
21175	St. Timothy's Abbey Church	1965
21177	Foundation for Science of Spiritual Law	1968
21179	Universal Christ Church, Inc.	1970
21181	Lotus Ashram	1971
21183	Holy Grail Foundation	194_
21185	Churches of Spiritual Revelation, Inc.	
21187	Christian Spirit Center	
21189	Society of Christ, Inc.	
21191	Cosmic Church of Life and Spiritual	
	Science, Inc.	
21193	Universal Church of Psychic Science	

Teaching Spiritualism (focuses in the revelations of spirit entities brought through one or, at most, a few mediums, usually called "channels"; emphasis is on the content and philosophy rather than contact with the dead)

21201	Universal Faithists of Kosmon	1883
21203	School of Natural Science	1883
21205	Kethra E'da Foundation, Inc.	1945
21207	Martinus Institute of Spiritual Science	1969
21209	Word Foundation	
21211	Urantia Foundation	1950
21213	American Grail Foundation	
21215	Morse Fellowship	1958
21217	Light of the Universe	1964
21219	Dena Foundation	
21221	Father's House	1968
21223	Spiritual Research Society	194_
21225	New Age Teaching	1967
21229	Robin's Return	1955
21231	Fellowship of Universal Guidance	1960
21233	Foundation Church of the New Birth	1958
21235	Divine Word Foundation	1962
21237	Cosmic Awareness Communications	1963
21239	Servants of Awareness	1967
21241	Anthropological Research Foundation	1967
21243	Organization of Awareness (Olympia)	196_
21245	Organization of Awareness (Federal Way, Wash.)	196_
21247	International Organization of Awareness	196_
21249	Radiant School of Seekers and Servers	1963
21251	Circle of Inner Truth	1970

```
21253    Association for the Understanding of Man       1971
21255    Cosmerism                                      1972
21257    Fellowship of the Inner Light                  1972
21259    Louis Foundation
21261    Forum of Cosmic Awareness
21265    International Community of Christ
```

Theosophy (follows the teachings of Madame Helene F.
Blavatsky and her successors)

```
21301    Theosophical Society (Covina)                  1875
21303    Theosophical Society (Hartley)                 1951
21305    Theosophical Society of America                1889
21307    United Lodge of Theosophists                   1909
21309    International Group of Theosophists
```

Alice Bailey (former theosophist with her own unique revelations from an ascended master, "the Tibetan")

```
21350    Arcane School                                  1925
21351    School of Esoteric Studies                     1950
21352    Meditation Group for the New Age               1950
21353    Full Moon Meditation Groups of Southern
         California
21354    Arcana Workshops                               196_
21355    Aquarian Educational Group                     1955
21356    School of Light and Realization                1969
```

Liberal Catholicism (theosophical, liturgical churches which
have orders derived from the Old Catholic bodies)

```
21401    The Liberal Catholic Church, Province of
         the United States of America                   1917
21402    Liberal Catholic Church                        1961
21404    International Liberal Catholic Church           1965
21405    Order of St. Germain/Ecclesia Catholica
         Liberalis                                      1969
21410    Church of Antioch, Malabar Rite                1957
21415    Brotherhood of the Pleroma (Pre-Nicean
         Christianity)                                  1953
21420    Aryo-Christian Church of St. George of
         Cappadocia
```

I AM (follow the revelation of Frank Ballard who built his
system on contact with the theosophical masters)

```
21501    Great I AM Movement                            1930
21502    Bridge to Freedom                              1952
21505    Summit Lighthouse                              1958
21510    Sacred Society of the Eth, Inc.
21515    Sologa, Inc.                                   1959
21520    Sanctuary of the Masters' Presence             196_
21522    Association of Sananda and Sanat Kumara        1954
21524    "Ruby Focus" of Magnificent Consumation        196_
```

21525	Christ's Truth Church and School of Wisdom	1968
21526	Teachings of the Angelic Host within the	
	Kingdom of Heaven	1973
21527	Ascended Master Fellowship	1972
21530	Order of the Circle Cross	

Miscellaneous Theosophical Groups (groups with a strong emphasis on various aspects of theosophical teachings and often a strong polemical relationship to the Theosophical Societies)

21550	The Christian Community (Anthroposophical	
	Society)	1920
21552	Interdenominational Divine Order	1936
21554	Amica Temple of Radiance	1937
21556	Church of Cosmic Origin and School of	
	Thought	1963
21558	Christward Ministry	
21560	Church of the Jesus Ethic	1953
21564	New Angelus (Great White Brotherhood)	1972
21566	Oasis Fellowship, Inc.	1956
21568	Bodha Society of America, Inc.	1892
21570	Philo-Polytechnical Center	
21572	Lighted Way	1966
21574	Agni Yoga Society	192_
21576	Open Way	196_
21580	Children of Light Society	

Occult Orders (teach the ancient wisdom of Egypt, the Kabbalah and Eastern mysticism, Rosicrucians)

21610	The Aeth Priesthood, Fraternitas Rosae Crucis/	
	Church of Illumination	1868
21612	Societas Rosicruciana in America	188_
21614	Rosicrucian Fellowship	1908
21616	Lectorium Rosicrucianum	1971
21618	Ancient and Mystical Order of the Rosae	
	Crucis (AMORC)	1915

Other Occult Orders

21630	Astara Foundation	1951
21632	Mayan Order	1928
21634	Brotherhood of the White Temple	1930
21636	Philosophical Research Society	1934
21638	Soulcraft Fellowship, Inc.	1950
21640	Church of Light	1932
21642	Lemurian Fellowship	1936
21644	Stelle Group	1963
21646	Holy Order of Mans	1961
21648	Sabian Assembly	1922

Flying Saucer Groups (receiving revelations from telepathic contact with UFOs)

21701	Mark-Age Meta-Center	1956
21705	Brotherhood of the Seven Rays	1956
21707	The Monka Retreat	197_
21710	Star Light Fellowship	1962
21711	Universariun Foundation	1958
21713	Cosmic Science Research Center	
21715	Ministry of Universal Wisdom	1958
21718	Orbit Family	
21720	White Star	1957
21722	Light Affiliates	
21725	Understanding, Inc.	1955
21730	Aetherius Society	1950
21735	Solar Light Center	196_
21740	Unarius-Science of Life	
21745	Cosmic Star Temple	1960
21750	Cosmic Circle of Fellowship	1954
21755	Last Day Messengers	196_
21759	Home Bible Study	
21761	Cosmic Communication Commune	
21775	Human Individual Metamorphosis (HIM)	196_
21780	New Age Foundation	196_
21782	Christ Brotherhood, Inc.	196_
21784	Reach Out (Hodan)	196_

Psychedelic Groups

21810	Native American Church	1906
21815	Church of the Awakening	1963
21820	Church of the Tree of Life	1971
21825	Neo-American Church	1965
21830	Lazy Nickels	
21835	Children of the Moon	

Miscellaneous Psychic Groups

21901	Chirothesian Church of Faith	1917
21903	Coptic Fellowship of America	1927
21905	Institute of Mentalphysics	1957
21907	Kingdom of Yahweh	1935
21909	Christ Ministry Foundation	1926
21911	Association for Research and Enlightenment	1931
21913	Ontological Society	1932
21915	Huna Research Associates	1936
21917	Church of Basic Truth	1963
21919	Quimby Center	1946
21921	Institute of Cosmic Wisdom	
21923	Scientology, Church of	1952
21924	Institute of Ability	1965
21927	Church of Spiritual Freedoms	1970
21929	People's Temple Christian (Disciples) Church	195_
21931	Theocentric Foundation	1959

265

21933	Holy Spirit Association for the Unification of World Christianity	1959
21935	New Age Samaritan Church	1961
21937	Inner Light Foundation	196_
21939	Church of the Christian Spiritual Alliance	1962
21941	The Process	1966
21943	Foundation Church of the Millennium	1974
21945	Inner Peace Movement	1965
21947	Society for the Teachings of the Inner Christ	1965
21949	Eckankar	1965
21951	Movement of Spiritual Inner Awareness	1970
21953	Etherian Religious Society of Universal Brotherhood	1965
21955	American Universalist Temple of Divine Wisdom	1966
21957	New Age Church of Truth	1967
21961	New Psychiana	1967
21963	Church (and Institute) of General Psionics	1968
21965	Congregational Church of Practical Theology	1969
21967	Love Project	1972
21969	Holy Order of Ezekiel	1968
21971	First Century Church (Buber)	1969
21972	Future Foundation	1969
21973	Arica Institute	1969
21974	Aletheia Foundation	1969
21975	Essene Center	1972
21976	Savitria	1970
21977	Only Fair Religion	197_
21978	Dawn of Truth	
21979	True Church of Christ, International	
21980	Universal Brotherhood	
21981	Embassy of the Gheez-Americans	
21982	World Catalyst Church	
21983	Hakim International Meditation Society	
21984	Church of the Gift of God	
21985	Church of the Lord Jesus Christ (Ishi Temple)	
21986	Church of the Gentle Brothers and Sisters	197_
21987	Astrological, Metaphysical, Occult, Revelatory, Enlightenment Church	1972
21988	Aum Temple of Universal Truth	1925
21990	International Church of Spiritual Vision	196_
21992	Doctrine of Truth Foundation	
21994	Fransisters and Brothers	1963
21995	Awareness Research Foundation, Inc.	
21996	Star of Truth Foundation	

The Magical Family

Magick is the art of employing cosmic, paranormal forces believed to underpin the universe in order to produce the desired effect at will.[20] Such a definition immediately relates the magical world to the religion of ancient Egypt and to alchemical practices. Taken together, the magical

266

religious community represents a significant minority tradition in American religion which 1) dates from the founding of the American colonies in the 1600s; 2) has experienced steady renewal and growth through the importation of African and European practitioners and literature; 3) shows a continuous history throughout American life both temporally and geographically, as in the present (1977); 4) has periodically played an important role in religious life; and 5) has possessed a leadership both intelligent and articulate as well as secretive and a clientele both large and largely ignored.

The magical life style is defined by the use of techniques to gain control of the self and the magical forces. Manipulation and a manipulative world view is of the essence of magical existence. Supernaturalism is denied and the universe is seen in a macrocosm-microcosm model. "As above, so below" is the Hermetic formula. Secrecy is a significant part of the shared life style and is the glue that binds the groups together in a form of elitism.

Apart from Indian religion, not included in this study, the first incident of magical religion in the colonies was the incident at Salem. Tituba, the Reverend Samuel Parrish's maid, was a voodoo practitioner, and her teaching magic to the Parrish children set off the Salem affair. All New England was home to a European folk witchcraft and to a witchhunt mentality.[22]

The magical community is divided into at least six discernable groupings, four of which have produced social groupings--lodges, covens, grottos, nests and groves.

Though a relatively new Family, ecumenical councils have emerged quickly. They include:

> Council of American Witches
> 476 Summit Avenue
> St. Paul, Minnesota 55102
>
> Council on Earth Religions
> c/o Stephen Bell
> 4445 36th Street
> San Diego, California 92116
>
> Council of Themis
> P.O. Box 691
> Altadena, California 91001

Magical Groups

Ritual Magick[23] (follows an alchemical tradition and an initiatory system of magical degrees)

22101   Builders of the Adytum   1956

22110	Ordo Templi Orientis (Ft. Myers, Florida)	
22111	Ordo Templi Orientis (Roanoke, Virginia)	
22112	Ordo Templi Orientis (Dublin, California)	
22113	Church of the Hermetic Sciences (Ordo Templi Astarte)	
22116	Bennu Phoenix Temple of the Hermetic Order of the Golden Dawn	197_
22117	Bavarian Illuminanti	
22119	Light of Truth Church	1973
22121	Order of Thelema	197_
22123	Shrine of Sothis	197_
22125	The Foundation, A Hermetic Society	196_
22127	Fellowship of Ma-Ion	
22129	The New England Institute of Metaphysical Studies	197_
22131	Order of the Lily and the Eagle	1972
22133	Neo-Pythagorean-Gnostic Church	1969
22150	Society of the Magians	197_
22155	Hermetic Educational Institute	197_
22165	Fellowship of Kouretes	197_

Voodoo and Related Groups[24]

22201	Yoruba (Orisha) Religion	1973
22205	Religious Order of Witchcraft	
22210	Afro-American Vodoun	

Witchcraft[25] (nature religion which worships the mother goddess and the horned god)

22301	New England Coven of Traditional Witches	196_
22303	Holywood Coven	1968
22305	Cymry Wicca, Association of	196_
22307	Church of the Wiccan Rede	196_
22309	Delphic Coven	
22310	New York Coven of Welch Traditional Witches	
22313	Dianic Wicca	1972
22315	Susan B. Anthony Coven	
22320	Witches International Craft Associates	1970
22325	American Order of the Brotherhood of Wicca	1973
22326	First Wiccan Church of Minnesota	1973
22329	Atlantion Wicca	
22330	Order of Osirus	196_
22340	Aquarian Family of Covens	
22343	Witchcraft & Pagan Institute	

Gardnerians

22350	Gardnerian Witchcraft	
22351	Alexandrian Witchcraft	
22352	Enchanted Moon Coven	
22353	Algard Wicca	1972
22355	Church of Wicca of Bakersfield	1970

268

| 22357 | New Reformed Order of the Golden Dawn | 197_ |
| 22359 | Open Goddess | 196_ |

Miscellaneous Traditions

22375	Church and School of Wicca	
22378	Miami Pagan Grove	
22379	Holy Order of Briget	196_
22380	Seax Wicca	1973
22383	Aquarius Spiritus Templum	
22385	Mental Science Institute	
22390	ESP Laboratory	1965
22395	Coven of the Mirrors	
22398	First Temple of the Craft of W.I.C.A.	197_

Satanism[26] (worship Satan)

22410	Our Lady of Endor Coven, The Ophite Cultus Satanas	
22415	Order of the Ram	196_
22425	Satanic Church in America	1966
22426	Church of Satanic Brotherhood	1972
22427	Ordo Templi Satanas	197_
22430	Order of the Black Ram	
22435	Thee Satanic Church of Nethilum Rites	197_
22436	Thee Satanic Church	
22450	Fellowship of Pan	

Neo-Paganism[27] (worship the earth mother and related female deities and celebrate nature; least magical of the magical groups)

22510	Fereferia	1967
22511	Dancers of the Sacred Circle	
22520	Church of All Worlds	1961
22525	Pagan Way	
22526	Uranus Temple	
22530	Neo-Dianic Faith	
22533	Nemeton	
22535	Reformed Druids of North America	1963
22537	Delphic Fellowship	

Egyptian Polytheists

22550	The Church of Eternal Source	1970
22552	Pristine Egyptian Orthodox Church	1961
22554	Congregation of Aten	1974
22555	Lady Sara's Coven	1971

Norse/Teutonic Paganism

22560	Viking Brotherhood	1972
22562	Teutonic Temple	
22564	Runic Society	1974
22566	Odinist Movement	

Miscellaneous

22580	Sabean Religious Order of Am'n	
22585	Psychedelic Venus Church	1970
22586	Kali Kong	
22589	Discordian Society	
22591	Huna International	

The Classical Non-Christian Family

One hestitates to consider Jews, Hindus, Buddhists, and Muslims as one family of American religion. At the minimum one would want to divide them into Eastern (India/China/Japan based) and Western (Mediterranean based) families. If heritage and the state of religious bodies around the world were the criteria for judging, such a distinction would be made. Yet in America there is not the full scope of any of the various faiths represented, and the American scene is <u>not</u> the reflector of the state of a particular tradition around the world. The American scene is normative for this study. With the possible exception of Judaism, whose situation was so dramatically altered by the Holocaust, the American manifestation of the non-Christian traditions is very much like the manifestation of Christianity in some Asian countries. There would be a smattering of representatives of the larger bodies, plus a large sampling from Pentecostal, Adventist, and various missionary-oriented bodies, plus some indigenous schisms of mission churches. Were one doing a study of a country like Afghanistan, all Christian groups would form a single family group.

The decision to designate a non-Christian family is based upon the following shared characteristics. First, each sub-family represents the American branch of a religious tradition which in some foreign country is dominant in the way that Christianity is in the United States, and each shares a drive to legitimize itself in the face of Christianity by drawing on long tradition and foreign ties. Secondly, each sub-family came to America to serve an ethnic group and is battling to keep alive religious and cultural forms in the face of constant pressure to Christianize and Americanize. Proselytization has come primarily among other alienated' segments of the population, namely black people (by the Jews and Moslems) and the counter-culture (by the Buddhists, Hindus and Sikhs).

Because of their peculiar relationship to the dominant faith, members of non-Christian groups have attempted to move toward Christianity. Some, like the Buddhist Churches in America and the Reformed Jewish congregations, are remodeling themselves on a Protestant Congregational model. The ashram was a prior Hindu adaptation of the Christian "church" concept. With only a few exceptions Jesus is assigned a positive, if lesser, role as an avatar, prophet, guru or yogi. Americanization, which forces the groups into a corporate model, is a further homogenizing force.

Of the forms of Judaism and Islam in America, the Eastern-Western distinction is least distinct. All but five of the Jewish bodies are Hassidic. The Hassidic form of Judaism is based heavily in mysticism, and the magical Kabbalah, and is not free from interaction with yogic forms and disciplines.[28] Islam in America is not based on Arab forms but on Indian (Ahamdiyya) and Persian (Sufi) forms.

In life style the non-Christian bodies share several forms, predominately "the teacher orientation." In all of the traditions the guru, the teacher of inner religious wisdom, is a key to the structure. He goes under various names--rabbe[29] or zaddik, shaikh, sensai, or swami--but his function is the same. He possesses the mystic truth and teaches the techniques--yoga, dancing, meditation, study and community--which lead to the truth.

The non-Christian groups have also found a world together in American life as they have expanded in the counter-culture community across the nation. They have emerged as the "spiritual communities," a term used to desig- nate the mystical/psychical groups now located across the United States. The Spiritual Community Guide, published by a Sikh group which is headed by Yogi Bhajan, included introductory articles by representatives of each of the major non-Christian faiths.

As with any family group, there is always the need for discernment as to when a sub-family becomes a family. With the non-Christian groups, their inclusion in one family emphasizes the shared characteristics peculiar to their American sojourn without negating their differences.

The Jewish community is well organized on a number of levels. A central focus, however, is:

American Jewish Committee
165 East 56th Street
New York, New York 10022

Forming networks for the new Eastern and mystical groups is:

The Spiritual Community
Box 1080
San Rafael, California 94502

Non-Christian Groups

Jewish Bodies

23010	Union or Orthodox Rabbis	1902
23011	Rabbinical Council of America (Conservative)	1935
23012	Central Conference of American Rabbis (Reform)	1889
23015	Rabbinical Assembly (Orthodox)	1919
23020	Jewish Reconstructionist Foundation	1935

Hassidism

23101	Novominsk	1925
23103	Stolin	1925
23105	Monastritsh	1928
23107	Lubavitch	
23109	Sighet	
23110	Satmar	1946
23113	Bratzlau	
23115	Cernobyl	
23117	Squira	
23119	Talnoye	
23121	Bobov	
23122	Klausenburg	1940
23123	Bluzherer	
23125	Radzyn	
23127	Spinka	
23128	Boston	
23129	Boyan	
23131	Kosienice	
23133	Amshinov	
23135	Kopyczynce	
23137	Lisker	
23139	Telem	
23141	Ziditshoiv	
23143	Work of the Chariot	1968

Havurat Communities

23201	House of Love and Prayer	1968
23203	Havurat Shalom	1968
23205	Community of Micah	

Miscellaneous

23220	United Israel World Union	1943
23225	Jewish Science Society	1922
23230	Society of the Bible in the Hands of its Creator	1943
23235	Little Synagogue	

Black Jews

23401	Church of God and Saints of Christ	1896
23405	Church of God (Black Jews)	
23410	Commandment Keepers Congregation of the Living God	1919
23415	Original Hebrew Israelite Nation	
23420	United Hebrew Congregation	
23425	House of Judah	
23430	Black Christian Nationalist Church	1972

Islamic Bodies[32]

23601	Islam/Orthodox, Islamic Center	
23710	Moorish Science Temple of America	1914
23715	Ahmidiyya Movement of Islam	1921
23716	Nation of Islam	1933
23720	Calistran Muslims	
23725	Sunni Muslims (Hanafi Movement)	
23730	Nubian Islamic Hebrew Mission	1970

Sufism

23801	Sufi Order	1910
23805	Habibiyya-Shadhiliyya Sufic Order	1973
23810	Institute for the Development of the Harmonious Human Being	
23815	Guru Bawa Fellowship	1971
23820	Sufism Reoriented (Meher Baba)	1931
23825	Gurdjieff Foundation	1953
23826	Institute for Religious Development	
24230	Prosperos	1960
24235	Subud	1957

Other

24301	Baha'i Faith	1912
24310	House of Mankind	1963

Hindu Bodies[33]

24001	Vedanta Society	1894
24050	Self-Realization Fellowship	1920
24051	Self-Revelation Church of Absolute Monism	1929
24052	Temple of Kriya Yoga	1960
24055	Prema Dharmasala	
24057	Ananda Meditation Retreat	1967
24059	All Faith Fellowship	197_
24110	Integral Yoga Institute	
24112	True World Order	1958
24114	Sivananda Conservatory of Yoga One Science	1964
24115	International School of Yoga and Vedanta	1968
24117	Yasodhara Ashram Society	1962
24151	Shree Gurudev Siddha Yoga Ashram	1970
24152	Shree Gurudev Rudananda Yoga Ashram	1970

24153	Dawn Horse Communion	1970
24155	Hohm, The Joyous Community	197_
24159	Kirpalu Yoga Ashram (Yoga Society of Penn.)	1969
24210	Subramuniya Yoga Order	1957
24212	Blue Mountain Center of Meditation	1960
24214	Divine Light Mission	1971
24216	International Society of Krishna	
	Consciousness	1965
24218	Sai Baba Movement	
24220	Sri Aurobindo Society	1953
24222	Yogiraj Sect	
24224	Yogi Grupta Association	1954
24226	Yoganta Meditation Center	
24228	Sri Chinmoy Center	1964
24230	Krishnamurti Foundation of America	
24232	Keshavashram International Order	1968
24234	International Kriya Babaji Yoga Sangam	
24236	International Meditation Society	
	(Transcendental Meditation)	1959
24238	Sonorama Society	1959
24239	Himalayan International Institute of Yoga	
	Science and Philosophy	1970
24242	Arunchala Ashrama	1964
24244	International Center for Self Analysis	
24246	Ananda Marga Yoga Society	1969
24248	New York Sacred Tantrics	1969
24252	Hanuman Foundation	1969
24253	Sanatana Dharma Foundation	
24254	Swami Kuvalayananda Yoga Foundation	
24255	Real Yoga Society	
24256	Kundalini Research Foundation	1971
24258	Light of Yoga Society	
24259	Sri Ram Ashram	1967
24262	Sri Sri Ma Ananda Mati Monastery	1969
24264	Rajneesh Meditation Center	
24266	American Vegan Society	
24268	Foundation of Revelation	1971
24272	Fivefold Path	
24275	Narayananda Universal Yoga Trust and Ashram	
	in America	

Jainism

| 24701 | Meditation International Center | 1975 |

Sikhs

24901	The Sikh Foundation	1904
24905	Healthy, Happy, Holy Organization	1968
24910	Radhasoami Spiritual Science Foundation	1911
24911	Ruhani Satsang	1955

Buddhist Bodies³⁵

Japanese:

25101	Neo-Dharma	1960
25103	Todaiji Hawaii Bekkaku Honzan	1941
25105	Shingon Mission	1902
25107	Gedatsu Church of America	1951
25109	Shinnyo-En	1971
25111	Stillpoint Institutes	1971
25113	Palalo Kannondo Temple	1935
25115	Nichiren Mission	1902
25116	Nichiren Shoshu of America	1950
25117	Rissho Kosai Kai	
25120	Jodo Mission	1898
25121	Higashi Hongwangi Buddhist Church	1899
25122	Buddhist Churches of America	1914
25150	Bodaiji Mission	1930
25190	Kailas Shugendo	

Zen:

Renzai:

25205	First Zen Institute of America	1930
25210	The Diamond Sangha	1959
25215	Zen Meditation Center (Rochester)	1966
25220	California Bosatsukai	1928
25225	Zen Studies Society	1956
25230	Cambridge Buddhist Association	1957

Soto:

25235	Zen Shiji Soto Mission	1915
25260	Zen Center of San Francisco	1959
25265	Zen Mission Society	1968

Other:

25275	International Buddhist Meditation Center	1970
25280	Kwan Yin Zen Temple, Inc.	1970
25281	Providence Zen Center	
25283	Zen Center of Los Angeles	1967
25285	Pyramid Zen Society	
25287	Zen Buddhist Temple of Chicago	
25290	Cimmaron Zen Center	

Chinese Buddhism

25305	Hawaii Chinese Buddhist Society	1955
25306	Chinese Buddhist Association	1953
25310	Buddha's Universal Church	1927
25315	Sino-American Buddhist Association	
25320	Jen Sen Association for Buddhist and	
	Taoist Teachings	1958

```
25325    On Tsu To Lin Buddhist Lecture Hall
25330    Buddhist Association of America
25335    Quong Ming Buddhist and Taoist Society          1958
25340    Buddhist Association of the United States        1964
25345    China Buddhist Association                       1963
25346    Kwan Yin Temple
25350    Eastern States Buddhist Temple of America        1962
25355    Buddha's Universal Church and Ch'an Buddhist
           Sangha

Tibetan Buddhism

25410    Tibetan Nyingmapa Meditation Center              1969
25412    Labsum Shedrub Ling Malamist Buddhist
           Monastery of America                          196_

25415    Karma Dzong                                      1970
25420    Ewan Choden Tibetan Buddhist Center              1971
25425    Home of the Dharma                               1967
25440    Panosophic Institute                             1973
25445    American Buddhist Society & Fellowship, Inc.

Other

25510    Buddhist Vihara Society                          1966
25515    Buddhist World Philosophical Group               1934
25517    American Buddhist Order
25520    Friends of Buddhism--Washington, D.C.
25525    Friends of Buddhism--New York City
25530    Buddhist Fellowship of New York                  1961
25535    Church of One Sermon
25540    Harmony Buddhist Mission
25544    Universal Buddhist Fellowship                    1951
25550    Shivapuram                                       1963
25555    Chowado Henjo Kyo                                1929
25560    American Buddhist Mission
```

Shinto[36]

```
25905    Honkyoku-Daijingu Temple                         1900
25910    Taishakyo-Hawaii Izumo Taisho                    1906
25915    Hawaii Ichizuchi Jinga
25920    Kotohira Jinsha Temple
25925    Tensho Kotai Jingu Kyo                           1959
25930    Tenrikyo                                         1929
25035    Konko-Kyo                                        1913
25940    Shinrei Kyo                                      1963
25945    Third Civilization
```

Other

Taoism:[37]

26005   Taoist Sanctuary
26010   Macrobiotics

Persian Bodies[38]

26050   Zoroaster--Mazdaznan   1902

Miscellaneous Religious Bodies

Some bodies are unclassifiable because either:
1) they are in such a state of religious ferment that their
future is uncertain and the present state is ambiguous;
2) there was not enough information to classify them; or
3) they are genuine "oddities" and do not fit into any
family group.

The Jesus People and the Gay Churches fit into the
first category. Both may still be absorbed in other family
groups or may adopt an adequate thought world to remain as
separate entities. The mail order groups are of doubtful
validity; while some are unquestionably serious, others
are probably fraudulent money-making front groups.

Miscellaneous Religious Bodies

Jesus People

30105   World Christian Liberation Front   1969
30106   Berkeley Christian Coalition   1975
30110   Jesus People, International   1969
30115   Christian Foundation   1967
30120   Way Biblical Research Center   1953
30125   Voice of Elijah   1970
30130   Avalon (and Related Jesus People
          Communities)   1970
30135   Harvest House Ministries   1970
30140   Fellowship of Christian Pilgrims   1971
30145   Jesus People USA   1969
30150   Christ Is The Answer   1972
30160   Chicago Metropolitan Jesus People Groups
30170   Christ's Household of Faith   1967
30190   Children of God   1969
30195   Church of Bible Understanding

Gay Churches

30201   Metropolitan Community Churches,
          Universal Fellowship of   1968
30210   Eucharistic Catholic Church   1970
30215   Orthodox Episcopal Church of God   1970

277

| 30220 | Gay Synagogues | 1973 |
| 20320 | The People's Church Collective (Jesuene Ek-Klesia) | 1960 |

Mail Order Churches

30301	Universal Life Church	1962
30302	Crown of Life Fellowship	1967
30305	Hilltop House Church	1970
30307	Life Science Church	1970
30309	Omniune Church	
30311	Universal Free Life Church	1969
30313	Apostolic Christian Church of the United States and Canada	1968
30315	Church of Universal Brotherhood	
30316	Missionaries of the New Truth	1969
30319	Calvary Grace Churches of Faith	1954
30321	Calvary Grace Christian Church	1961
30325	Brotherhood of Peace and Tranquility	
30330	International Clergy Association	
30335	God's Kingdom on Earth	

Social Action Churches

30401	Humanity Benefactor Foundation of Detroit	1931
30410	People's Institute of Applied Religion	1934
30415	Ecumenical Institute	1962
30420	Church for the Fellowship of All People	1943
30421	Berkeley Free Church	1968
30425	Church of What's Happening Now	1968
30450	Assembly of Christian Soldiers	1971
30455	Church of the Christian Crusade	1966
30457	Fellowship of Christian Men	
30459	Church of the Creator	

Miscellaneous

30901	All-One-Faith-In-One-God-State	1969
30903	American Mission for Opening Closed Churches	1943
30905	Apostolic Christian Church (Nazarean)	1850
30907	Apostolic Christian Churches of America	1847
30909	Christian Catholic Church	1896
30911	Christian Union	1864
30913	Church of the New Song	1970
30915	Followers of Christ	1889
30917	Full Salvation Union	1934
30918	JFK Memorial Temples	
30921	Moral ReArmament	1913
30923	Mt. Zion Sanctuary	1882
30925	Perfect Liberty	1960
30927	The Church of World Messianity/Sekai Kyusei Kyo	1953
30929	Smithvenner	
30931	United Christian Church	

| 30933 | Universal Christian Churches of America | 1960 |
| 30935 | Gospel of Regeneration | 1947 |

Hawaiian Family Churches

30955	Hoomana Naauoa O Hawaii	1853
30957	Church of the Living God	1911
30958	Ka Hale Hoano Hou O Ke Akua	1948
30959	Kealaokalamalama	1935

30965	All Freedom Church
30970	Universal Great Brotherhood
30975	Apostolic Christian Church
30976	New Apostolic Church of North America
30977	Christian Apostolic Church (Kansas)
30978	Christian Apostolic Church (Illinois)
30979	German Christian Apostolic Church
30980	Evangelical Fellowship Chapels
30981	House of Prayer for All People
30982	Peace Mission, Universal

NOTES

Chapter I

[1] For a summary of the use of such terms see David O. Moberg, The Church as a Social Institution (Englewood Cliffs, N.J.: Prentice-Hall, Inc., 1962), pp. 73-99.

[2] See the recent studies in fringe movements edited by Irving I. Zaretsky and Mark P. Leone, Religious Movements in Contemporary America (Princeton, N.J.: Princeton University Press, 1974).

[3] David St. Clair, The Psychic World of California (Garden City, N.Y.: Doubleday & Company, 1972), p. 313.

[4] J. Gordon Melton, "The Chicago Psychic/Metaphysical/ Occult/New Age Community: A Directory and Guide," in Psychic City Chicago by Brad Steiger (Garden City, N.Y.: Doubleday & Company, 1976), pp. 161-186.

[5] In order to complete any picture of religious structures in the United States, the tribal religious life and structures of the Native Americans must be given their proper consideration. Unfortunately, ISAR has only begun the major project of incorporating such data into its avenue of research. Instead of doing a poor and incomplete job of the type too often done in this area, we decided to omit the area of Native American tribal religion. It is hoped that this area will be incorporated in a later edition of this directory or in a separately published summary.

NOTES

Chapter II

[1]All quotes are from the English translation by Olive
Wyon, The Social Teachings of the Christian Churches   (New
York: Harper & Brothers, 1960).

[2]Ibid., I, p. 21.

[3]Ibid., II, p. 993.

[4]Ibid., I, p. 59.

[5]Ibid., I, p. 331.

[6]Archiv fur Sozialwissenschaft und Sozialpolitik, XX
(1904) and XXI (1905), later reprinted in Gesammelte Aufsatze
zur Religions-soziologie (Tubingen: 1921), trans. Talcott
Parsons, The Protestant Ethic and the Spirit of Capitalism
(London: G. Allen & Unwin, Ltd., 1930).

[7]Troeltsch, op. cit., I, p. 333.

[8]Ibid., I, p. 339.

[9]Ibid., I, pp. 89, 329. Mysticism was mentioned in
passing in I, p. 376.

[10]Ibid., II, P. 693.

[11]The only actual establishments were in Colonial New
England prior to the establishment of King's Chapel in Boston
and in Utah in the 1850s and 1860s in the Mormon theocracy.

[12]The Psychology of Religious Sects   (New York: Fleming
H. Revell Company, 1912), p. 97.

[13](St. Louis: Concordia Publishing House, 1961).

[14]Joachim Wach, Sociology of Religion   (Chicago:
University of Chicago Press, 1944), p. 17.

[15]The lack of concern for the role of ideas is due possibly to the overemphasis on theology in nineteenth-century
sect studies.

[16] Howard Becker, Systematic Sociology (New York: John Wiley & Sons, 1932), pp. 613-642.

[17] J. Milton Yinger, Religion, Society and the Individual (New York: MacMillan Company, 1957), pp. 156-194.

[18] Ibid., p. 144.

[19] Benton Johnson, "On Church and Sect," American Sociological Review, XXXVIII (August, 1963): 539-549. See also Peter L. Berger, "The Sociological Study of Sectarianism," Social Research XXI (Winter, 1954): 473-476; Russell R. Dynes, "Church-Sect Typology and Socio-Economic Status," American Sociological Review XXI (October, 1955): 555-560; and Nicholas J. Demerath, III, "Social Stratification and Church Involvement," Review of Religious Research II (Spring, 1961): 151.

[20] Erich Goode, "Some Critical Observations on the Church-Sect Dimension," Journal for the Scientific Study of Religion VI (September, 1967): 77.

[21] Nicholas J. Demerath, III, "In a Sow's Ear: A Reply to Goode," Journal for the Scientific Study of Religion VI (September, 1967): 83.

[22] Allen W. Eister, "Toward a Radical Critique of Church-Sect Typologizing," Journal for the Scientific Study of Religion VI (September, 1967): 85.

[23] Robert Friedmann, "Conception of the Anabaptists," Church History IX (December, 1940): 355-365.

[24] Johannes Kuhn, Toleranz und Offenbarung (Leipzig: 1923).

[25] Friedmann, op. cit., p. 359.

[26] Leland Jameson, "Religions on the Christian Perimeter," in The Shaping of American Religion (Princeton: Princeton University Press, 1961), pp. 162-231.

[27] Elmer T. Clark, The Small Sects in America (New York: Abingdon-Cokesbury Press, 1949), pp. 11-25.

[28] Elmer T. Clark, The Psychology of Religious Awakening (New York: The MacMillan Company, 1929).

[29] Bryan Wilson, Religious Sects (New York: McGraw-Hill Book Company, 1970), pp. 36-47.

[30] Ralph Linton, "Nativistic Movements," American Anthropologist XLV, 2 (April, 1943):230; Simone Clemhout, "Typology of Nativistic Movements," Man LXVI (January-February, 1964): 14-15; Marion W. Smith, "Toward a

Classification of Cult Movements," Man LIX (January, 1959):
8-12; and Fred W. Voget, "Toward a Classification of Cult
Movements: Some Further Considerations," Man LIX (February,
1959): 25-28.

[31]Igor Kopytoff, "Classification of Religious Movements:
Analytical and Synthetic," Proceedings, American Ethnological
Society (1964), 77-90.

[32]Ibid., p. 85.

[33]Robert Ellwood, Religious and Spiritual Groups in
Modern America (Englewood Cliffs, N.J.: Prentice-Hall,
Inc., 1973), pp. 31-36.

[34]A striking instance of a child continuing the forms of
its parent is demonstrated by the Mormons. They are an
eclectic body but draw heavily from the non-instrumental
Church of Christ. Alexander Campbell reflecting on the
Mormons noted:

> 7. This prophet Smith, through his stone spectacles,
> wrote on the plates of Nephi, in his book of Mormons,
> every error and almost every truth discussed in N. York
> for the last ten years. He decides all the great con-
> troversies--infant baptism, ordination, the trinity,
> regeneration, repentance, justification, the fall of
> man, the atonement, transubstantiation, fasting, penance,
> church government, religious experience, the call to
> the ministry, the general resurrection, eternal punish-
> ment, who may baptize, and even the question of free-
> masonry, republican government, and the rights of man.
> All these topics are repeatedly alluded to. How much
> more benevolent and intelligent this American Apostle,
> than were the holy twelve, and Paul to assist them!!!
> He prophesied of all these topics, and of the apostacy,
> and infallibly decides, by his authority, every question.
> How easy to prophescy of the past or of the present time!!

An Analysis of the Book of Mormon (Boston: Benjamin H.
Greene, 1832), p. 13.

[35]These three characteristics have been extracted from
the works discussed above. Life style relates to religious
response to the world (Wilson); acceptance/rejection of the
social order (Johnson); and social form (Yinger). Thought
world relates to view of the Bible (Friedmann, Jameson);
doctrine (Mayer and Piepkorn); and theoretical expressions
(Wach). Heritage relates to the external characteristics
(McComas) and doctrine (Mayer and Piepkorn).

[36]Paul Tillich, Dynamics of Faith (New York: Harper &
Row, Publishers, 1956); and Carl G. Jung, Man and His Symbols
(London: Aldus Books, 1964).

[37]Donald Dayton, "Theological Roots of Pentecostalism," (ditto, 18 pages, 1974).

[38]The Family Group idea has already shown the ability to meaningfully replace the rather inadequate Library of Congress Classification System which has in its alphabetical classification not allowed room for materials published by these bodies.

[39]See Troeltsch, op. cit., I, pp. 23-34.

[40]Charles G. Finney, Lectures on Systematic Theology (New York: G.H. Doran, 1878); and Timothy L. Smith, Revivalism and Social Reform (New York: Abingdon Press, 1957).

Those who seek a direct basis for social involvement by the Church in the actions of Jesus or the Apostolic Church will find little, if any, material to build upon. It is obvious that the early Church sought only to affect society enough to allow itself to live without persecution. The contemporary social imperative is as much a new response to changed conditions as the missionary movement was to the rediscovery of the outside world. Historically and sociologically speaking, such action cannot be found in early Christianity.

[41]One of the obstacles to the convergence of those bodies which accept the social gospel is the broad span of opinions usually held on any given social issue. Thus, while groups may accept the necessity of social involvement, they may still be at odds over the particular nature of such involvement relative to a given war or social movement or political issue.

[42]Such as the Ecumenical Institute and the Church of the Christian Crusade.

[43]Troeltsch, op. cit., I, p. 336.

[44]The Wesleyan Church has changed from Pietist to Holiness. The Missionary Church has left behind its Mennonite heritage. The name of a group is often, but by no means always, an indicator of the family group. Such terms as Methodist, Baptist and Presbyterian do identify bodies that tend to share a common tradition but there are notable exceptions, particularly with such terms as Catholic, Orthodox, Spiritual, and Metaphysical.

[45]The affirmation or denial by a group of its "religious" basis or orientation has not been a factor in exclusion or inclusion in this study. Groups which adhere to the definitions proposed in Chapter III have been included.

284

[46]See a recent attempt to trace the rituals of witch-craft by the use of form criticism. C. Taliesin Edwards, "Textual Criticism to the Craft Laws," Gnostica News IV, 1 (September 1974), 3: 35-37.

[47]The definition of the content of the "dominant reli-gious faith" has come from a survey of the consensus of those groups included in Chapter V of this work, with added refer-ence to Martin E. Marty, The New Shape of American Religion (New York: Harper & Brothers, 1958); Rodney Stark and Charles Y. Glock, American Piety: The Nature of Religious Commitment (Berkeley: University of California Press, 1968); and W. Seward Salisbury, Religion in American Culture (Homewood, Ill.: The Dorsey Press, 1964).

[48]Within recent years the Hare Krishna Movement, the Divine Light Mission of Guru Maharaj Ji, and the Unification Church of the Reverend Sun Myung Moon have been able to generate considerable media coverage.

[49]The Methodist Episcopal Church ⟶ African Methodist Episcopal Church ⟶ African Methodist Episcopal Zion Church.

NOTES

CHAPTER IV

[1]The description of the liturgical family is drawn from
Konrad Algermissen, Christian Denominations (St. Louis:
B. Herder Book Co., 1946), pp. 93-556; Dennis Meadows, A
Short History of the Catholic Church (London: Robert Hale,
Ltd., 1959); and George Brantl, ed., Catholicism (New York:
Washington Square Press, Inc., 1962).

[2]The Eastern Orthodox traditions are described in Donald
Attwater, The Christian Churches of the East (Milwaukee:
Bruce Publishing Company, 1962); and Aziz S. Atiya, A History of Eastern Christianity (London: Methuen & Co., Ltd.,
1968).

[3]The Anglican tradition in America is fully discussed in
William B. Williamson, A Handbook for Episcopalians (New
York: Morehouse-Barlow Co., 1961); Raymond W. Albright, A
History of the Protestant Episcopal Church (New York:
MacMillan Company, 1964); and W. Norman Pittenger, The
Episcopalian Way of Life (Englewood Cliffs, N.J.: Prentice
Hall, 1957). The Old Catholic tradition is discussed at
great length in Peter F. Anson, Bishops at Large (London:
Faber and Faber, 1964); Henry R.T. Brandreth, Episcopi
Vagantes and the Anglican Church (London: SPCK, 1961); and
Karl Pruter, A History of the Old Catholic Church
(Scottsdale, Ariz.: St. Willibrord's Press, 1973).

[4]For a general picture of Lutheranism, see the Lutheran
World Federation, Lutheran Churches of the World
(Minneapolis: Augsburg Publishing House, 1957). For a
survey of Lutheran organizations in the United States of
America, see Robert C. Wiederaenders and Walter G. Tillmanns,
The Synods of American Lutheranism (St. Louis: Concordia
Seminary Printshop, 1968). The recent Lutheranism in North
America, 1914-1970, by E. Clifford Nelson (Minneapolis:
Augsburg Publishing House, 1972) is valuable also.

[5]For delineation of the Reformed-Presbyterian tradition,
see in particular Max Weber, Die Protestantische Ethik und
der Geist des Kapitalismus, (Archiv für Sozialwissenschaft
und Sozialpolitik), XX (1904) and XXI (1905). For discussions of particular aspects see Arthur C. Cochrane, ed., The
Reformed Confessions of the Sixteenth Century (Philadelphia:
Westminister Press, 1966); Bard Thompson and others, Essays
on the Heidelberg Catechism (Philadelphia: United Church

286

Press, 1963); James Hastings Nichols, Corporate Worship in
the Reformed Tradition (Philadelphia: Westminster Press,
1968); and Walter L. Lingle, Presbyterians: Their History
and Beliefs (Richmond, Va.: John Knox Press, 1944).

[6]Congregationalism is discussed in Douglas Horton, The
United Church of Christ: Its Origin, Organization and Role
in the World Today (New York: Thomas Nelson & Sons, 1962).
For the particular intrafamily issue of the true nature of
Congregational polity see Harry M. Butman, The Lord's Free
People (Wauwatosa, Wis.: The Swannet Press, 1968).

[7]See Stow Parsons, Free Religion (Boston: Beacon Press,
1947); George E. MacDonald, Fifty Years of Free Thought
(New York: The Truth Seeker Co., 1929); Sidney Warren,
American Free Thought, 1860-1914 (New York: Gordian Press,
1966); Madalyn Murray O'Hair, What on Earth Is An Atheist!
(Austin, Texas: American Atheist Press, 1969); and Jack
Mendelsohn, Why I Am A Unitarian Universalist (New York:
Thomas Nelson & Sons, 1969).

[8]For texts of the two "Humanist Manifestos" see Corliss
Lamont, The Philosophy of Humanism (London: Barrie &
Rockliff, 1965); and Humanist Manifestos I and II (Buffalo,
N.Y.: Prometheus Books, 1975).

[9]For a description of classical Pietism see E. Ernest
Stoeffler, German Pietism During the Eighteenth Century
(Leiden: E.J. Brille, 1973). The British phase is best
seen through a biography of its leading exponent in a book
by Martin Schmidt, John Wesley, A Theological Biography
(New York: Abingdon Press, 1962-1972), 2 vols. The
Moravians have recently published a lengthy history, J.
Taylor Hamilton and Kenneth G. Hamilton, A History of the
Moravian Church--The Unitas Fratrum, 1722-1957 (Bethlehem,
Pa.: Interprovincial Board of Christian Education/Moravian
Church in America, 1957). Scandinavian pietism is best
viewed through the work of Karl A. Olsson, By One Spirit
(Chicago: Covenant Press, 1962). For added perspective on
the American scene see George J. Eisenach, Pietism and the
Russian Germans in the United States (Berne, Ind.: Berne
Publishers, 1948).

[10]Discussions of modern Pietism and of its representa-
tive body in the United States are illumined by Egon W.
Gerdes, "Pietism: Classical and Modern," Concordia Theological Journal, Vol. XXXIX, No. 4, April 1968, pp. 257-268.

[11]The emergence of the Holiness movement is traced in
Timothy Smith, Called Unto Holiness (Kansas City, Mo.:
Nazarene Publishing House, 1962). Other items include
Delbert R. Rose, A Theology of Christian Experience

287

(Minneapolis: Bethany Fellowship, Inc., 1965); and Charles
Edwin Jones, A Guide to the Study of the Holiness Movement
(Metuchen, N.J.: Scarecrow Press, 1974). No comprehensive
history of the Holiness Movement has been produced as yet,
but available materials are listed in Donald W. Dayton, The
American Holiness Movement/A Bibliographic Introduction
(Wilmore, Ky.: B.L. Fisher Library/Asbury Theological
Seminary, 1971).

[12]The scant material on the Glenn Griffith movement can
be found in Jones, op.cit., and the Manual of the Bible
Missionary Church (n.p., 1971).

[13]The amount of material on Pentecostalism is staggering,
but central items in capturing its essence would include
John L. Sherrill, They Speak in Other Tongues (New York:
McGraw-Hill Book Company, 1964); Walter J. Hollenweger,
Handbuch de Pfingstbewegung (Typescript, 1965-1967, Microfilm,
10 reels); Stanley H. Frodsham, With Signs Following
(Springfield, Mo.: Gospel Publishing House, 1926).

[14]The history of the Oneness churches is found in Fred
J. Foster, Think It Not Strange (St. Louis: Pentecostal
Publishing House, 1965).

[15]"The Story of the Great Restoration Revival," Worldwide
Revival, Vol. XI, 1958 (appeared as a series of five arti-
cles). See also Gordon Lindsey, The Gordon Lindsey Story
(Dallas, Texas: Voice of Healing Publishing Co., n.p.).

[16]James S. Tinney, "Black Origins of the Pentecostal
Movement," Christianity Today, XVI, 1, October 8, 1971, pp.
4-6. Walter J. Hollenweger, "Black Pentecostal Concept,"
Concept, special issue #30, June 1970.

[17]Weston LaBarre, They Shall Take Up Serpents (New York:
Schocken Books, 1969).

[18]Homer A. Tomlinson, Miracles of Healing in the Minis-
try of Rev. Francisco Olazabal (Queen's Village, N.Y.: Homer
A. Tomlinson, 1939); Fourteenth Anniversary of the Spanish
Defender Churches in the United States (n.p., 1959).

[19]David J. Du Plessis, The Spirit Bade Me Go (Oakland,
Calif.: David J. Du Plessis, 1960).

[20]The European Free Church tradition has been one seemingly to produce more historians for its size than any and
some excellent explorations of their life. The major work
by George H. Williams, The Radical Reformation (Philadelphia:
The Westminister Press, 1962) has done much to shift the
negative attitude of many earlier studies. Donald F.

Durnbaugh has emerged as the major historian of the Brethren
and his The Believer's Church (New York: The MacMillan Co.,
1968) is helpful. Henry C. Smith's The Mennonites (Berne,
Ind.: Mennonite Book Concern, 1920) remains useful even
after half a century. The Quaker bodies are surveyed in
Handbook of the Religious Society of Friends (Birmingham,
England: Friend's World Committee for Consultation, 1967).

[21]The traditional interpretation of Quaker history can be
found in Rufus Jones, The Spiritual Reformers of the Sixteenth and Seventeenth Century (Boston: Beacon Press, 1914).
Among those who assert that Quakers were essentially Puritans
is Geoffrey F. Nuttall, The Holy Spirit in Puritan Faith and
and Experience (Oxford: Basil Blackwell, 1946). The entire
debate is summarized in Donald F. Durnbaugh, "Baptists and
Quakers--Left-wing Puritans?" Quaker History, Vol. 62, No. 2,
Autumn 1973, pp. 67-82.

[22]For a general picture of the Baptists, the excellent
study by Robert G. Tolbert is the best, A History of the
Baptists (Philadelphia: The Judson Press, 1950). The problem of Baptist origins and distinctives in relation to both
Continental Anabaptists and Puritans is treated.

[23]The various issues which have led to schism can be
found in Cushing Biggs Hassell and Sylvester Hassell,
History of the Church of God from Creation to A.D. 1885
(Atlanta: Turner Lassiter, 1962); Owen C. Pelt and Ralph
Lee Smith, The Story of the National Baptists (New York:
Vantage Press, 1960); The Seventh Day Baptists In Europe and
America (Plainfield, N.J.: The Seventh Day Baptist General
Conference, 1910).

[24]Varying perspectives on the Restoration Movement can be
found in Winifred Garrison, Heritage and Destiny (St. Louis:
The Bethany Press, 1961); A.T. DeGroot, New Possibilities for
Disciples and Independents (St. Louis: Bethany Press, 1963);
and James DeForest Murch, Christians Only (Cincinnati:
Standard Publishing Co., 1962).

[25]Of course, some forms of dispensationalism are quite
old. The division of Christian history into three periods
was associated with such men as Saballius and Joachim of
Flores. Darby seems, however, to be the first to pose the
pretribulation-premillennialism accompanied by the seven
dispensational divisions of history. See Dave McPherson,
The Unbelievable Pre-Trib Origin (Kansas City, Mo.: Heart
of American Bible Society, 1973); and Arnold D. Ehlert, A
Bibliographic History of Dispensationalism (Grand Rapids,
Mich.: Baker Book House, 1965).

[26]Numerous editions since its first publication in 1886.

[27]Edited by C.I. Scofield (New York: 1909).

[28]Light on the emergence of fundamentalism in the late nineteenth century from Darbyism is found in Ernest R. Sandeen, The Roots of Fundamentalism (Chicago: University of Chicago Press, 1970) and a more recent effort in George W. Dollar, A History of Fundamentalism in America (Greenville, S.C.: Bob Jones University Press, 1973).

[29]Ultra-dispensationalism is dated from the work of E.W. Bullinger. See his The Foundations of Dispensational Truth (London: Camp Press, third edition, 1959). In America, J.C. O'Hair was the pioneer. The story of its emergence is told in C.R. Stam, The Controversy (Chicago: Berean Bible Society, 1963).

[30]British-Israel has been the subject of much polemical literature. For both sides of the issues see J.H. Allen, Judah's Sceptre and Joseph's Birthright (Boston: A.A. Beauchamp, Publishers, 1930); P.S. McKillop, Britain and America/The Lost Israelites (St. Albans, Vt.: n.p., 1902); and Anton Darms, The Delusion of British-Israelism (New York: Loizeaux Brothers, Bible Truth Depot, n.d.). The latter is a Plymouth Brethren publication.

[31]Adventism is yet to be treated in its broadest scope in a non-polemical manner, and there is no single text which traces the development of Millerism in its various phases especially from the time of the Great Disappointment to the emergence of main Millerite groups in the early twentieth century. The story can be put together from Rene Noorbergen, Ellen G. White/Prophet of Destiny (New Canaan, Conn.: Keats Publishing, Inc., 1972); Francis D. Nichols, The Midnight Cry (Washington, D.C.: Review and Herald Publishing Company Association, 1965-1966); Seventh Day Adventist Encyclopedia (Washington, D.C.: Review and Herald Publishing Association, 1966). The Sacred Name Movement is covered briefly in A.N. Dugger and C.O. Dodd, A History of the True Religion (Jerusalem, Israel: Mt. Zion Reporter, 1968). The Southcottites are given extensive treatment in C.R. Balleine, Past Finding Out (New York: The MacMillan Company, 1956).

[32]Leon Festinger, Henry W. Riecken, and Stanley Schachter, When Prophecy Fails (New York: Harper and Row, Publishers, 1964).

[33]From the mass of literature on the Jehovah's Witnesses, several stand out, including two written by ex-Witnesses: Edmund Charles Gruss, Apostles of Denial (n.p., Presbyterian and Reformed Publishing Co., 1970); Alan Rogerson, Millions Now Living Will Never Die (London: Constable, 1969); Timothy White, A People For His Name (New York: Vantage Press, 1968).

290

NOTES

CHAPTER V

[1]An unbiased history of Joseph Smith has not yet been
produced, but of the many books about him a good start at
understanding the issues surrounding his life can be found
in Murder of An American Prophet, edited by Keith Huntress
(San Francisco: Chandler Publishing Company, 1960); Fawn M.
Brodie, No Man Knows My History (New York: Alfred A. Knopf,
1945); and Hugh Nibley, No Ma'am That's Not History (Salt
Lake City: Bookcraft, 1946).

[2]The Mormon scriptures have appeared in numerous editions,
and at least four different sets are being used by the
various groups. For a discussion of the issues concerning
their authenticity, see Francis W. Kirkham, A New Witness for
Christ in America/The Book of Mormon (Independence, Mo.:
Zion's Printing and Publishing Company, 1951); and Jerald and
Sandra Tanner, The Case Against Mormonism (Salt Lake City:
Modern Microfilm Company, 1967).

[3]For an overall view of Mormonism see Robert Mullen, The
Latter-Day Saints: The Mormons Yesterday and Today (Garden
City, N.Y.: Doubleday & Company, Inc., 1966); and Wallace
Turner, The Mormon Establishment (Boston: Houghton Mifflin
Company, 1966). The most popular presentation of present
Mormon theology is in LeGrand Richards, A Marvelous Work and
a Wonder (Salt Lake City: Deseret Book Company, 1968).

[4]The various alternatives to the Utah Church are discussed
in George Bartholomew Arbaugh, Revelation in Mormonism
(Chicago: University of Chicago Press, 1932); Kate Carter,
Denominations that Base their Beliefs on the Teachings of
Joseph Smith (Salt Lake City: Daughters of Utah Pioneers, 1969);
Russell Rich, Those Who Would Be Leaders (Provo, Utah:
Brigham Young University, 1967); and Russell Rich, Little
Known Schisms of the Restoration (Provo, Utah: Brigham Young
University, 1967).

[5]B.C. Flint, An Outline History of the Church of Christ
(Temple Lot) (Independence, Mo.: Church of Christ [Temple
Lot], 1953); and Daniel MacGregor, A Marvelous Work and a
Wonder (n.p., 1911).

[6]Fundamentalists are operating openly in Utah, and their
material can be purchased in most bookstores. Main items

291

include Joseph H. Musser, Celestial or Plural Marriage (Salt Lake City: Truth Publishing Co., 1944); and Mormon Fundamentalism and the L.D.S. Church (Salt Lake City: "The Watchmen on the Towers of Israel," 1969).

[7]Communal literature is vast and growing. Concerning the nineteenth century, start with William Alfred Hinds, American Communities (Oneida, N.Y.: American Socialist, 1878). For the twentieth century see William Hedgepeth and Dennis Stock, The Alternative/Communal Life in America (New York: The MacMillan Company, 1970) and Dave and Neta Jackson, Living Together in a World Falling Apart (Carol Stream, Ill.: Creation House, 1974). The Hutterites have been the single most influential force as an American communal model. The best single volume on them is John A. Hostetler, Hutterite Society (Baltimore, Md.: Johns Hopkins University Press, 1974).

[8]See J. Stillson Judah, The History and Philosophy of the Metaphysical Movements in America (Philadelphia: Westminister Press, 1967); Charles S. Braden, Spirits in Rebellion (Dallas: Southern Methodist University Press, 1963); and Horatio W. Dresser, History of the New Thought Movement (New York: Thomas Y. Crowell Co., 1919).

[9]Charles S. Braden, Christian Science Today (Dallas: Southern Methodist University Press, 1958); Frank Podmore, Mesmerism and Christian Science (London: Methuen, 1909); and Israel R. Regardie, The Romance of Metaphysics (Chicago: Aries Press, 1946).

[10]Geoffrey Nelson, Spiritualism and Society (New York: Schocken Books, 1969).

[11]George Trowbridge, Swedenborg: Life and Teaching (New York: Schocken Books, 1969); Judah, op.cit.

[12]Slater Brown, The Heyday of Spiritualism (New York: Hawthorne Books, 1970); World Centennial Celebration of Modern Spiritualism (San Antonio: Federation of Spiritual Churches and Associations, Inc., 1948).

[13]No more influential books in the psychic realm have been written than the massive volumes by Madame H.P. Blavatsky Isis Unveiled (Pasadena: Theosophical University Press, 1960) and The Secret Doctrine (Pasadena: Theosophical University Press, 1963) which laid out modern theosophy. See also Alvin Boyd Kuhn, Theosophy (New York: Henry Holt and Company, 1930).

[14]LaRoy Sunderland, Book of Psychology (New York: 1853) and Pathetism (Boston: 1848).

[15]The most widely circulated of the antipsychic books
are Raphael Gasson, The Challenging Counterfeit (Plainfield,
N.J.: Logos International, 1966) and Hobart E. Freeman,
Angels of Light? (Plainfield, N.J.: Logos International,
1969).

[16]Judah, op.cit., pp. 119-132.

[17]Charles S. Braden, "The I AM Movement," in These Also
Believe (New York: MacMillan Company, 1949), pp. 257-307.

[18]J. Gordon Melton, "The Flying Saucer Movement as a New
Form of Spiritualism/An Outline, History and Survey" (unpub-
lished manuscript in ISAR collection).

[19]Art Kleps, The Boo Hoo Bible (San Cristobal, N.M.:
Toad Books, 1971).

[20]This definition is taken from Aleister Crowley, Magick
without Tears (St. Paul: Llewellyn Publications, 1973),
p. 27.

[21]J. Gordon Melton, "Toward a History of Magical Religion
in the United States," Listening, (Autumn 1974),
pp. 105-111.

[22]Chadwick Hansen, Witchcraft at Salem (New York: George
Braziller, Inc., 1969).

[23]Francis King, Ritual Magic in England (London: Neville
Spearman, 1970) and Kenneth Grant, The Magical Revival (New
York: Samuel Weiser, 1973). "Magick" has become the common
spelling of the magical art. The new spelling emphasizes the
distinction between Magick and stage illusions.

[24]Robert Tallant, Voodoo in New Orleans (New York:
MacMillan Company, 1946) and Leo Louis Martello, Witchcraft/
The Old Religion (Secaucus, N.J.: University Press, 1973).

[25]Susan Roberts, Witches U.S.A. (Hollywood, Cal.: Phoenix
House, 1974) and Leo Louis Martello, Witchcraft, op.cit.

[26]Jason Michaels, The Devil Is Alive and Well and Living
in America Today (New York: Avon Books, 1969) and Arthur
Lyons, Jr., The Second Coming: Satanism in America (New
York: Dodd, Mead, 1920).

[27]See Hans Holzer, The New Pagans (Garden City, N.Y.:
Doubleday & Company, Inc., 1972); A Book of Pagan Rituals
(Brooklyn: Earth Religious Supplies, 1974); David L. Miller,
The New Polytheism (New York: Harper & Row, 1974); Robert
Graves, The White Goddess (New York: Farrar, Strauss, and
Giroux, 1966).

293

[28]Gershom Scholem, Kabbalah (New York: Quadrangle/The
New York Times Book Co., 1974), p. 180.

[29]Not to be confused with "rabbi" or teacher, the rabbe
may be a rabbi but is essentially the charismatic leader of
an Hassidic community.

[30](San Rafael: Spiritual Community Publications, 1974).

[31]Lee J. Levinger, A History of the Jews in the United
States (New York: Union of American Hebrew Congregations,
1949); Norman Glazer, American Judaism (Chicago: University
of Chicago Press, 1957); Theodore Friedman and Robert Gordis,
eds., Jewish Life in America (New York: Horizon Press, 1955);
Daniel Goldstein, Jewish Panorama (St. Paul: Radio Replies
Press, 1940); Howard Brotz, The Black Jews of Harlem (New
York: Schocken Books, 1964); Solomon Poll, The Hasidic
Community of Williamsburg (New York: Schocken Books, 1969);
and Herbert Weiner, 9-1/2 Mystics (New York: Collier Books,
1969).

[32]Abdo A. Elkholy, The Arab Moslems in the United States
(New Haven: College and University Press, n.d.); Pir Vilayat
Inayat-Khan, Toward the One (New York: Harper & Row, Pub-
lishers, 1974); Sufism (San Francisco: Sufism Reoriented,
Inc., 1971); Gloria Faizi, The Bahai Faith (n.p., 1971);
E.U. Essien-Udom, Black Nationalism (Chicago: University of
Chicago Press, 1962); and Eric Lincoln, The Black Muslims in
America (Boston: Beacon Press, 1961).

[33]Wendell Thomas, Hinduism Invades America (New York: The
Beacon Press, Inc., 1930); Marvin Henry Harper, Gurus,
Swamis and Avatars (Philadelphia: Westminster Press, 1972);
H.H. Wilson, Religious Sects of the Hindus (Calcutta: Susil
Gupta [India] Private Limited, 1958); and Vedanta in Chicago
(Chicago: Vivekananda Society, 1968).

[34]Sardarni Premka Kaur, Guru for the Aquarian Age (San
Rafael: Spiritual Community, 1972); Maharaj Charan Singh,
The Path (Delhi, India: Radha Soami Satsang, Beas, 1969).

[35]Louise H. Hunter, Buddhism in Hawaii (Honolulu: Univer-
sity of Hawaii Press, 1971); E. Dale Saunders, Buddhism in
Japan (Philadelphia: University of Pennsylvania Press, 1964);
Agehananda Bharati, The Tantric Tradition (Garden City, N.Y.:
Doubleday & Company, Inc., 1965); and Harry Thomsen, The New
Religions of Japan (Rutland, Vt.:   Charles E. Tuttle Company,
Publishers, 1963).

[36]"The Shinto Shrines of Hawaii," (8 pp. typescript);
Marcus Bach, "Shinto Religion of the Way of the Gods," in
Major Religions of the World (Nashville, Tenn.:   The Graded
Press, 1959).

[37]R.B. Blakney, trans., The Way of Life/Lao Tzu (New York: New American Library, 1955); Arthur Waley, The Way and Its Power (New York: Grove Press, Inc., 1958); James Legge, trans., I Ching/Book of Changes (New Hyde Park, N.Y.: University Books, 1964).

[38]Henry L. Sorge, ed., The Philosophy of Mazdaznan (Los Angeles: Mazdaznan Press, 1960).

BIBLIOGRAPHY

The sources listed below form a highly selective bibliography of materials concerning American Religious bodies. Items included are in addition to those referred to in the footnotes and were selected for their breadth of coverage of religious bodies or their offering hard to find information on important topics.

General

Acheson Jr., Louis K., ed. Directory, International Council. Northridge, Ca: International Cooperation Council, Revised Annually.

Algermissen, Konrad. Christian Sects. New York: Hawthorn Books, 1962. 1051 pp.

Biteaux, Armand. The New Consciousness. Willits, Ca: Oliver Press, 1975. 168 pp.

Braden, Charles Samuel. These Also Believe. New York: MacMillan Co., 1949. 491 pp.

Directory of Sabbath-Observing Groups. Fairview, Ok: The Bible Sabbath Association, 1974. 258 pp.

Ellwood, Robert S. Religious and Spiritual Groups in Modern America. Englewood Cliffs, NJ: Prentice-Hall, Inc., 1973. 334 pp.

Gardner, Martin. Fads and Fallacies in the Name of Science. New York: Dover Publications, Inc., 1957. pp.

Jacquet Jr., Constant H., ed. Yearbook of American Churches. Nashville: Abingdon Press, Revised Annually.

Mead, Frank Spencer. Handbook of Denominations in the United States. New York: Abingdon Press, 1970. 265 pp.

O'Hair, J.C. Isms and Schisms. Chicago: J.C. O'Hair, n.d. 84 pp.

Rowley, Peter. New Gods in America. New York: David McKay Company, Inc., 1971. 207 pp.

Smith, Hannah (Whitall). Group Movements of the Past
and Experiments in Guidance. London: Faber & Faber,
Ltd., 1934. 270 pp.

United States Bureau of the Census. Religious Bodies:
1936. Washington: U.S. Govt. Printing Office,
1941. 3 volumes.

Van Baalen, Jan Karel. The Chaos of Cults. Grand Rapids.
Eerdmans, 1956. 409 pp.

Family Groups

Liturgical

Bolshakoff, Serge. Russian Non-Conformity. Philadelphia:
Westminster Press, 1950. 192 pp.

Berger, Monroe. "America's Syrian Community." Commentary,
Vol. XXV, No. 4 (April, 1958), pp. 314-323.

Fox, Paul. The Polish National Catholic Church. Scranton,
PA: School of Christian Living, n.d., 146 pp.

Manross, William Wilson. A History of the American
Episcopal Church. New York: Morehouse-Gorham Co.,
1950. 415 pp.

Pittenger, W. Norman. The Episcopalian Way of Life.
Englewood Cliffs, N.J.: Prentice Hall, Inc., 1957.
188 pp.

Presbyterian

Campbell, Thomas A. Good News on the Frontier. Memphis,
Tenn.: Frontier Press, 1965. 172 pp.

Centennial Committee of the Christian Reformed Church.
One Hundred Years in the New World. Grand Rapids:
Publication Section of the Centennial Committee,
1957. 218 pp.

Harden, Margaret G., Comp. A Brief History of the Bible
Presbyterian Church. N.p. n.d.

Hoeksema, Herman. The Protestant Reformed Churches in
America. Grand Rapids, n.p., 1947. 418 pp.

King, Roy A. A History of the Associate Reformed
Presbyterian Church. Charlotte, N.C.: Covenant Life
Curriculum, 1966. 132 pp.

Loetscher, Leffants A. A Brief History of the
Presbyterians. Philadelphia: The Westminster Press,
1958.

Liberals

Warren, Sidney. American Free Thought/1860-1914. New
York: Goodion Press, Inc., 1966.

Wilbur, Earl Morse. A History of Unitarianism. Cambridge,
Mass.: Harvard University Press, 1946.

Pietism

Neisser, Georg. A History of the Beginnings of Moravian
Work in America. Translated by William N. Schwarze
and Samuel H. Gapp. Bethleham, Pa.: Archives of the
Moravian Church, No. 1, 1955. 192 pp.

Bucke, Emory Stevens, ed. The History of American
Methodism. Nashville: Abingdon Press, 1964. 3 vols.

Holiness

Marston, Leslie R. From Age to Age a Living Witness.
Winona Lake, Ind.: Light and Life Press, 1960.
608 pp.

Redford, M.E. The Rise of the Church of the Nazarene.
Kansas City: Nazarene Publishing House, 1951.
108 pp.

Pentecostal

Campbell, Joseph E. The Pentecostal Holiness Church/1898-
1948. Franklin Springs, Ga.: Pentecostal Holiness
Church, 1951. 573 pp.

Conn, Charles W. Like A Mighty Army. Cleveland, Tenn.:
Church of God Publishing House, 1955. 380 pp.

Kendrick, Klaude. The Promise Fulfilled. Springfield,
Mo.: Gospel Publishing House, 1961. 237 pp.

Left Wing Reformation

Bender, Harold S., ed. The Mennonite Encyclopedia.
Scottsdale, Pa.: Herald Press, 1955-59. 4 vols.

Durnbaugh, Donald F., and Schultz, Lawrence W. "A Brethren Bibliography, 1713-1963." Brethren Life, Vol. IX, Nos. 1 & 2 (Winter and Spring 1964), pp. 3-177.

Hostetler, John A. Mennonite Life. Scottsdale, Pa.: Herald Press, 1954. 39 pp.

_____. Amish Life. Scottsdale, Pa.: Herald Press, 1952. 39 pp.

Mallot, Floyd E. Studies in Brethren History. Elgin, Ill.: Brethren Publishing House, 1954. 382 pp.

Westin, Gunnar. The Free Church Through The Ages. Nashville: Broadman Press, 1958. 33 pp.

Baptist

Baptist Advance. Forest Park, Ill. Roger Williams Press, 1964. 512 pp.

Barnes, W.W. The Southern Baptist Convention 1845-1853. Nashville: Broadman Press, 1954.

Boyd, Jesse L. A History of the Baptists in America. New York: The American Press, 1957. 205 pp.

Dowling, Enos. E. The Restoration Movement. Cincinnati: Standard Publishing, 1964. 128 pp.

Latch, Ollie. History of the General Baptists. Poplar Bluff, Mo.: The General Baptist Press, 1954. 428 pp.

Independent Fundamentalists

Bass, Clarence B. Backgrounds to Dispensationalism: Its Historical Genesis and Ecclesiastical Implications. Grand Rapids: Wm. B. Eerdmans Publishing Company, 1960.

Ryrie, Charles Caldwell. Dispensationalism Today. Chicago: Moddy Press, 1965.

Adventist

Froom, Leroy E. The Conditionalist Faith of Our Fathers. Washington, D.C.: Review and Herald Publishing Assocation, 1965-1966. 2 vols.

Jehovah's Witnesses in the Divine Purpose. Brooklyn:
Watchtower Bible and Tract Society, 1959.

Communal

Desroche, Henri. The American Shakers. Amherst: The
University of Massachusetts Press, 1971. 357 pp.

Hine, Robert R. California's Utopian Communities.
Chicago: Charles H. Kerr & Co., 1902.

Holloway, Mark. Heavens on Earth: Utopian Communities
in America 1680-1880. New York: Dover Publications,
1966. 240 pp.

Hostetler, John. Hutterite Life. Scottsdale, Pa.:
Herald Press, 1965. 39 pp.

Houriet, Robert. Getting Back Together. New York:
Avon Publisher, 1969. 408 pp.

Periodicals:

   Communities: Louisa, Va.
   Modern Utopian

New Thought

Braden, Charles S. Spirits in Rebellion. Dallas: Southern
Methodist University Press, 1963. 571 pp.

Corey, Arthur. Behind the Scenes   with the Metaphysicians
Los Angeles: DeVorss & Company, 1968. 261 pp.

Merritt, Robert E., and Corey, Arthur. Christian Science
and Liberty. Los Angeles: DeVorss and Company, 1970.
225 pp.

Psychial

de Camp, L. Sprague and Catherine C. de Camp, Spirits,
Stars and Spells. New York: Canaveral Press, 1966.
348 pp.

Flammonde, Paris. The Age of Flying Saucers. New York:
Hawthorn Books, 1971. 288 pp.

Hardinge, Emma. Modern American Spiritualism. New York:
By the author, 1870. 565 pp.

Nethercot, Arthur H. The First Five Lives of Annie
Besant. Chicago, University of Chicago Press, 1960.
419 pp.

_____. The Last Four Lives of Annie Besant. Chicago:
University of Chicago Press, 1963. 483 pp.

St. Clair, David. The Psychic World of California.
Garden City, N.Y.: Doubleday & Company, 1972. 323
pp.

Magical

Bonewits, P.E.I. Real Magic. New York: Coward, McCann
& Geoghegan, Inc., 1971, 236 pp.

Conway, David. Magic, An Occult Primer. New York:
E.P. Dutton & Co., Inc., 1972. 286 pp.

Farrar, Stewart. What Witches Do. New York: Coward,
McCann & Geoghegan, Inc., 1971. 211 pp.

Galbreath, Robert, ed. The Occult: Studies and
Evaluations. Bowling Green: Bowling Green University
Press, 1972. 126 pp.

Gonzaloz-Wippler, Migene. Santeria/African Magic in Latin
America. New York: Julian Press, 1973. 181 pp.

King, Francis. Sexuality, Magic and Perversion. Secacus,
N.J.: The Citadel Press, 1972. 207 pp.

Melton, J. Gordon. "Sources and Resources for Teaching
The Occult" Paper delivered at the 1976 Meeting of the
Midwest Popular Culture Association at Bowling Green
State University.

McTeer, J.E. High Sheriff of the Low County. Beaufort
S.C.: Beaufort Book Co., Inc., 1970. 101 pp.

Puckett, Newbell Niles. The Magic and Folk Beliefs of
the Southern Negro. New York: Dover Publications,
Inc., 1969. 644 pp.

Daraul, Arkon. A History of Secret Societies. New York:
Citadel Press, 1962.

Periodicals:

    The Green Egg   St. Louis, Missouri.
    Gnostica News   St. Paul, Minnesota

302

Non Christian - General

Dasgupta, Shashibhusan. Obscure Religious Sects
   Calcutta: Firma, K.L. Mukhopadhyay, 1969. 436 pp.

Friedlander, Ira, ed. Year One Catalog. New York:
   Harper and Row Publishers, 1972. 152 pp.

Spiritual Community. Spiritual Community Directory. San
   Rafael, Cal.: Spiritual Community, 1973. 208 pp.

Jewish

Ben Yehuda, Shaleak. Black Hebrew Israelites From America
   to the Promised Land. New York: Vantage Press,
   1975. 357 pp.

Crombach, Abraham. Reform Movements in Judaism. New
   York: Bookman Associates, Inc., 1963. 138 pp.

Ehrman, Albert. "Black Judaism in New York." Journal
   of Ecumenical Studies, VIII (Winter, 1971) 103-114.

Landes, Ruth. "Negro Jews of Harlem." Jewish Journal
   of Sociology, IX (December, 1967), pp. 175-189.

Skir, Leo. "Shlomo Carlebach and the House of Love and
   Prayer." Midstream, XVI, (February, 1920), 27-42.

Tinney, James S. "Black Jews: A House Divided."
   Christianity Today, Vol. XVIII, No. 5 (December 1973),
   pp. 52-53.

Hindu

A Western Disciple. With the Swamis in America. Chicago:
   Vivekananda Vedanta Society, 1946. 138 pp.

Prabhavananda, Swami, and Isherwood, Christopher. How
   to Know God/The Yoga Aphorisms of Patanjal. New
   York: New American Library, 1969. 156 pp.

Buddhist

Hunt, Ernest Shinkaku. Gleanings from Soto-Zen. Honolulu:
   n.p., 1953. 58 pp.

Wilson, H.H. Religious Sects of the Hindus, Calcutta:
   Susit Gupta (India) Private Limited, 1958. 221 pp.

Kapleau, Philip. The Three Pillars of Zen. New York: Harper & Row, 1966. 363 pp.

Kubose, Gyomay M., American Buddhism. Chicago: The Dharma House, 1976. 36 pp.

Linsen, Robert. Living Zen. New York: Grove Press, Inc., 1958. 348 pp.

Salanave, Miriam. A Buddhist Role Call. n.p., n.d. 18 pp.

Saunders, E. Dale. Buddhism in Japan. Philadelphia: University of Pennsylvania Press, 1964. 328 pp.

The Fall 1969 issue of Windbell (Vol, VIII, Nos. 1-2) was entirely devoted to a history of the Zen groups in America.

Japan

Bach, Marcus. The Power of Perfect Liberty. Englewood Cliffs, N.J.: Prentice-Hall, Inc., 1971. 163 pp.

MacFarland, H. Neill. The Rush Hour of the Gods. New York: The MacMillan Company, 1967. 267 pp.

Offner, Clark B. and Straelen, Henry von. Modern Japanese Religions with Special Emphasis Upon Their Doctrine of Healing. New York: Twayne Publishers, 1963. 296 pp.

Moslem

Hassen, Selma Al-Faqih. "A Short History of Sufism" in Suffism. San Francisco: Sufism Reoriented, Inc., 1971, pp. 3-22.

Speeth, Kathleen Riordan. The Gurdjieff Work. Berkeley, Ca.: And/or Press, 1976. 154 pp.

Miscellaneous

Ellwood, Robert S. One Way/The Jesus Movement and Its Meaning. Englewood Cliffs, N.J.: Prentice-Hall, 1973. 150 pp.

Hunter, John Francis. The Gay Insiders. New York: Stonehill Publishing Company, 1972.

Kamakau, Samuel Manaiakulani. Ka Poe Kahiko/The People
    of Old. Honolulu: The Bishop Museum Press, 1964.
    165 pp.

LaBarre, Weston. The Peyote Cult. New York: Schocken
    Books, 1969. 260 pp.

Whalen, William J. Handbook of Secret Organizations.
    Milwaukee: The Bruce Publishing Company, 1966.
    169 pp.